WOMEN, WRITING, HISTORY

1640 – 1740

WOMEN, WRITING, HISTORY

1640–1740

Edited by
Isobel Grundy and
Susan Wiseman

B.T. Batsford Ltd · London

Typeset by Servis Filmsetting Ltd, Manchester

and printed in Great Britain
by Dotesios Ltd, Trowbridge, Wilts

for the publishers
B. T. Batsford Ltd
4 Fitzhardinge Street
London W1H 0AH

ISBN 0 7134 5793 7

Contents

Acknowledgements

Isobel Grundy would like to thank her co-workers on *The Feminist Companion to Literature in English*, since that project produced the work which made this one possible.

Susan Wiseman would like to thank Barbara Rosenbaum, and staff in the School of Literature and Media Studies at the Polytechnic of North London, especially John Thieme.

We would both like to thank the contributors for their patience, and special thanks to Kate Lilley and Diane Purkiss.

Notes on contributors

Ros Ballaster is a lecturer in English at the University of East Anglia. She has recently completed her doctoral work on amatory fiction 1684–1740, and has published on eighteenth-century women's fiction. She is co-author of a forthcoming book on women's magazines.

Carol Barash is a professor of English at Rutgers University, New Brunswick, New Jersey. She is currently working on a book-length study, 'Feminist Fictions of Difference: Formations of Gender and Culture in Eighteenth-Century Narrative', and a new, standard edition of the poems and plays of Anne Finch, Countess of Winchilsea. She is author of *English Women Writers and the Body of Monarchy* (forthcoming, Oxford University Press) and editor of *An Olive Schreiner Reader: Writings on Women and South Africa* (Methuen, 1987).

Isobel Grundy moved in 1990 from Queen Mary and Westfield College, London University, to the University of Alberta, Edmonton, Canada, as Henry Marshall Tory Professor. She has published on Lady Mary Wortley Montagu, Samuel Johnson and others, and is, with Virginia Blain and Patricia Clements, editor of *The Feminist Companion to Literature in English: Women Writers from the Middle Ages to the Present* (Batsford, 1990).

Elaine Hobby is a socialist, a feminist and a lesbian, who has been working on seventeenth-century women's writing ever since being told at Essex University in 1978 that 'there weren't any women then'. She is lecturer in Women's Studies, English and Drama Department, Loughborough University, and has published *Virtue of Necessity: English*

Women's Writing 1649–1688 (Virago, 1988), and edited (with Elspeth-Graham, Hilary Hinds and Helen Wilcox) *Her Own Life: Autobiographical Writings By Seventeenth-Century Englishwomen* (Routledge, 1989).

Kate Lilley did her BA at the University of Sydney, and her Ph.D. at University College, London, on 'Masculine Elegy'. From 1986 to 1989 she was a Junior Research Fellow of St Hilda's College, Oxford, working on 'The Genres of Seventeenth-Century Women's Writing'. She is now lecturer in English at the University of Sydney. Her poetry is widely published in Australia.

Jeslyn Medoff holds a BA from Simmons College, an MA from the University of Massachusetts, and is presently completing a Ph.D. thesis entitled 'After Aphra: Women Writers and Their Public Personae, 1660–1740' at Rutgers University. She has co-edited *Kissing the Rod: An Anthology of Seventeenth Century Women's Verse* (Virago, 1988) and has published articles on women writers in *Notes and Queries, Tulsa Studies in Women's Literature, Modern Fiction Studies, British Women Writers* (Routledge, 1989), *Modern American Women Writers* (Scribner's, 1990) and elsewhere.

Diane Purkiss is a lecturer in English at the University of East Anglia. She has published articles on women's writing in the early modern period, and has edited an essay collection *Women, Texts and Histories 1558–1760*, with Clare Brant.

Valerie Rumbold is lecturer in English in the University of Wales, Bangor. Her *Women's Place in Pope's World* was published by Cambridge University Press in 1989. She is now working on an edition of Pope's 1743 *Dunciad*, and on women's poetry of the early eighteenth century.

Catherine Sharrock is a lecturer at the University of Nottingham. Having worked on Jonathan Swift she is now engaged on a project on linguistic and political authority in eighteenth-century England.

Susan Wiseman is a lecturer in English at the University of Kent at Canterbury.

Introduction

The title of this book indicates its central concerns; it also outlines the areas in which contributors to this volume are often arguing from quite different assumptions. The divisions in the title *Women, Writing, History* are as important as the words. They indicate some of the contradictions in the material under discussion, but also in methodology and approach.

In defining the field of study as writing by women in the early modern period, we find ourselves tracing imperatives and counter-imperatives in writing by women. We wanted to ask how we can begin to map the interrelationships of writing, gender and historical circumstances through the inevitable contradictions in the writings of early modern women.

The feminist scholars and critics writing in this volume ask what were the social and discursive forces constituting women in the early modern period, and investigate women's participation and intervention in writing practices. Our aim, as editors, was to bring together questions about gender as focused by the idea of 'women' and questions about time, place and discourse as focused by the idea of 'history'. The word 'writing' which links these two ('women' and 'history') signals a further problem in the categories: does a 'woman' write her self in (or into) history, or is she written by (or out of) it?

We set out to bring together literary scholars and critics who were investigating these questions in different ways in relation to the early modern period. We also decided that the division literary history creates between the seventeenth and eighteenth centuries was a construct of periodization that in this case seemed unhelpful. The year 1699–1700 marks no significant boundary in terms of genre or gender, or of politics as it affects these two. We wanted to concentrate on the period after print became the dominant mode of literary production and to include writing from a range of literary and political perspectives. For this reason, the period from the final years of Charles I's personal rule to the second Hanoverian reign seemed to us to bring together a range of political, religious and economic changes. In literary terms, it covers the period from the lifting of restrictions on presses at the outbreak of the Civil War to the end of what might be seen as women's dominance in the field of prose fiction. Therefore, this period enabled us to contrast genres and positions that are very different and sometimes in open conflict, and to begin to compare, for example, literary production by women during the Civil War and Interregnum with their relations to the market for poetry in the early eighteenth century. Cultural production both registers and helps to shape such social transformations and divisions.

Disputes about meaning, genre and politics exist in the past, but equally important disputes exist in the present which structure differences of methodology and topic. No volume of writing on such topics would present a singular feminist approach; one of the advantages of current feminist work is the coincidence of a shared enterprise with fruitful methodological argument. The essays presented here do not share a single methodology or approach. Feminisms there are, and there is therefore a recurrence to particular questions as central to feminist scholarship and criticism on the early modern period. Disputed, in the essays and in the gaps between the essays, are three central ideas which we have chosen to categorize as 'women', 'writing' and 'history'; these are the terms in play, differently, in each essay.

To begin with 'women'. This is a fundamental category of feminist work, some would say *the* fundamental category. But its precise meaning, or what it can be taken to signify, depends on its context, and is implicitly an issue in each essay in this book. As Denise Riley points out, the past suggests that in feminist thinking 'both a concentration on and a refusal of the identity of "women" are essential to feminism'.[1] When we asked contributors for essays on writing by English women, we left open the question as to what such a person as a 'woman' was, is or might be. Some contributors (such as Catherine Sharrock) investigate the early modern meanings of the category 'women' in relation to ideology, subjectivity and emergent feminist discourses. Sharrock's analysis of the difficult connection between Mary Astell's feminist prose and political and religious discourses calls into question the relationship between female agency in writing and predetermined structures of thought. Ros

Ballaster, writing about fiction in similar terms, investigates women as subjects in discourse and woman as objects of novelistic discourse. Ballaster also implicates the reader in novelistic *mise-en-scène* and points out the subversive potential in the seduction of the reader by the text. Where Ballaster explores questions of identification in fiction, Diane Purkiss and Isobel Grundy write about the role of feminine identity in religious writing. Purkiss's reading of the part played by the female body in seventeenth-century women's prophetic writing, and the interrelationship between religious symbolism and the transgression of the norms of femininity, elucidates some of the ways in which religious writing speaks the position of women not only in relation to a deity but also to their social circumstances. The writing of a 'life' and the way women writing might establish a female identity within religious discourse is the topic of Grundy's essay, together with the uses of writing in refashioning a social self. Furthermore, the concerns shared by Grundy and Purkiss alert us to the multiple traditions of writing from Catholic to radical Protestant. They also begin to explore the relationships between feminine identity and a range of political and religious positions, both central and marginalized, over a century of rapid and often violent social and doctrinal shifts.

The uneasy intervention of 'women' in politics, especially marginalized political positions, is the subject of Valerie Rumbold's essay on Mary Caesar's 'book', in which Caesar recorded her political opinions but which, inevitably, bears traces of her marginality with respect to the political world she was basically excluded from. Sue Wiseman engages with some similar issues in tracing the relationship of theatre to gender and status in the plays of Margaret Cavendish. Mary Caesar's manuscript book and the self-determined, even fetishistic, symbology of her art collection suggest the problem of where a female 'I' might be in masculist discourse, and serve to suggest that the term 'women' representing a felt identity is not only fragmented (suggesting accident), but structured as contradictory by social, political, religious and other circumstances and discourses.

Some contributors take the category of 'women' as a positive given and see the critic's activity as uncovering the struggle for the representation of a female self which already existed but which needed to be revealed in writing. Carol Barash explores the way the figure of Queen Anne enabled poets to form a sorority united by the simultaneously Amazonian and maternal image of the queen. Barash shows women beginning to use poetic devices differently once the queen gave them psychic and writerly space to do so. Elsewhere, Jeslyn Medoff traces some of the problems involved in the shaping of a woman's reputation, and that of her writing. Once again, a periodized division between the seventeenth and eighteenth centuries is exposed as obfuscatory: Medoff shows how Aphra Behn and Katherine Philips left opposed images of the female poet to ensuing generations. While Behn came to stand for sexual freedom and transgression, Philips was increasingly imagined as her polar opposite: morally spotless and supportive of traditional roles. Medoff traces the way changing times, taste and morality affected the construction of a poetic identity for eighteenth-century women poets and shows how these identities were manipulated by authors, publishers and editors.

In different ways, Elaine Hobby and Kate Lilley address the question of genre. Hobby examines the genres in which women wrote during one decade. She finds women participating (or intervening) in all kinds of religious discourse, from nonconformist prophecy and conversion narrative to Roman Catholic devotional poetry. As her slice of literary production suggests, women were busy everywhere in the 1650s writing prose, poetry and even drama. Hobby notes the maternal relation between women and their literary production as suggested in the title *Eliza's Babes*. This is something which Lilley analyses in her essay on women's writing of elegy. Lilley identifies dominant tropes and modes across a wide range of women's elegies and in doing so suggests a methodology for examining the relationship between gender and genre which moves with facility between detail and overview.

In dispute among these different essays is the question of whether feminine identity is artificial, fluctuating, transformed by historical accident and exegesis, or whether the various texts produced by women in (masculist) society constitute what might be called a coherent 'selection of counter-identities'. We hope, therefore, that this collection puts the category of 'women' helpfully into question – and shows readers some of the different ways contributors answer it. Once 'women' is accepted as an unstable and disputed category, 'writing' ceases to be something obvious or given. Further questions are generated by asking, Who is doing the writing? Or, in Barthes's terms, 'Who speaks?' We must further ask, Who is spoken? And, as Ros Ballaster reminds us, Who reads? As Lilley notes, changes of tropes suggest the centrality of gender to the material instance of genre. And these questions are in part generated by a reader, and a reader's social and generic horizon of expectation.

Just as writing was something that early modern women were both doing and being done by, it also both describes what we are doing now and formulates the way we do it. 'History' shapes the way we write but the category of 'history' raises a new set of questions. For some contributors, 'history' can exist only as our own interpretation of earlier discursive practices, made for our own 'interests' in the present. Furthermore, there is no outside to that which may be read or interpreted. Elsewhere in the volume, at the other end of an imagined spectrum of attitudes to historical discourse, 'history' appears as the legitimate object of our quest for knowledge: the past is seen as (within whatever limitations) knowable. In each case there remain disputes: Does this idea of history as currently constituted as a legitimate field of knowledge merely endorse patriarchal structures? Whose history is it that might be reconstructed, and by whom? In relation to these disputes, Elaine Hobby maps two rival versions of the history of women's writing during part of the seventeenth century, and demonstrates that many genres not previously considered as 'literary' go to make up the cultural production of the period, and therefore affect any 'tradition' we choose to construct.

Inevitably, this collection itself has made choices about what it discusses and what it leaves out. Some choices we would have liked to be different. Regretfully, we have left out writings from those parts of Britain and related islands furthest removed from the metropolis, and this means that a range of Irish and Scottish writings are excluded. Similarly, our investigations focus on available evidence. Of the women making their voices heard by contemporaries during the years 1640 to 1740 a small minority used the written word; from that minority we can engage only with the smaller minority whose writing was preserved either by collectors (in convents, family archives) or by publication and survival of the printed copy. Some degree of privilege or influence has been involved in every writing down and every passing down, and this operates as the centripetal force drawing scholarship and criticism back towards the simultaneously chimerical and powerful centrality of what survives. However, several streams *are* represented here: the writings of aristocrats and gentlewomen, marked by the dominant, though sometimes defensive, discourses of monarchist and Tory politics; the writings of women engaged with the cultural marketplace; and the writings of women in religious or political opposition to the status quo – in print and manuscript. Inevitably we need to go on asking, What 'women'? Whose 'writing'? Which 'history'?

WOMEN

'Discourse so unsavoury'

Women's published writings of the 1650s

Elaine Hobby

What is spoken of Maids, may be properly applyed by a useful consequence to all women: They should be seene, and not heard: A Traveller sets himselfe best out by discourse, whereas their best setting-out is silence.[1]

The 1650s were a period of experimentation and change in Britain. After the beheading of Charles I in 1649, a series of attempts was made to establish a new governmental structure for the country, and the radical religious sects that had grown up through the years of civil war continued to argue, split and realign themselves as they examined the social implications of the belief that each individual could communicate directly with God. Because the Quakers, in particular, made a practice of attending church services to argue with ministers, and of preaching in public spaces such as marketplaces, far more people came into contact with their ideas than ever joined their organizations. At the same time, various groups petitioned parliament for legal changes, whilst many royalists fled overseas or withdrew from public life for safety's sake. In the resulting confusion, the intermittent attempts to revive state control over publishing were largely ineffective, and many groups and individuals found a public voice.[2]

Perhaps it is not surprising, therefore, that despite oft-cited injunctions to women's silence, including William Brathwait's remark quoted above, the 1650s produced the first great outpouring of women's published writings in English: some 130 texts, written by more than 70 women.[3] Although recent anthologies of seventeenth-century women's writing might lead us to expect that their authors were either poets or instantly recognizable 'feminists',[4] a more detailed examination of the decade's output reveals a far wider range of genres and concerns. What their authors shared, by and large, was a keen recognition that women in the period were expected to be too modest to vaunt themselves in print. A woman's primary concern was supposed to be with her family, and its good name or 'honour'. If her reputation for 'modesty' was brought into question in any way – either in its modern sense or in its specific seventeenth-century sense of 'female chastity' – both she and her relatives would meet social condemnation. Women writing for publication in the period exposed themselves to adverse judgment, and their writings therefore commonly included justifications for their unfeminine bold-ness. It is this consciousness of the need to justify their activity that unites the writings of the decade.[5]

Their differences, however, were legion, and whilst I make reference here to the majority of the decade's works, several dozen others are omitted. Those neglected include the large number of petitions to parliament published by women in 1650 to 1651 and 1654 to 1655, the almanacs of Sarah Jinner and the translation into English of writings by a French midwife, Louise Bourgeois. It is also important to realize that whilst we can find connections between the writings of this decade and of those that precede and follow it, it would be wrong to look for any overarching 'women's experience' or 'female voice'. Women's access to education, writing and publishing varies from one period to another, as does the specific inflexion of injunctions to silence or to other 'feminine' characteristics. I hope that this essay will indicate the need for future feminist research to pay closer attention to the details of history than has recently been customary, or perhaps even possible.

I Poets and 'feminists'

Certain women writers of the 1650s are beginning to receive some attention, either because they wrote in 'literary' forms, especially poetry, or because their works include polemical statements attractive to modern feminists. The poets include, most obviously, Anne Bradstreet, whose *The Tenth Muse* (1650) is being embraced as the United States' first published volume of verse; and Katherine Philips, whose first printed poems were included in William Cartwright's *Comedies* (1651) and in Henry Lawes's *Second Book of Ayres* (1655).[6] Most noted amongst the 'feminists' is Margaret Cavendish, the Marchioness (later Duchess) of Newcastle, whose works ran to more than a dozen titles between 1653 and 1668, several of them in more than one edition.

It is easy to see why Cavendish's works should hold immediate appeal for present-day feminists. A much-quoted preface to her *Philosophical and Physical Opinions* (1655), addressed to the two universities, attacks male scorn of women's abilities and attributes female subordination to social circumstances: circumstances engineered by men.

> We are become like worms that onely live in the dull earth of ignorance, winding ourselves sometimes out, by the help of some refreshing rain of good educations which seldom is given us; for we are kept like birds in cages to hop up and down in our houses, not sufferd to fly abroad to see the several changes of fortune, and the various humours, ordained and created by nature; thus wanting the experiences of nature, we must needs want the understanding and knowledge and so consequently prudence, and invention of men: thus by an opinion, which I hope is but an erronious one in men, we are shut out of all power, and Authority by reason we are never imployed either in civil or marshall affaires, our counsels are despised, and laught at, the best of our actions are troden down with scorn, by the overweening conceit men have of themselves and through a despisement of us. (sig. B2ᵛ)

There is an abundance of such angry, analytical statements in Cavendish's works, and their existence is eloquent testimony to the fact that women in the period did not necessarily accept their subordinate station as God-given, whatever the evidence from contemporary conduct books might seem to be.[7]

Other aspects of Cavendish's work also offer immediate interest to today's woman reader interested in finding evidence of female defiance in earlier centuries. The main body of her *Philosophical and Physical Opinions* is an implicit defence of women's right to intellectual endeavour, consisting of an extended attempt to account for natural and supernatural phenomena, and explicitly defending her right to speculate on such matters. *Poems and Fancies* (1653) provides much material for an analysis of what might be called 'female' imagery, since it makes wide use of metaphors comparing writing to spinning, embroidery and childbearing. (Poetry-writing is 'Spinning with the braine . . . to Spin a Garment of Memory' (sig. A2); she has chosen her 'Silke with fresh contours, and matcht them in good shadows' (sig. A3); she explains her pride in her work, 'True, it [the world] may taxe my Indiscretion, being so fond of my Book, as to make it as if it were my Child, and striving to shew here to the World, in hopes Some may like her, although no Beauty to Admire, yet may praise her Behaviour, as not being wanton, nor rude' (sig. A8).) *The Worlds Olio* (1655) dismisses male claims to superiority and disputes the usefulness of their book-learning, and *Natures Pictures* (1656) includes stories of female heroism and intelligence, as well as the author's autobiography. Between them, these books can be seen as a diverse exploration of literary activity, and a defence of women's right to write. Cavendish's forays into print met with derision,[8] and again and again in these works she laments how few opportunities she has to make a name for herself, asserting her determination to disregard the dismissive responses of her critics: 'The Worlds dispraises cannot make me a mourning garment: my mind's too big, and I had rather venture an indiscretion, then loose the hopes of a Fame' (*Poems and Fancies*, sig. A4).

Such sentiments can be explained as a call for her personal glory, but can also be interpreted as a desire for independence from a woman's identity with her husband:[9]

> Give me that Wit, whose Fancy's not confin'd,
> That buildeth on it selfe, not two Braines joyn'd.
> For that's like Oxen yoak'd, and forc'd to draw,
> Or two Witnesses for one Deed in Law.
> But like the Sun that need no help to rise,
> Or like a Bird in Aire which freely flies.
> (*Poems and Fancies*, p. 133)

This reference to the general state of women is not, however, the only resonance of her call for fame. In her autobiography she explains her 'delight in a singularity, even in acoutrements of habits' (*Natures Pictures*, p. 387), and in 'An Epistle to my Readers' prefacing *Natures Pictures* she extends this into a wish to be appreciated as a unique talent unlike and superior to all others:

> I have not read much History to inform me of the past Ages, indeed I dare not examin the former times, for fear I should meet with such of my Sex, that have outdone all the glory I can aime at, or hope to attain; for I confess my Ambition is restless, and not ordinary; because it would have an extra-ordinary fame: And since all heroick Actions, publick Imployments, powerfull Governments, and eloquent Pleadings are denied our Sex in this age, or at least would be condemned for want of custome, is the cause I write so much.

This statement, like so many of Cavendish's dedicatory epistles, is more than a little disingenuous.[10] Cavendish's first published book, *Poems and Fancies*, was apparently written during the 15 months she spent in England (an interlude in her voluntary exile on the continent that had begun at the court of Henrietta Maria in Oxford), when she was petitioning for a share in the estate of her outlawed royalist husband, the Marquess of Newcastle. It is likely that during her sojourn in London she would have heard of the 'bands of clamouring women' who frequently petitioned parliament,[11] and possible that she would have known about the activities of other royalist women like herself, who were publishing their appeals for restitution of property.[12] It was not exactly true that 'eloquent Pleadings' were denied women, although working in the legal profession was, and many, like Cavendish herself, were unsuccessful in their appeals.

In the light of her treatment of such phenomena in her writings, it also seems certain that during her stay in England, Cavendish came to realize that many women were gaining public notoriety through their activities as preachers, and that increasing numbers of them were having their work published. This last and most significant aspect of women's activities in England in that decade presented a dilemma for her: if other women could make a name for themselves as thinkers and have their works published, perhaps she could too. On the other hand, as a committed royalist married to a peer, she was profoundly opposed to the civil disorder, insubordination and revolution that such women were involved in. This conflict makes its appearance many times in her writings of the 1650s. In *Poems and Fancies*, for example, she justifies her publishing by asserting that it was better for her to be so immodest as to write than 'to busie my self out of the Sphear of our Sex, as in Politicks of State, or to Preach false Doctrine in a Tub' (sig. A4). In her address 'To all Writing Ladies' she teeters back and forth between defending and attacking the status quo. The monarchy and social order are threatened by the increase in 'spirits of the Faeminine Gender', but the same development seems to make greater female activity possible. Reflecting on the possibility of social change, she refers to

> Some Ages, as in Aristocracy, when some part did rule; and other Ages a pure Monarchy, when but one rules; and in some Ages, it seemes as if all those spirits were at defiance, who should have most power, which makes them in confusion, and War; so confused are some Ages, and it seemes as if there were spirits of the Faeminine Gender, as also the Masculine. There will be many Heroick Women in some Ages, in others very Propheticall; in some ages very pious, and devout: For our Sex is wonderfully addicted to the spirits. But this Age hath produced many effeminate Writers, as well as Preachers, and many effeminate Rulers, as well as Actors. And if it be an Age when the effeminate spirits rule, as most visibly they doe in every Kingdome, let us take the advantage, and make the best of our time, for feare their reigne should not last long. (*Poems and Fancies*, sig. Aa)

This conflict, between the desire to maintain social order, and the need to overturn a system that denies her the right of access to publishing and acclaim, is also manifested in her treatment of questions of sexual politics, producing the dynamic of many of Cavendish's fictional works. Many of these alternate between violent overthrow (such as shooting an unwelcome suitor and leaving him for dead) and acceptance of things the way they are (marrying the same man at his recovery).[13]

Committed by her political and class allegiances to the re-establishment of social order, Cavendish's analysis of women's position necessarily excludes the activities of unruly 'effeminate spirits', and rarely extends beyond the bounds of the ruling class. *The Worlds Olio* includes a pessimistic assessment of women's achievements to date, which was written before her more famous address to the two universities. At that time she could find no satisfactory social explanation of the origins of female subordination, believing that 'Thoughts are free, those can never be inslaved' (sig. A5). Her description there of the female leisure-time that would enable women to study if they wished to bears no relation to the lives of most of her contemporaries: 'we are not hindered from studying, since we are allowed so much idle time that we know not how to pass it away'.[14] Just how limited her analysis of women's oppression was by constraints of class is demonstrated by the fact that the condemnation of 'discourse so unsavory', which provides the title of my essay, is not an attack by men on women's writing, but a Lady's attack on the language of working people:

> The meaner sort of people are not onely ignorant of the purity of their native Language, but corrupteth what they have, and being always groveling in the dung of the earth, where all their thoughts are imployed, which makes their discourse so unsavory. (*The Worlds Olio*, pp. 17–18)

II Women commanded by God

It is relatively easy to establish a list of Margaret Cavendish's published works, to read them and gain a sense of the scope of her concerns. Much women's writing of the period, however, belongs to ephemeral forms, making it impossible to know how representative is what has survived. More than one half of the extant writings of the decade, for instance – some 70 texts – are politico-religious tracts which address the key social concerns of the Interregnum. The great majority of these were written by members of the Society of Friends (Quakers), which might seem to indicate that women were more visible there than in the contemporary sects of the Baptists, Seekers or Muggletonians. The figures are skewed, though, by the Quaker decision in 1672 to collect and preserve two copies of all writings produced by their movement since its inception.[15] Other groups made no such attempt, and we shall never know how many pamphlets were lost as a result. Bearing in mind these reservations, however, some general observations can be made concerning the religio-political tracts that have survived.

Of these 70 texts, written by 34 women (some of whom wrote jointly with one another or with men), only four went into more than one edition. Lady Eleanor Douglas's *The Benediction* was published three times in 1651, and her *Given to the Elector Prince Charles* [1651], like Mary Cary's *The Resurrection of the Witnesses* (1653), was a new edition of an original that had come out in 1648. Martha Simmons's *A Lamentation For the Lost Sheep* was brought out in both 1655 and 1656, and Anne Audland's *A True Declaration of the Suffering of the Innocent* was printed both as a separate and as part of the collective *The Saints Testimony Finishing through Suffering* in 1655. The rarity of a woman's writing being reprinted, combined with the fact that two-thirds (i.e., 22) of the religio-political tract writers of the period each published only a single text, might indicate how difficult it was for women to have such writings published. Judging by the frequency with which St Paul's instruction to the Corinthians, 'Let your women keep silence in the churches' (1 Corinthinians 14.34–5), appears in the writings of the period, it seems likely that a specific religious embargo was added to the general social pressures for feminine modesty to discourage women from writing such works. None the less, eleven of the women publishing tracts in the 1650s went on to publish again in later years.

What were these writings about? The most prolific woman writer of the seventeenth century, and specifically of the 1650s, was Lady Eleanor Douglas (earlier Davies, née Touchett).[16] The 13 titles she published in the 1650s include *The Appearance or Presence Of The Son of Man* (1650), which survives only in a fragment, breaking off at the point where the author is tracing her claim to be a 'She-Counsellor . . . Made like unto the Son of God' (p. 8), related to or identical with the female deity of a 'woman clothed with the sun' found in Revelation 12. It is fitting that a text which appears to have been destroyed because of its blasphemous implication of the author's divinity should make use of imagery that alludes to a punishment inflicted on 'seditious' printers, the destruction of their near-irreplaceable type.[17] Lady Eleanor's (and God's) enemies are threatened with becoming 'Those Heathen Potentates, but like to Potters brittle Vessels broken in pieces, scattered, suddenly a Printers Press like' (p. 4). In the years before the revolution, when state control over the press was thoroughly policed, the government might have been able to destroy the printer's work and stop the writer publishing, but Lady Eleanor reminds the present authorities that they are themselves answerable to a God whose vengeance will shatter them.

The extreme condensation of Lady Eleanor's language here, and the implicit assumption that the reader is entirely conversant with biblical text and commentaries, are typical of her work. (The phrase 'Potters brittle Vessels broken in pieces' alludes to God's threat to punish 'rebellious children' who disregard his prophet, Isaiah 30.14.) Similar imagery and themes appear in *Of Times and Seasons Their Mystery* (1651) which is likewise concerned to establish the author's claims to blessedness;[18] and in *The Benediction* (1651) she makes use of anagrams (a favoured device) and dense biblical allusion to celebrate Oliver Cromwell's return from his murderous expedition to Ireland. A cursory reading of these materials makes it evident that she offers us a closely argued interpretation of the events of the civil war period. Far more detailed study of her pamphlets and their relationship with the Bible will have to be made if we are to produce a properly informed account of our most prolific seventeenth-century woman writer.

Even such a fleeting acquaintance with Lady Eleanor's prophecies alerts us to the condensed language and implicit political imperatives that are to be found in the religio-political writings of the time. Her social position – she was by birth and marriage an aristocrat, with the financial means to have her works published abroad during the 1630s, as well as to see more than 60 of her works into print between 1640 and 1650 – was, however, unusual. If her position as a female member of the ruling class gave her some sense of a right to write and publish, the great majority of women prophets of the decade, like their male counterparts, were of the 'middling sort' of people.[19] Taking on an identity as God's handmaidens and servants, however, they were able to publish pamphlets concerning local and national justice and affairs of state, explaining their activities as the inevitable outcome of God's command. (See, for example, the writings of Dorothy White and Rebeckah Travers, Jeane Bettris's *A Lamentation*, Sarah Blackborow's *A Visit To The Spirit*, Mary Howgill's *A Remarkable Letter of Mary Howgill To Oliver Cromwell*, and Margaret Killin and Barbara Patison's *A Warning from the Lord to the Teachers & People of Plimouth*.) In common with many people of the time, they believed that they were living through the last days before the second coming of Christ, and the title-pages and marginalia of their writings make frequent reference to the promise in Joel 2.28–9:

> I will pour out of my spirit upon all flesh; and your sons and your daughters shall prophesy, your old men shall dream dreams, your young men shall see visions: And also upon the servants and upon the handmaids in those days will I pour out my spirit.[20]

Inspired by hopes of the coming millennium, women sectaries (Quakers, Baptist, Seekers) argued in church against ministers' interpretations of the Bible, some even leaving their families to travel and spread God's message. In *A Lamentation For the Lost Sheep Of the House of Israel* (1655), Martha Simmons recalls her many years of seeking for insight into God's will, during which time, 'he kept me still from running after men' (p. 6). Having realized that she needs to turn to God's light within her rather than looking to others for spiritual guidance, she ends her pamphlet calling on her women readers to follow her example, telling them, 'and this is my beloved, and this is my friend O daughters of Jerusalem' (p. 6).

Such behaviour was not presented by these women prophets as an unfeminine rejection of subservience, but as a response to God's undeniable command. Dorothy White's *A Diligent Search* (1659), for instance, opens with her explanation of the origin of her writing:

> Upon the 25th day of the second moneth, 59. as I was passing along the street, I heard a cry in me; again on the 26th day of the same Moneth, the same cry in me; againe on the 27th day, the same cry in me, And I was waiting upon the Lord in silence, the word of the Lord came unto me, saying, write, and again I say write. (p. 1)

A similar passage appears in Anna Trapnel's *The Cry of a Stone* (1654), where the prophet, in one of her famous trances, reflects that her opponents

> will say the spirit of madness and distraction is upon her, and that it is immodesty; but thou knowest Lord, that it is thy Spirit; for thou cast thy servant where she would not, and hast taken her contrary to all her thoughts. (p. 67)

This apparent passivity could be reconciled with women's traditional silence, but the explanation did not always impress those who arrested and jailed travelling preachers. After Anna Trapnel visited Cornwall to preach, sent there, she claims, by God against her will, she was imprisoned and spent some time in Bridewell, publishing her *Legacy* there.[21] In 1655 Dorothy Waugh was sentenced to the scold's bridle (a punishment traditionally reserved for nagging wives) when she was arrested for preaching,[22] and the collectively written *The Saints Testimony* (1655) includes descriptions of the prosecution for preaching of various Quakers including Anne Audland, Margaret Vivers and Sarah Tims, the last of whom was reimprisoned when refusing to be bound over to good behaviour:

> Then she desired to know by what law they committed her; and one *John Austine*, called Mayor, answered, *that sweeping the house, and washing dishes was the first point of law to her* (or words to that effect) so sent her back to prison. (p. 8)

It is not surprising that many pamphlets of the period focus on the rage of those unjustly imprisoned.[23]

Male church ministers and magistrates sought to silence such women but, clear in their conviction that they were obeying a higher master, women sectaries expressed their fury time and again, often having their works published whilst in prison for their activities. Priscilla Cotton's single-sheet broadside *As I was in the Prison-house* (1656), for instance, ends by referring her reader to the words of (female) wisdom in Proverbs 1, predicting that at Christ's arrival, 'I also will laugh at your Calamity, I will mock when your fear cometh'. Dorothy White concludes in similar vein: 'the Lord God is coming to shake you like a leaf, & to break down your invented imagined Laws, made by your evil hearts' (*Upon the 22 day*, p. 2).

Though their opponents often identified unwomanly behaviour as a crucial component in the crimes of such women, a straightforward concern with women's role was by no means the central element of their writings. Many of them, like their male contemporaries, were concerned with the 'great overturning' that was to come, that Christ at his arrival would 'turne the World upside down. That that which hath ruled over may be brought down under, and that which hath been of low degree may be raised up in the power of God, to rule and have dominion' (Dorothy White, *A Diligent Search*, p. 4, alluding to Isaiah 24 and Acts 17.6).

One of the most extended analyses of such ideas written in the period is found in the books of Mary Cary. A Fifth Monarchist, she was actively engaged in preparing the way for the 'fifth monarchy', the predicted period of Christ's personal reign on earth. She was a gentlewoman, and her carefully structured books – *The Resurrection of the Witnesses* (1648 and 1653) reads like a catechism or logic exercise, and is peppered with extensive marginal references – led to her being favourably compared in the work's dedicatory epistles to the two most famous of contemporary learned ladies, Queen Elizabeth of Bohemia and Anna Maria van Schurman. Elsewhere, having demonstrated at length the grounds for her belief that the second coming of Christ was at hand and should be fought for with 'the material sword', she goes on to recommend to the Parliament of Saints a wide range of specific legal reforms 'concerning The Propagation of the Gospel, New modling of the Universities, Reformation of the Laws, supply of necessities to the poor' (*Twelve Humble Proposals*, 1653, title-page). In the second half of *The Little Horns Doom and Downfall* (1651), she also included a utopian vision entitled *A New and More Exact Mappe or, Description of New Jerusalems Glory when Jesus Christ and his Saints with him shall reign on earth a Thousand years*. Her vision for the imminently expected future includes the ending of the idleness of the rich (that idleness which Margaret Cavendish connected with her sex rather than her class) – 'such idle and profane creatures shall then have no allowance or sufferance to live such lives as now they do' (p. 308) – and a promise that:

> No infant of days shall die; none shall die while they are young; all shall come to a good old age. They shall not be afflicted for the loss of their children . . . . And old men and women shall live till they come to a good old age till they walk with a staff in their hand for age. (pp. 289–90)

In shorter pamphlets, other prophets (like Margaret Fell) call Jews to convert to Christianity (believed to be a necessary precondition for the second coming), criticize the way in which enclosure is robbing the poor of land (Margret Braidley), and rebuke Cromwell for allying himself with his erstwhile enemies (Anna Trapnel, Mary Howgill). On God's behalf, Margaret Killin declares, 'Wo to all you proud and lustfull ones, who feeds on dainty dishes, and spends the creation upon your lusts. Cumber not the ground ye fruitless trees, for the Lord God of life and power is come' (A Warning from the Lord, 1655, p. 6).

Such protests are linked to extensive criticism of the church hierarchy, and repeated calls for an end to 'preaching for hire', the support of church ministers by tithes (a tax of ten per cent on everyone, ostensibly used to support the ministers of the national church, though monies were often lawfully pocketed by local landlords).[24] Sectaries saw the continuation of the imposition of tithes after the supposed abolition of a national church as clear evidence that the state was maintaining centralized ideological control. Arguing for 'freedom of conscience', they believed that it was especially unjust that they be required to provide financial support for ministers whose services they avoided and whose opinions they abhorred. Many individual pamphlets argue against this 'filthie and horrible thing',[25] including Grace Barwick's appeal To all present Rulers in 1659; and in that same year Quakers organized a mass women's petition, containing many thousands of signatures demanding the abolition of tithes and the implementation of other wide-ranging legal reforms.[26] These include a call for the abolition of the universities, the training-ground of church ministers and lawyers, echoing earlier individual protests against an over-dependence on book-learning in theological disputes, something that had traditionally excluded women and other 'uneducated people' from debating. In 1655, for instance, Hester Biddle threatened, in God's name, to burn to the ground the two university towns, and in the following year Ann Gargill's Of That Which is called the Popish Religion repeated the suggestion. Gargill analyses at length the connections between Roman Catholicism and the tithe-supported ministers, asserting that 'the Spirit of Christ is plainness, it cometh not by study' (p. 24), and threatening her opponents:

The Son of righteousness will arise, and consume the works of your hands, and burn up your Schools of learning, and and [sic] your Libraries of Books, and all your compleated subtlety: against the living God of life have you acted confusion, and builded Babylon. This is the whore that sitteth upon many waters, the floods of iniquity you have suckt in, swiftly to the destruction of your souls. (p. 30)

Gargill's reference here to the Whore of Babylon, a biblical image commonly interpreted at the time as signifying the Catholic church and/ or the Anglican church under Charles I's Archbishop Laud, draws attention to the fact that, whilst questions of gender might not have been central to the sectaries' writings, an analysis of femininity was none the less an abiding concern. In several women's pamphlets, the Whore of Babylon is specifically compared to the pride and idleness of ruling-class women, and in particular to the queen (who was also a Catholic). Starting from the language of Revelation 18.7, which refers to the Whore as 'a queen', Priscilla Cotton and Mary Cole challenge their religious and political opponents:

> Thou sittest as a Queen and Lady over all, and will have the pre-eminence, and hast got into the seat of God, the consciences of the people, and what thou sayest must not be contradicted: if thou bid them fight and war, they obey it; if thou bid them persecute and imprison, they do it; so that they venture their Bodies and Souls to fulfil thy lusts of envy and pride. (*To the Priests*, 1655, p. 6)[27]

This attack on the ruling powers and on a class-specific femininity develops into an extended justification of women's activities as radical preachers and writers. Cotton and Cole show how the biblical assurance that 'we are all one both male and female in Christ Jesus' (p. 7, citing Galatians 3.28) can be taken to prove that it is not real live women who are forbidden, in St Paul's words, to speak in church. ('Let your women keep silence in the churches . . .', 1 Cor. 14.34–5.) The scriptures require a metaphorical interpretation, they insist. Just as the national church can be compared to the Whore of Babylon and thereby to the queen, the proper interpretation of 'women' in Paul's injunction is 'weakness whether male or female'. It is not women who may not preach, but those who are 'weak' because they are not inspired by God: most likely, the male church ministers who had visited Cotton and Cole in prison and whose behaviour had inspired them to write their pamphlet.

> Indeed, you your selves are the women, that are forbidden to speak in the Church, that are become women; for two of your Priests came to speak with us; and when they could not bear sound reproof and wholesome Doctrine, that did concern them, they railed on us with filthy speeches, as no other they can give to us, that deal plainly and simply with them, and so ran from us. (pp. 7–8)[28]

It is clear that these radical pamphlets merit a closer linguistic study than they have yet been afforded, one that would attend to the attempts made by women writers to analyse the inter-connections between gender, writing and politics of state.

III Devotional writings

These direct addresses to matters of state were not the only product of the development of the idea that each individual had a direct relationship with God. Several of the pamphlets discussed above also contain autobiographical passages, explaining how a woman's activities had led to her imprisonment and her experiences in gaol.[29] Other practices of the radical sects also prompted an increase in women's writing. Particularly important are the facts that those joining various Independent churches would often have passed through several years of religious doubt and isolation before finding like-minded people, and that new members of such congregations were expected to make a public declaration, sometimes in writing, of how they had come to their present beliefs. This requirement, allied to a more general interest in people's relationships with God, promoted the publication of spiritual autobiographies, and a number of women in the decade wrote accounts of their lives.[30]

The procedure for joining a church common to many Independent congregations is described by Susanna Parr in *Susanna's Apologie against the Elders. Or A Vindication* (1659). This closely argued book, which is presented as a refutation of charges brought against her by an Independent congregation of which she had been a founder member, opens with an explanation of her original reasons for seeking to leave the national church and a description of how the newly separated congregation was established. People wishing to join this group must give an autobiographical account, she explains, detailing their reasons for believing themselves to be amongst the elect, and therefore assured of a place in heaven: 'We must have an account of a change from a naturall and legall estate, into an estate of grace and believing, of those whom we admitted into communion with us' (p. 10).[31] Church members were expected to express their opinions of the accounts given and vote on whether to admit the applicant. To make such decisions unanimous, women had to speak in church, and Susanna Parr asserts that she was shocked at this unfamiliar behaviour:

> Though I pleaded my Sex, my naturall and sinfull infirmities, which made me unfit to speak unto others, yet he [Lewis Stuckley, the congregation's minister] pressed it on me as my duty. (pp. 9–10)

It would seem that this matter swiftly became the topic of another debate: when Parr and other women began to express opinions not welcomed by male church elders, the congregation's policy, she tells us, was reversed – one of the charges brought against Parr by Stuckley was that she had contended for women's speaking. These events suggest that the issue of women's access to language and the relationship of this to their social position was a major site of struggle in the period, as do observations made by John Rogers in 1653 when he published a collection of 'confessions of faith' by both women and men, *Ohel or Beth-shemesh.* There, he asserts women's 'right to vote, offer, object, concurre in and consent to all things that concern the benefit of the whole body' (p. 468), whilst carefully adding that men must still maintain authority outside this realm.

Susanna's Apologie is armed not only with biblical allusions to justify Parr's behaviour and beliefs but also with detailed references to major theological works of the day. Many other such texts of the decade demonstrate careful and detailed study over many years, as women passed through periods of religious doubt and, often, devastating feelings of isolation. (Although, to some extent, the progression from 'a naturall and legall estate, into an estate of grace and believing' was a formulaic one, imposing on women and men a need to find and emphasize such experiences in their pasts, the variety of these accounts is sufficient to indicate that they cannot be simply explained away by the idea that women were merely using a religious 'format'.)[32] Jane Turner's *Choice Experiences Of The Kind dealings of God before, in, and after Conversion* (1653), for instance, gives a detailed record and analysis of her search for kindred spirits, describing the books she read, meetings she attended, and recording her emotions. All this appears to have been conducted independently of her husband, though she records as one of her greatest blessings that he had, on his own initiative, come to the same religious conclusions as herself. On her return to a Baptist congregation after a period as a Quaker she celebrates the fact

> that the Lord should vouchsafe this mercy to both of us, & that at one & the same time; and that at our return he should manifest such a sweet acceptance of us, melting our hearts into tears of joy, to our mutual comfort in the Lord, and in each other. (pp. 131–2)[33]

A comparable independence from male judgment is displayed in *A Wise Virgins Lamp Burning, Or, God's sweet incomes of Love to a gracious soul waiting for him,* by Anne Venn. The daughter of John Venn the political radical and regicide, she accompanied her parents to Puritan meetings in the 1630s, taking more and more responsibility for her own spiritual well-being as she passed through long years of doubt and isolation, and recording details of her changes of heart in notebooks used as a basis for her autobiographical account. Whilst she always writes of her father with respect, expressing obedience, she none the less presents herself as the initiator of their mutual decision to leave an unsatisfactory congregation (p. 21), and her narrative ends with her account of her role in establishing a separatist church.

These narratives indicate how threatening spiritual independence could be to the hierarchy of the family, where the father or husband had traditionally held moral authority. An Collins's *Divine Songs and Meditacions* of 1653 (a remarkable collection of poetry that makes imaginative use of nature imagery and experimental verse forms) opens with a long poem exploring the affects on families of religious and political differences.

> This is the cause of home debates,
>   And much domestick woes,
> That one may find his houshold mates
>   To be his greatest foes.

The anonymous poet of *Eliza's Babes* is less distressed by such eventualities, celebrating a personal relationship with God as a welcome escape from the demands of courtship and marriage. She addresses a suitor:

> My heart I will still keep, take thou thine own,
> My heart is happy when disturb'd by none.
> Without a heart I know you cannot live,
> Therefore your own I freely to you give.
> Mine is in heaven, and will admit no change,
> To leave my rest in heaven, on earth to range.
> I'd have it written in my happy story,
> None had my heart but heav'ns great prince of glory. (p. 30)

When marriage looms none the less, she reflects sardonically of her husband-to-be: 'My body here he may retain,/My heart in heaven, with thee must reigne' (p. 42). It is scarcely surprising that the sects were seen as so disruptive to social order and family hierarchy, or that John Rogers, whilst asserting women's right to an active role in the church, should add, 'In a word, I say to all, Those whom God hath joyned together, let no man put asunder' (*Ohel*, p. 477).

In recognizing this, it might seem that my analysis of the period has come full circle, and that I am suggesting that such writings are assimilable to a modern definition of feminism. Such a reading is a distortion, since neither these texts, nor the experiences that preceded them, in any straightforward way represent women's autonomy, or offer us a 'feminist' message simply recognizable in twentieth-century terms. The process of transition to a 'state of grace' often entailed an abandonment of the self, a turning over of everything to God. Sarah Wight's *A Wonderful Pleasant and Profitable Letter* (1656) records the reappearance[34] of religious doubt in her mind after the death of her dearly loved brother. She has had to learn to accept God's will in all things, bowing to his instruction that 'he or she that loves any thing more than mee, is not worthy of me' (p. 47). Elizabeth Major, too, writes to warn her reader to take her experiences as a lesson and not question God's will. She explains how she was struck down by a painful and cripping illness 'in the prime of my years' (*Honey on the Rod*, sig. A4). She was forced to return home to her father's house from her service in 'a great and honourable Family', and spent all her savings trying to find a medical cure, 'and this, O this, was my great evil' (sig. h2ᵛ). God has punished her like a naughty child for her presumption – 'he was pleased to own me as one of the poor Scholars in the Schooll, of the lowest Form, and according to my weakness he dealt with me' (sig. A5) – and she has had to learn to accept her crippled state and not struggle to recover. This acceptance has made it possible for her to write her *Honey on the Rod: Or a comfortable Contemplation for one in Affliction* (1656), in which she explores with authority many moral issues, ending her book with a series of poems which, being acrostics, represent her name (like her body), broken and remade into an object to teach others:

> On the Authors Name
> E ternal God, open my blinded eyes,
> L ighten my sadded heart that in me lies:
> I ncrease thy grace in me, indear my heart,
> S avior, to thee, by faith to have a part
> A bove with thee in glory, there to shine,
> B eloved with that lasting love of thine:
> E vil is my life, I walk in earthen ways,
> T each me thy path, in it to spend my days;
> H ear me in him on whom hopes Anchor stays.
> M ercy, O Savior, teach me to ask aright,
> A nd then for comfort, 'tis thy chief delight:
> I beg and faint, I fear and hope again,
> O Lord, I see all self, and earth is vain,
> R enouncing all, on thee Lord, I remain.

This annihilation of the self as a necessary precondition for a woman's appearance in print is also suggested in other ways in many of these books. Anne Venn's account of her experiences was not published until after her death, and the version of her life made available by her male editors is a partial one, offered to the reader as a moral example of self-denial. Jane Turner's book appeared prefaced by lengthy recommendations to the reader from her husband and other men. Sarah Wight's was apparently published without her prior consent; it too is prefaced by male interpretations of its significance. An account of Elizabeth Moore's life, her *Evidences for Heaven*, appeared only as part of Edmund Calamy's argument against separation from the national church, and was again probably heavily edited, since his explicit purpose was to present her as a model of suffering and forbearance.[35]

What these texts do offer us, however, is a complex account of the interrelationships between femininity and religious belief in the decade: a more complex picture indeed than there is space to trace here, as I have not analysed the differences introduced by the women's class origins, or by the different sects to which they belonged.[36] What is clear, though, is that these writings are a fruitful source of information about how women at the time understood the constraints of gender and its connections to other matters. To attempt to account for the period without examining these texts is seriously to distort women's concerns at that time, imposing on the decade an anachronistic sense of what was or was not a 'woman's issue'.[37]

The daughters of Behn

and the problem of reputation

Jeslyn Medoff

In 1680 John Dryden praised Aphra Behn's paraphrase of the Ovidian epistle 'Oenone to Paris', by generously excusing her inability to read Latin, claiming that she put better-educated translators to shame. Nine years later his epilogue to Behn's posthumously published play, *The Widow Ranter*, importuned the audience to receive kindly her 'orphan child'. A few months before his death in 1700, however, Dryden advised the aspiring poet Elizabeth Thomas (1675–1731) against emulating Behn:

> avoid . . . the Licenses which Mrs. *Behn* allowed her self, of writing loosely, and giving, (if I may have leave to say so) *some Scandal to the Modesty of her Sex*. I confess, I am the last Man who ought, in Justice to arraign her, who have been myself too much a Libertine in most of my Poems, which I should be well contented *I had time either to purge or to see them fairly burned.*[1]

Dryden's ostensibly self-deprecating gesture and his new attitude toward Behn point to what has traditionally been defined as a change in English literary and theatrical taste, a movement away from the 'licence' of the age and towards a more 'moral' and sentimental outlook. Reaction to 'Libertinism and Profaneness . . . Idleness and Gallantry' had begun long before King William III found satisfaction in Jeremy Collier's *A Short View of the Immorality and Profaneness of the English Stage* (1698).[2] In analysing the demise of an era which redefined sexual boundaries, it makes sense to highlight the death of Aphra Behn on 16 April 1689, an event usually ignored or slighted in mainstream literary histories. As Behn's life and works reflect upheaval in the worlds of politics and letters, so her death, coming within weeks of the 'Glorious Revolution', signalled a kind of 'Inglorious Revolution' for women writers.

Women poets of Behn's own time – Elizabeth Taylor (later Mrs

Wythens and then Mrs Colepepper), whose poems appear in Behn's 1685 *Miscellany*; the still-unidentified 'Ephelia'; and Rochester's niece, Anne Wharton – regarded her with respect, even though her work was read as autobiography and used against her personal reputation. Matthew Prior equated Behn with her courtesan heroine, Angellica Bianca of *The Rover* (1677), and suggested that she was best suited for writing sex comedies since she could 'describe the cunning of a Jilting Whore' from first-hand experience.[3] Gilbert Burnet, a man of great power, warned Anne Wharton in 1682 to stop corresponding with Behn, pronouncing her an 'abominably vile' woman who 'rallies not only all Religion but all Virtue in so odious and obscene a manner . . . .'[4] Near the time of her death, Behn and her emulator 'Ephelia', author of *Female Poems on Several Occasions* (1679 and 1682), were vilified in lines that might deter any would-be woman writer:

> Their wants by prostitution were supplied;
> Show but a tester you might up and ride:
> For punk and poetess agree so pat
> You cannot well be this, and not be that.[5]

In spite of 'Punk and Poetess' equations, Behn wrote and published without apologizing for her sex, disclaiming any interest in fame, or feigning an unwillingness to appear in the public eye. In her own words, she valued fame as if she had been born a hero.

Behn's association with actresses like Nell Gwynn, for whom she wrote, and with noted rakes and wits like Rochester and Buckingham, combined with her subject matter, made it possible for subsequent generations to devalue her status and defuse the impact of her words. Although her male contemporaries were also subject to neutralizing refashioning (Burnet's story of Rochester's death-bed repentance is one example) or to reactive condemnation after their deaths, the effect was greater in Behn's case. Her life, works and reputation stood as both an encouragement and a warning to the women writing after her, who could not evaluate her work without the spectre of the 'Punk Poetess' hovering before them. Behn's last years were marred by poverty and illness, and her reputation, particularly as a woman, declined rapidly in the 1690s and the early eighteenth century. The term 'Inglorious Revolution' signifies the changes that took place after Behn's death. Women writers who followed in her wake would have to make conscious decisions about accepting, rejecting or refashioning her precedents, not only in style and subject matter but in the personae of their writings, in the personae they, as authors, would assume in public (in formal letters, prefaces, dedications and the like), and in the way they tried to control their reputations as women, which were essentially inseparable from their reputations as writers.

The effect of Behn's influence on her successors is not so much Bloomian 'anxiety' about usurping the position of the father (or mother) figure as it is a self-consciousness determined largely by the fate of Behn's reputation. The women who wrote in the generation after Aphra Behn were strongly affected by society's reception (or rejection) of her, well aware that they were writing in a new era that required different methods for coping with the problem of combining femaleness and fame.[6] As the eighteenth century progressed, Behn's daughters (in their late years) and granddaughters continued to assail (as Behn had done) the 'mistaken rules' that held them back, but they no longer employed the terms of heroic 'valour' common in her era.[7] Instead, they used rhetorical questions and lengthy conditional clauses to present their case, with the emphasis on argumentation and reason, writing like persuaders rather than warriors. While reflecting an overall conversion from seventeenth-century militaristic, zealous discourse to the eighteenth-century language of balance and logic, this approach also demonstrates the special situation of women writers at this later date, writers who were aware of the forms of expression available to them and sensitive to the limitations in their range of options. The present study examines how some of these women revealed this awareness through their published works and letters, through their manner of suppressing early notoriety that might prove embarrassing in their mature years, and through the tactics they employed in a new age that operated with a new set of 'rules'.

For the women after Aphra, the immaculate image of Behn's predecessor, Katherine Philips, 'The Matchless Orinda', seemed the sole alternative to that of the 'Punk Poetess'. Philips was particularly skilful in establishing and maintaining a public persona that became a model to female successors. Unlike Behn, she assiduously claimed to be averse to fame; her poetry exalted platonic friendship and country refinement in the politest, most acceptable terms, and productions of her translations of Corneille were well received. Unlike Behn and her successors in the theatre, Philips did not write for profit nor was her position in society questioned. Only recently has her celebration of love between women been regarded by some as subversive. For nearly a century after her death, women poets were sure to be compared to 'Orinda'. Though she said nothing about Philips's persona, Behn herself expressed hope that her work would become immortal like that of Sappho and Orinda.[8]

A kind of immortality is claimed for Behn in 'An Elegy Upon The Death of Mrs. A. Behn; The Incomparable Astrea. By a Young Lady of

Quality', perhaps Delarivier Manley, which appeared as a broadside within days of Behn's death.[9] The 'young lady' grants Behn a hero's commemoration. For her, Behn's death is an event of epic proportions, moving her 'untaught, unpractis'd' Muse to poetry for the first time, to praise 'wise' Behn's 'moving' numbers and 'Charming Accents'. As the poet sees it, Behn stepped into Orinda's position as 'the' woman writer but now there is no one qualified to wear Behn's mantle:

> Who now, of all the inspired Race,
> Shall take *Orinda*'s Place?
>   Or who the Hero's Fame shall raise?
>   Who now shall fill the Vacant Throne?
>   The bright *Astrea*'s gone . . . .
> Of her own Sex, not one is found
>   Who dares her Laurel wear,
>   Withheld by Impotence or Fear . . . .

The poem signals the end of an era; Behn's laurels are 'intomb'd with her, and never to return'. Although Behn's death inspired the author of this elegy to pick up her pen in tribute, she predicts that now there will be no poetical female successors with enough 'Presumption' or 'Courage' to replace Astrea. Daughters, it seems, there are none, except the self-deprecating poet herself.

Behn's praises are sung in true heroic fashion; she is depicted as a military hero, a monarch, a saint, and the champion of her sex. With her death, 'Aspiring Man has now regain'd the Sway / To them we've lost the Dismal Day . . . to them with Grief we yield / The Glorious envy'd Field'. Her passing is cause for 'all our Hopes [to] despair and dye, / Our Sex for ever shall neglected lye'. This elegy substitutes the entire female sex for the customary figure of the bereaved homeland, in a significant variation on the traditional lament for the irreplaceable bard or hero. In addition, the author complicates the elegiac convention of bemoaning the lack of a fitting successor by displaying 'anxiety' over filling her throne. However, the elegy is more intricate than that. Embedded within the encomium lies overt criticism of Behn's personal lack of 'Virtue'. In the penultimate stanza, the author attributes to Behn 'the softest sense' in Love, but finds 'failure' and 'sin' in Astrea for practising 'what she taught'. 'Too much Wit' in describing the 'Mysteries of Love' is seen as a 'fault'. Astrea will be greeted in Elysium not only by Orinda but also by 'Amorous Lovers' since she surpasses even Ovid in paying homage to 'Sacred Love'. The Behn of this elegy is certainly important as a model but she also functions as a Great Warning.

Unlike other critics, Behn's daughter does not assume that Astrea's unchastity disqualifies her as a poet; in fact, she salutes her in terms like those used to pay homage to Orinda. The language of power and competition used in this elegy, the purposeful location within a literary battle of the sexes, is similar to a remarkable commendatory poem by one of Orinda's early admirers, an Irishwoman known only as 'Philo-Philippa', who proclaims Philips to be 'the glory of our Sex, envy of men' and declares that her 'more than masculine Pen hath rear'd / Our Sex; first to be prais'd, next to be fear'd'. Because of Philips, 'Phoebus to Cynthia must his beams resigne, / The rule of Day, and Wit's now Feminine'.[10] The pens of both Orinda and Astrea are seen as mighty weapons in the struggle. This mode of heroic celebration survives as far as a poem by Elizabeth Thomas in praise of Lady Chudleigh ('Rise! Rise ye Heroins, secure the Field') which again doubts whether other women are equal to the challenge.[11] According to their women admirers, these female 'champions' are forces which cannot be easily dismissed or replaced.

Critical acclaim for Orinda's poetry and widespread approval of her chaste and modest persona, combined with the proliferation of religious and political publications by women during the Interregnum and the popularity of Behn's work during the Restoration, made it relatively unproblematic for women writers in the late seventeenth century to get their works published.[12] Booksellers of the time were quite willing to attach a female designation to a romance, play or love lyric, preferably a young woman's full name. A woman was safer from notoriety when she was published as 'A Young Lady' or 'A Lady of Quality'; the problems began once her name became public. If her name appeared on the title-page, preface or dedication of a secular work and she gave the appearance of actively seeking fame, a woman risked having her name bandied about in lampoons and scandal fiction, touted about town by ambitious booksellers, and used in 'commendatory' poems that flattered her in compromisingly light tones.

For example, one of many male-authored commendatory poems prefaced to Jane Barker's 1688 Poetical Recreations (published in a format closely resembling Behn's 1685 Miscellany) is particularly awkward. 'S.C., Esquire' begins by comparing Barker (whose full name appears on the title-page) to Orinda, but he actually uses the occasion as a pretext for a satirical attack on male poets of the age, including 'Revolting Jack' Dryden, who is outdone by Barker's 'modest Style' and 'chast Lines'.[13] The poem's birth imagery carries demeaning implications, surpassing Cowley's well-intentioned 'Upon Mrs Philips Her Poems' (which finds 'so much room/In the unexhausted and unfathom'd womb' of Orinda's brain, and claims that the 'birth' of Philips's poems, her 'immortal Progeny', avoids 'th' ancient Curse to Woman-kind' by causing her no pain, travail, or labour).[14] In 'S.C.'s' verses, poets Thomas Shadwell and Elkanah Settle 'yield' to Barker's ability to bring forth 'Fancy well-shap't' with 'less noise and pain' than male poets. Barker's male counterparts, after great 'din', can give birth only to 'some poor crude Sooterkin' which makes Jacob Tonson, the noted bookseller, 'vex't he e'er put in' (sig. a). Such a tone, which betrays a perception of writing women as primarily sexual beings, can only have caused difficulty for a woman whose literary persona was chaste and emphatically un-Behnlike. About a decade later, correcting the early published poems 'by her own hand', Barker asserted in an Orinda-like fashion that they had been published 'without her consent' and deleted passages which presumably had been inserted by other hands or were now considered inappropriate for public view.[15] In Barker's later novels, addressed to female readers, revised versions of her early poems are ostensibly written by a heroine who emulates the Matchless Orinda and disparages Behn.[16] Yet Barker's actions lean towards Behn: she publishes with her full name on the title page.

An extreme case of a woman writer whose reputation suffered by association with a disreputable bookseller is that of Elizabeth Thomas, who had been warned early in her writing career against emulating Behn, and who shared with her the financial need that inspired literary production. Her *Miscellany Poems on Several Subjects* (1722) seems designed to present its author as an educated, opinionated, yet still respectable woman, but her association with Edmund Curll counteracted whatever her poetry might have said for her. The poems pay polite homage to dead women friends, influential poets (male and female) and family members. Acknowledging inspiration from Mary Astell and Lady Chudleigh, they gently but firmly urge women to devote their time to 'the Culture of the Mind', admitting that women who have 'resign'd' their power to husbands have 'little time' for this, but suggesting that women hold the right to acquire learning before marriage (pp. 117; 182–3).

The poems, reissued in 1726 and appearing in a second edition in 1727, did not prevent Thomas from being imprisoned for debt in 1727. Her friends and family long dead, Thomas now became a 'creature' of Edmund Curll: that is, she wrote for hire for him, as Behn had for the theatres. She assisted him in publishing Pope's correspondence, probably in writing *Codrus, or the Dunciad Dissected* (1729), and in publishing a fabricated account of Dryden's funeral. To this day, she has been overwhelmed by ill repute ever since Pope portrayed 'Curll's Corinna' as a physically incontinent whore (*Dunciad*, II, II. 69–72), making cruel, perverted use of Thomas's painful and life-threatening intestinal ailments, reported in an appendix to *Pylades and Corinna* (1731–2), Curll's collection of Thomas's posthumously published letters. With no substantiation, she is still assumed to have been the mistress of Henry Cromwell, one of Pope's friends. Ironically, she had never cultivated a radically defiant or liberated literary persona. In accordance with Dryden's advice, Thomas had approved of the 'Cadence' of Behn's verse, but disapproved of the 'Licentiousness of her Morals'.[17] The 'evidence' of Thomas's poems has long been forgotten, but her reputation, tarnished beyond that of Behn, remains.[18] More clearly than Barker, she shows what dangers were courted by the woman writer.

Unlike Thomas, the women playwrights whose works appeared on the London stage just seven years after Behn's death – Delarivier Manley, Mary Pix and, to a lesser extent, Catharine Trotter (later Cockburn) – had obvious qualifications for the title of 'Daughters of Behn'. Pix and Manley seem to have been unconcerned to retrieve their reputations as 'respectable' women, or quickly became too much a part of the world of theatre, politics, intrigue and public scandal to attempt it. As soon as their first plays were produced in 1696, satires attacked them for daring to emerge on the scene after Philips and Behn ('Astrea' or 'Sappho'). Pix was condemned for 'very pertinaciously, malipertly, unjustly, and peremptorily . . . unworthily, fraudulently, and sacriligiously' writing fiction and plays.[19] Manley was seen as 'usurp[ing] that Province of Poetry no ways belonging or appertaining to her, for few *Sappho*'s or *Orinda*'s appear now upon the stage' (p. 39). Her 'Fame' was found to be 'none of the best, by reason she keeps very unseasonable Hours, and is a great frequenter of Taverns and Musick-Houses, and the like places . . . she writes like a self-conceited, and opinionative Female' (pp. 40–1).

In spite of Behn's precedent (or perhaps because of it), as women writers for the stage Manley, Pix and Trotter were seen as pioneers, resented for their activity (and success) in the profession. Richard Steele's *Spectator* essay of 28 April 1711 demonstrates the disparity between the treatment of male and female playwrights in the years following Behn's death. Declaring that 'no one ever writ Bawdry for any other Reason but Dearth of Invention', Steele lit on *She Would if She Could* (1668) by 'Polite Sir George Etherege'. He observes that Etherege made 'the Desire of Multiplying our Species' the entire basis of the play but notes that 'the Play has always been well received'. Pix and Behn are then discussed in a different tone: 'It is remarkable, that the Writers of least Learning are best skill'd in the luscious Way. The Poetesses of the Age have done Wonders in this kind . . . .' 'Female Compositions' by Pix and Behn are cited by their titles, Pix's *Ibrahim* (1696) and Behn's *The Rover* (1677), but the authors remain nameless.[20] Although Pix and Manley appear to have been impervious to *ad feminam* attacks, the young Catharine Trotter, like her contemporary the neophyte poet Elizabeth Singer (later Rowe), moved quickly to detach herself from the Behn-Manley 'school' of public personae.

While Manley embraced the concept of woman writer as threateningly sexual (see the essay by Ros Ballaster in this volume), Trotter and Singer strove to create public images that would be acceptable in the post-Restoration era. Close in age, both Trotter and Singer began their careers in the 1690s, but within a decade both came to regret their early publications and affiliations. They asserted their status in the lower gentry and clerical classes and struggled to extricate themselves from potentially damaging youthful associations, adopting similar strategies for creating new images of themselves as women in the public eye. Their marriages, in 1708 and 1710 respectively, underscored their acceptable status and marked a change in their publishing patterns. Rowe, who was childless, wrote and published more frequently and with greater success; but in each case collected works were published two years after death, Rowe's edited by male relations, Cockburn's by a male family friend.[21] The two writers tried to preserve their works selectively (as did the editors of their posthumously published works), and in so doing, sought to form an image of the woman writer as exemplum to other women, a female in the public sphere who reinforces the private, domestic role of woman as moral guide and guardian. Rowe's strategies worked well: she was famous in her lifetime and for some generations afterwards as a moral and religious writer, her earliest works forgotten. Trotter, too, was successful in suppressing her early, risqué reputation, but the more acceptable, far more limited 'fame' she achieved died soon after her.

After an early debut in prose fiction, *Olinda's Adventures*, Trotter based her first play, *Agnes de Castro* (produced in December 1695), on Aphra Behn's translation of a French novel with the same title, but she never acknowledged her debt to Behn, unlike Thomas Southerne, another adapter of Behn's fiction.[22] The play was published anonymously; Trotter distanced herself from Behn by describing herself in the dedication as 'one who Conceals her Name, to shun that of Poetress'.[23] However, her authorship became common knowledge, and subsequent plays appeared with signed dedications or, in one case, with her name on the title-page. Soon after the production of *Agnes de Castro*, 16-year-old Trotter received a letter from a woman identified only as 'E.B.'

concerning Trotter's association with sister-playwright Delarivier Manley. The undated letter suggests that Trotter should not write a verse
commendation for the publication of Manley's comedy, *The Lost Lover*
(produced in March 1696), even though 'E.B.' has not yet seen the play. If
Trotter feels herself 'oblig'd' to praise Manley's work, 'E.B.' recommends *The Royal Mischief* (produced in April 1696), having heard that it
is 'something better'. She does 'not indeed suspect [Manley] should ever
prove a Rivall' to Trotter, who 'may dispute the Laurells with some of the
most noted of Our Sex'.[24] The tone and content of this letter are similar to
the warnings Anne Wharton and Elizabeth Thomas received about Behn.
'E.B.' seems to object to Manley on both moral and aesthetic grounds,
inseparable issues for women writers.

'E.B.'s' concerns about Trotter's associations are echoed in the known
letters of Trotter's friend Elizabeth Burnet, third wife of Bishop Gilbert
Burnet and author of a popular book of meditations and possibly of the
'E.B.' letters. When Trotter published *A Defence of Mr. Locke's Essay of
Human Understanding* (1702) anonymously, Mrs Burnet revealed to
Locke the identity of his young champion, but expressed great
reservations about the playwright's reputation, associations and her
conversion from the Church of England to the Church of Rome. After
attributing Trotter's writing for the stage to her 'mean circumstances' as
the daughter of a Scottish naval officer's impoverished widow, her friend
described Trotter as having 'a more then comon genius' and found it a
'great pety her studys are not better directed'.[25] When Locke indicated
that he wanted to present a gift to Trotter, she expressed more
reservations: 'the fassion of her religion which allows great libertys, her
stract curcumstances, and being forced as it were to write plays, and
consequently to contract Idle acquantance, has left great blemishes on
her reputation, and tho I am very willing to think her in great measure
injured, yet my charity will be laughed at if not sencured should I show
that regard that is due to her good understanding . . .' (*Correspondence*,
VII, pp. 650–1). In her next letter to Locke, Burnet retracted her
condemnation, pronounced herself 'more severe in my Caracture then I
ought to have ben', and, citing Trotter's 'great poverty', recommended
that they send her four or five guineas (VII, p. 702). Locke did in fact give
Trotter a gift of books and the Burnets provided financial assistance to
her and her indigent mother. Trotter, in turn, returned to the Church of
England, publishing an explanation of her conversion with an anonymous preface by Bishop Burnet.

Trotter also took 'E.B.'s' advice in writing for *The Royal Mischief*,
using the same tropes that Manley had used in her own commendatory

poem for Trotter's *Agnes de Castro*. Manley's poem envisages competition with men in phrases that echo the elegy on Behn and exhibit Manley's ambition to fill Astrea's 'vacant throne':

> *Orinda*, and the fair *Astrea* gone,
> Not one was found to fill the Vacant Throne:
> Aspiring man had quite regain'd the Sway,
> Again had taught us humbly to obey; . . .
> O! How I long in the Poetick Race,
> To loose the Reigns and give their Glory Chase;
> For thus Encourag'd, and thus led by you,
> Methinks we might more Crowns than theirs Subdue [sig. A2v].

Trotter's poem introduces an element of modesty not found in Manley's tribute. Finding her own 'force' to be 'too weak' to invade 'the Borders of [Men's] Empire', Trotter claims that she incited Manley's 'greater Genius' to assist her and to become the true champion of their sex.[26] She continued her association with Manley by contributing to *The Nine Muses* (1700), Manley's collection of elegies on Dryden, and by obtaining a contribution to that collection from Sarah, Lady Piers, but the Trotter-Manley friendship came to an end soon thereafter and 'E.B.'s' warning proved prescient.[27]

Of all Behn's daughters, Manley is the true heir. Unlike others of her time, Manley consistently worked in all the areas most dangerous for women writers (theatre, political pamphleteering, journalism and scandal fiction) and did not employ the self-protective tactics of Barker, Thomas, Trotter or Rowe. Just as 'gay Astrea' had got entangled with the authorities for an epilogue criticizing the Duke of Monmouth (and, unofficially, for anti-Whig sentiments), so Manley was arrested for writing *The New Atalantis* (1709), in which she characterized the sexual lives of prominent Whigs; she was probably inspired by the success of Behn's key novel, *Love-Letters from a Nobleman to His Sister* (1684-7). Like Behn, Manley combined the political with the sexual.

Manley's critics, like Behn's, used the same device of conflating politics and sexuality to castigate her. Soon after the publication of *The New Atalantis* she was described as 'formerly belonging to ye Play-house, and an Old Sinner'.[28] The Whigs called her 'the Lewdest Wretch in the Island . . . amidst her Lewdness and Infamy, is the greatest Fury of a Zealot . . . ever produced.'[29] Like Behn, Manley was perceived as a 'Great Warning' by many of her contemporaries.[30]

In the process of converting from a 'female poetess' to a Tory propagandist, Manley abandoned the sisterhood exhibited in her poem to Trotter. No longer interested in reinforcing the renown of her sex,

Manley disparaged not only prominent Whigs, but the very women she had once praised and supported, including Pix, Sarah Fyge Egerton, Piers and particularly Trotter. It appears that not even Behn was spared. In *Memoirs of Europe* (1710), we find Manley attacking her predecessor on moral grounds: '*Sapho* the Younger ... when living, was Owner of a Soul as amorous as the elder, yet wanted much of that Delicacy and all that nice, yet darting Spirit (of which hers is but a faint Imitation) so applauded in *Phaon*'s Mistress'.[31] Although keys to Manley's novels indentify 'Sapho the Younger' as Behn and it is possible that Behn is meant in this passage, there is a problem. In *The Memoirs of Europe*, 'Sapho the Younger' along with 'Cassius' (Wycherley), 'Corvino' (Congreve), 'Maro' (Addison), 'Gallus' (Prior), 'Lais' (Trotter) and 'Clarinda' (Sarah Fyge Egerton) are named as people whose portraits hang in the 'gallery' of 'Julius Sergius' (Charles Montagu, Earl of Halifax, 1661–1715). Halifax was well known as one of the most prominent patrons of his age; the 'gallery' is a figure for his patronage. Trotter dedicated *The Unhappy Penitent* (1701) to Halifax, as did Egerton her *Poems on Several Occasions* [1703]. Richard Basset, the publisher of *The Nine Muses* (1700), edited by Manley, dedicated that collection to him as well, but no work by Behn was dedicated to Halifax nor is there any known connection between Halifax and Behn.

On the other hand, 'Sapho' may indeed signify Behn, since this apparently gratuitous slap is not much different from the damning implications of the elegy that Manley probably wrote for her. Here Behn is not delicate (therefore, she is coarse) nor is she nice (therefore, she is undiscriminating), and certainly she is 'amorous'. The passage takes on even more importance when viewed in context; the tilt at 'Sapho the Younger' is used to introduce vilifications of two more women writers, former friends of Manley, whom she attacks both as women and as writers. Catharine Trotter, or 'Lais', is described as 'another of the Sex' who 'intrude[s] her self' as a 'Pretender' to the title of 'Master of the Muses'. She is presented as some kind of monster, 'this Thing without a Name', whose addresses to 'numerous Coxcombs' are often rejected. Her charms are 'the Leavings of the Multitude' (*Memoirs of Europe*, I, p. 289). Manley follows with a quick swipe at Sarah Fyge Egerton, who, for dedicating her *Poems on Several Occasions* [1703] to the Earl of Halifax, is described as 'so forbidding ... so shockingly ugly' and likened to a Fury (I, p. 290). In attacking these three women on the grounds of their physical appearance, their morality and their roles as writers, Manley incorporates the idea of Behn as negative model into her fiction and assumes an arch-masculine position. In her writing and perhaps in the example of her own reputation, Manley did as much as any male satirist to warn off her less audacious sister-writers.

Although Trotter was generally perceived as less audacious than Manley and Pix, she was not spared from being attacked along with them. In *The Female Wits* (produced in September 1696; published in 1704), a comedy aimed primarily at Manley, she was parodied as 'Calista, a lady that pretends to the learned languages, and assumes to herself the name of critic'.[32] Two years later, when Trotter and Pix became protégées of Congreve, they came in for a misogynist attack, replete with sexual innuendoes, as 'the two Female things . . . who flant in town / And flutter loosely but to tumble down'.[33] Trotter had more to lose by these attacks than Manley or Pix. She was young and unmarried, dancing on the edge of two worlds, flirting with danger in the public worlds of theatre and letters, and maintaining a hold on safer ground by keeping up relationships with women like Lady Piers and Elizabeth Burnet whose positions in life were higher and more secure.

Like other productions of the period, Trotter's plays dealt with sexual subject matter, but unlike Behn, Manley or Pix, Trotter presented herself as a reformer of the stage. Trotter's signed dedication of *Fatal Friendship* (1698) claimed that the play's 'End is the most noble, to discourage Vice, and recommend a firm unshaken Virtue', but in her representations of 'Vice' Trotter also satisfied her audience's taste for female characters of unbounded passion.[34] Lamira, a young widow and the villainess of the plot, upbraids her beloved, who is secretly married. Sensing that she faces insurmountable competition, she threatens to ruin the reputation of her unknown rival:

> . . . Dare not to see her,
> For if thou dost, I'll find the Strumpet out;
> Confusion! Slighted, for another too!
> O how I'll be reveng'd! I'll know this Sorceress,
> Make her most infamous;
> I'll be your plague, anticipate your Hell. . . .
> I'll haunt your Steps, and interrupt your Joys;
> Fright you with Curses from your Minions arms;
> Pursue you with Reproaches, blast her Fame;
> I'll be the constant Bane of all your Pleasures,
> A Jarring, Clamorous, very Wife to thee,
> To her a greater Plague, than thou to me. (pp. 25–6)

Trotter's desire to 'discourage Vice' created a character whose fervent language, with its trope of women as contending witches and its implied criticism of 'clamorous' wives (pandering to gender stereotypes), is the most compelling in the play.

In Trotter's early days a woman playwright might create a powerful, sexual, female character with impunity if the character was presented as evil and if she remained unsuccessful in her lustful machinations. An anonymous ally of the stage reformer Jeremy Collier, one self-described 'Friend to Religion and . . . good Poetry', found that the unnamed 'celebrated Female' author of *Fatal Friendship* had proved 'that 'tis possible to entertain, with all Judgement, Wit, and Beauty of Poetry; without *shocking our senses*, with intollerable prophaneness or obscenity'.[35] Likewise, Sarah, Lady Piers praised Trotter's *The Unhappy Penitent* (1701) by commending her 'judicious rules' for the stage, rules by which she teaches virgins to be bashful, wives to be prudent, friends to be sincere, youths to be temperate, lovers to be chaste, statesmen to be honest; in effect, instructing all types to fulfil their expected social and gender roles. Piers used the concept of 'Champion of the Sex' and the image of 'Orinda' in a prescriptive manner, citing 'Astrea' with caution and recommending to women writers a less combative and ambitious posture:

> Thus like the Morning Star *Orinda* rose
> A Champion for her Sex, and wisely chose,
> Conscious of Female weakness, humble wais
> T'insinuate for applause, not storm the Bays.
> Next gay *Astrea* briskly won the Prize,
> Yet left a spacious room to Criticise.[36]

According to Piers, who was not a playwright and belonged to a higher social echelon than Trotter, Manley and Pix, the best method for a woman writer to achieve acclaim is by 'insinuation', by subtle, circuitous means, a far cry from conquering male dominions.

Although Trotter's plays were accepted as reforming in their own time, their explicitly stated moral intent did not save them from later criticism. As the eighteenth century progressed, and as 'the rules' for playwriting, women's writing and women's behaviour changed, her plays were regarded as, at best, unfashionable, at worst, shocking and inappropriate for a woman's pen. In later years, when she discussed the theatre of her youth, Trotter, now Mrs Cockburn, often sounded like Jeremy Collier:

> I was always so bent upon doing my part towards reforming the abuses of the Stage, that it must have been by some strange oversight if I contributed to it, tho' I might not think much in the heat of writing of putting some levities in the mouths of disapprov'd characters. 'Tis faults of another nature that have made plays in general so much run down; comedies especially were for a long time vicious in their very foundation, the fine gentlemen are Debauchees, intrigues of married people are the business of the Play, & coming off with

success in deceiving a good natur'd or jealous Husband, the happy Event. (BL Add. MS 4265, fol. 85b)

Nearly a century after *Fatal Friendship* was written, James Beattie, the Scottish poet and philosopher, said that the play

> ought to have been suppressed; for it does her no credit, and shows her to have been at eighteen a greater adept at love matters than unmarried women of that age are commonly supposed to be: There are passages in that play, which I could not have the face to read, or hear, in a lady's company. But her youth, and the licentiousness of the English stage in the end of the last century, may be pleaded, and ought to be admitted, as an apology, in behalf of one, who was undoubtedly an ornament to her sex, and an honour to her country.[37]

Beattie was able to attack the play (in terms similar to those used against Behn's work) but praise the creator as 'an ornament to her sex' because he had been reading Thomas Birch's *Works of Mrs Catherine Cockburn, Theological, Moral, Dramatic, and Poetical* (1751).[38] Birch's efforts to establish Cockburn as a model woman writer in the mid-eighteenth century included an introductory biography which presented her as an exemplary, self-sacrificing wife and mother, whose character was 'unexceptionable . . . in all respects, from a conduct throughout life strictly conformable to those principles of morality and religion, of which she had the fullest and most rational conviction' (Birch, I, p. xlvii). The biography quotes a letter to Pope (which was never sent), in which Cockburn describes getting married as 'retiring' from the world, becoming 'in a manner dead' to the world of poetry and letters:

> Being married in 1708, I bid adieu to the muses, and so wholly gave myself up to the cares of a family, and the education of my children, that I scarce knew, whether there was any such thing as books, plays, or poems stirring in *Great Britain*. (Birch, I, p. xl)

Birch construed these lines as an admission of willing self-sacrifice. As he tells the story, Cockburn and her family were haunted by political persecution and poverty for much of her married life, until 1726, when the non-juring Reverend Patrick Cockburn, who had finally agreed to take the oath of allegiance to King George, was given an appointment at St Paul's Episcopal chapel in Aberdeen. From that year until her death in 1749, she concerned herself almost exclusively with philosophical questions, except for revisions of earlier works and a few new poems. Birch's biography and his process of selection, as well as Cockburn's unpublished correspondence and Birch's manuscript notes for the edition, all shed light on the efforts of both author and editor to ensure her status as a respectable woman writer.

As early as 1728, Cockburn had planned to publish a collection of her works, but at her death in Northumberland on 11 May 1749, the project, still incomplete, devolved to Thomas Birch, a family friend and editor of Bacon, Milton and Spenser.[39] Cockburn's obituary in the *Gentleman's Magazine* carried an advertisement for the collection: 'Her exalted virtue and understanding will be more generally known, when her writings, now in the press, shall be published' (XIX, p. 236).

According to the correspondence of Cockburn's son John, as well as a copy of a letter written by the Reverend Patrick Cockburn while his wife was alive, she had not kept printed versions of her plays and early poetry on hand. At the time she first began to think of collecting her work, she had available only her last play, *The Revolution of Sweden*, and a revised manuscript copy of her sole comedy, *Love at a Loss*.[40] The Cockburns anticipated 'some trouble' in assembling her early material; the three remaining tragedies were 'not to be had in Booksellers shops' (BL Add. MS 4265, ff. 108–9). Cockburn's suppression of her early career, deliberate or not, was successful at the immediate level; her own children were not familiar with her early work. When he sent published copies of his mother's philosophical essays and manuscript copies of her poetry to Birch after her death, John pronounced himself unqualified to judge whether some poems were 'worth making publick' and explained that none of her children knew whether a particular elegy on Dryden's death was the one published 50 years earlier in *The Nine Muses* (BL Add. MS 4302, ff. 290–1).

Careful construction of the respectable woman author via her collected works required not only that the editor create a validating biography, but that he choose to include works generically appropriate to the task. Birch seems to have had copies of Cockburn's five plays at his disposal, but included only *Fatal Friendship*, finding her essays to be 'superior in their kind to the most perfect of her poetical [writings], and of a more general and lasting use to the world' (Birch I, p. xlvi). He obviously considered 'works moral' to be more desirable for the collection than 'works dramatic'. In making such a judgement, he undoubtedly exercised the taste of his own age, which did not look fondly on the high-flown rhetoric of heroic tragedy. Birch also omitted Cockburn's 1693 autobiographical fiction, *Olinda's Adventures*, though he knew about it.[41] (Potentially embarrassing fan letters from effusive male admirers, one of whom claimed that *Agnes de Castro* had 'by a kind of Magick Power wrought a Reformation' in his opinion of women, as well as the warm epistles of Trotter's devoted friend, Lady Piers, were also available to Birch, but excluded.)[42] Birch assumed that Cockburn's 'mature productions' would be more likely to service both 'the world' and her own reputation than her early works, a different view from those held by critics today, who find in *Olinda's Adventures* a foreshadowing of 'new breadth and realism in the English novel', see 'great promise' in the plays, and consider Trotter's comedy to be 'a dashing play of wit'.[43]

Though Cockburn planned to include all of the plays in her projected collection, according to Birch she would have omitted most of her letters, many of which he chose to publish (in an edited version): '[H]er own modesty would have restrained her from permitting [them] to see the light' (Birch, I, pp. xlv–xlvi). Birch refers particularly to her correspondence with suitors, including her future husband, written while she was in transition from the late stage of her play-writing career to her new interest in philosophy and religion. Birch printed, among others, letters in which Cockburn played moral and intellectual mentor to her niece. In recommending Molière, she considered 'the worst' of his plays likely to improve her niece's French without hurting her morals (6 December 1731; Birch, II, p. 258). Though Cockburn might have hesitated to publish her own epistles, Birch preferred the letter to amorous fiction or heroic tragedy as an acceptable genre for the 'modest' woman writer.

Birch's collection was initially successful in drawing attention to Cockburn's life and work. John Duncombe's long poem on women writers, *The Feminiad* (1754), attested to the success of the *Works* in defining Cockburn as a neglected writer worthy of respect. Noting that 'her works . . . have lately been collected and generally admired', Duncombe reiterated Birch's version of her life:

> Tho' long, to dark, oblivious want a prey,
> Thy aged worth past unperceiv'd away,
> Yet Scotland now shall ever boast thy fame,
> While England mourns thy undistinguish'd name,
> And views with wonder, in a female mind,
> Philosopher, Divine, and Poet join'd!

Judging from Duncombe's response, the attempt to establish Cockburn as a woman writer of an entirely different species from Behn took hold. In contrast to Cockburn, Duncombe proffered 'the bold unblushing Mein/ Of modern Manley, [Susanna] Centlivre, and Behn . . . Vice's Friends and Virtue's Female Foes'. Duncombe warned:

> Tho' harmony thro' all their numbers flow'd,
> And genuine wit its ev'ry grace bestow'd,
> Nor genuine wit nor harmony excuse
> The dang'rous sallies of a wanton Muse:
> Nor can such tuneful, but immoral lays,
> Expect the tribute of impartial praise . . .[44]

In spite of the flurry of interest in Cockburn in the 1750s, by 1789 no one in Aberdeen, where she had lived for many years, ever spoke of her, though they did of her husband.[45] Although her works, early or late, were no longer widely read, Birch's all-too-successful version of the self-sacrificing lady author did become a legacy for subsequent generations. In the next century when Cockburn appeared briefly in reference works and anthologies of women's poetry, where critics focused on her life rather than on her works, she was seen as the epitome of the admirable woman who neglects her talents and intellectual growth for the demands of a family. Sarah Hale said of Cockburn's life as wife and mother: 'This is the true way for a woman to live contentedly, to grow old gracefully, and to die happily'.[46] John Doran's Annals of the English Stage (1888) described her as 'a valiant woman . . . one whom asthma and the ills of life could not deter from labour'.[47] Like Duncombe, Doran contrasted Behn and Cockburn, describing them respectively as, 'the most shameless woman who ever took pen in hand, designedly to corrupt the public' (p. 238), and '[S]he is remembered in the history of literature as a good and well-accomplished woman – the very opposite of Mrs. Behn and all her heroines' (p. 242).

In her own lifetime and even afterwards, Elizabeth Singer Rowe was far more successful than Cockburn in negotiating the narrowing range of genres, public personae and ways of living open to woman writers between the 1690s and the mid-eighteenth century. Her male relations, Henry Grove and Theophilus Rowe, exercised the same values as Birch in editing an authorized edition of her works, The Miscellaneous Works in Prose and Verse of Mrs Elizabeth Rowe (1739), published two years after Rowe's death, but with even better results, since they were dealing with a reputation already solidly in place. Particularly noticeable in the edition is the omission of most of Rowe's early poems, first published anonymously in John Dunton's periodical The Athenian Mercury (1691–7). The verses of 'The Poetic Lady' or 'The Pindaric Lady', who remained anonymous for a time even to her publisher, accounted for a great deal of the publication's popularity. The preface to Dunton's collection of the early poems, Poems on Several Occasions by Philomela (1696), claims that the author's name would have appeared on the title-page, 'had not her own Modesty absolutely forbidden it'.[48] Despite her desire to remain anonymous, Singer did allow her name to be attached to mostly devout poems in various miscellanies of the first decade of the eighteenth century.[49] In addition, Dunton revealed the identity of 'Philomela' in his 1705 autobiography, in which he says that Mrs Singer 'knows the purity of our Tongue and converses with all the Briskness and the Gayety that she writes. Her Stil is noble and flowing, and her Images are very vivid and shining. To finish her Character, she's as Beautiful as she's Witty.'[50]

Dunton's use of her name in those early years could only have been a source of pain to Singer, and her entanglement with him seen as a regrettable youthful folly. His *Athenianism* (1710), published in the year of her marriage to Thomas Rowe, opened with a 60-page narrative, 'The Double Courtship; or Dunton's Character of Madam Singer'. He presented her as an irresistible young lady whose steadfast adherence to the principles of platonic friendship could not prevent him from proposing marriage to her or from using her as a 'character' in his 'Character'. In Dunton's hands, the 'beautiful Body of Philomela' became the subject of a *carpe diem* admonition, 'so soon does Death change the fairest Beauty into Loathing'.[51] According to Dunton, when Singer found out about the characterization in-progress, she expressed great regret at being unable to 'have [her] Character rescu'd', and begged him to write nothing like it again without her knowledge, since she wished to 'die in Oblivion' (p. 23). Dunton responded by promising never to publish any of the letters she wrote to him, 'save under *borrow'd* Names', unless she tried to disown anything in the 'Character', in which case he would publish their entire correspondence (p. 24). He then proceeded, in the rest of the 'Character', to quote a number of her letters. Eight years later, when she was a well-known author and respected widow, a letter from a Mr 'J. W.' warned Dunton to stop using Mrs Rowe's name in print.[52]

In a calculated effort to reinforce the status Rowe enjoyed in her lifetime, the editors excluded from the *Miscellaneous Works* all of Singer's poems published by Dunton, deliberately omitted mentioning Dunton's name in the 'Life' of Rowe which prefaces the collection, and said of her early verses:

> Tho' many of these poems are of the religious kind, and all of them consistent with the strictest regard to the rules of virtue; yet some things in them gave her no little uneasiness in advanced life. To a mind that had so entirely subdued its passions, or devoted them to the honour of its maker, and endued with that tenderest *moral sense*, what she could not absolutely approve, appear'd unpardonable; and, not satisfied to have done nothing that injur'd the sacred cause of virtue, she was displeas'd with herself for having written any thing that did not directly promote it. (Rowe, I, pp. xvi–xvii)

Just as her 'character' as a lively young charmer was discomforting, so were the products of those early years. Some of Rowe's early poems demonstrate strong political viewpoints, adamantly supporting King William III and attacking his opponents as 'ungrateful Vipers'.[53] Others boast of romantic conquests or complain of unfaithful lovers, vowing to 'contemn/The treacherous and deluding Arts,/Of those *base things call'd men*' and seek the company of her adored friend, Celinda.[54] 'To one that perswades me to leave the Muses', one of the many poems which were not included in the *Works*, is a spirited defence of her poetry, first published in the *Athenian Mercury* in 1695, when she was not yet 21:

> Forgo the *charming Muses!* No, in spight
> Of your ill-natur'd Prophecy, I'le write . . .
> . . . I'm so scurvily inclin'd to Rhiming,
> That undesign'ed my thoughts *burst out a chiming*;
> My *active Genius* will by no means sleep,
> And let it then its proper channel keep.
> I've told you, and you may believe me, too
> That I must this, or greater mischief do;
> And let the world think me *inspir'd, or mad*,
> I'le surely write whilst paper's to be had . . .[55]

She bids farewell to her boarding school, where the mistress bans the plays of Dryden and Sedley as well as novels and the *Athenian Mercury* 'for study's sake', meaning dancing, singing, drawing and various decorative arts. Singer welcomes her rural environment and other sources of inspiration '[t]hat please my *genius*, suit my make and years,/ Unburden'd yet with all but lovers cares'. In later years Rowe perhaps viewed this poem as not promoting 'the sacred cause of virtue'.

The editors who chose not to reproduce this poem were working with an already well-established reputation; their job was to underscore a pre-existing, firmly grounded image. After 1710, when she married Thomas Rowe, son of a well-known Dissenting minister and himself an author, Rowe no longer wrote polemic; her expressions of passion were limited to those of a devoted wife to her husband or a devout woman to her God; and she resumed publishing only anonymously (though her authorship was common knowledge). She became famous as an author of Biblical paraphases and pious fiction, particularly *Friendship in Death: In Twenty Letters from the Dead to the Living* (1728). Her elegy on Thomas Rowe was especially popular, the admitted inspiration for Pope's *Eloisa to Abelard*. Maintaining active intellectual relationships with literary and religious figures of the day in spite of life in a secluded country village, Rowe enjoyed a reputation that lasted well into the nineteenth century. As a literary widow of exemplary piety and virtue, she was held up to aspiring young women poets in much the same way that Orinda had been held up to her.

The kind of attitude that helped shape the eminent Mrs Rowe can be found in a poem Thomas Rowe addressed to her in 1710, comparing her to Astrea and Orinda, but so qualifying his praise of 'the charmer' Behn's 'amazing force' and 'moving lays' as to render Behn a sort of 'Bogey-Woman', the subject of a sermon on the woman-poet-gone wrong:

> *Astraea* well *Orinda*'s place supply'd.
> *Phoebus* did ne'er before a breast inspire
> With larger portions of poetic fire:
> On ev'ry subject she her art could prove,
> Well on each subject sung, but best of love . . .
> O! had chaste transports fill'd her virtuous mind,
> And to permitted pleasures most inclin'd,
> *Sappho* had yielded to her nobler fame,
> And only *Philomel*'s had been a brighter name:
> But while too oft her guilty fancy roves
> To loose desires, and wild, disorder'd loves;
> Unheeding minds with lewd ideas warms,
> And gives adultery and incest charms;
> The good and chaste abhor the vitious lays,
> And hate the beauties they are forc'd to praise . . . (Rowe, II, p. 279)

Thomas's brother, Theophilus Rowe, who took over the job of editing the *Works* upon the death of Henry Grove, did his best to illuminate Philomela's 'brighter name', prompted by good reasons for maintaining his sister-in-law's memory as she would have wished it. Just as John Dunton had done in her youth, so the infamous bookseller Edmund Curll posed a threat to Mrs Rowe's pristine reputation in her final days, recalling, perhaps, the tragic spectre of Elizabeth Thomas. To Mrs Rowe's horror, in 1736 Curll announced a second edition of Dunton's collection of Philomela's poems, and according to a letter to her friend Lady Hertford, she could do nothing about it:

> I am entirely ignorant of *Curl*'s romance of my life and writings; only what I have seen in an advertisement. I was told of his design indeed, and wrote, and postively deny'd him the liberty of printing any thing of mine: But they tell me he is a mere savage, and has no regard to truth and humanity; and as he has treated people of greater consequence in the same manner, I am advis'd to suffer no friend to take the least notice of his collection; and for my own peace, if ever it comes my way, I never intend to see what is in it. I have often secur'd my happiness, by governing my curiosity; and I am sure of doing it in this case, because I am so perfectly indifferent to the trifles I have writ, and have at present no manner of ambition . . . I can look on the various events of human things with indifference, as I know I shall very soon quit the changing scenes of mortality, and enter on a more lasting and important state. (Rowe, II, pp. 177–8)

She died in February 1737; Curll brought out the abhorred second edition in the same year. In spite of Rowe's protests to the contrary, one might speculate that she was not as averse to the reappearance of the early poems as she would have Lady Hertford believe, as long as she was not implicated in the republication. Curll prefaced the book with a 'letter' supposedly written by Rowe, promising that no one would 'dispute his Right, or give him any Opposition' if he would admit that the edition was inspired by his 'partiality to [her] Writing' and not by her 'Vanity'.[56] Curll triumphantly crowed, 'PHILOMELA long Dead, / Now re-warbles her Throat, again lifts up her Head' (p. xi). In the dedication to Alexander Pope, in which he incorrectly dated various events in Rowe's life, Curll admitted to making 'a little Reformation in the Numbers' of some of the poems, and to substituting some of Rowe's later poems for those which 'the Writer's *Friends* were desirous of having omitted, as favouring of *Party-Reflection* and the *Heat* of *Youth*, since *cooled* by a stricter *Judgment*' (p. xvii). 'To a Friend who persuades me to leave the Muses' was included; Singer's panegyrics on William and Mary were not. Theophilus Rowe pronounced Curll 'entirely ignorant of every thing relating to the person whose memoirs he attempted to compose' (Rowe, II, p. 177).

When the works of Rowe and her female contemporaries were criticized, in their own time and later, moral considerations, intertwined with issues of gender and genre, were always at the forefront. As John Duncombe, Thomas Rowe and others indicated (invoking Astrea's case as their bugbear), no matter how intense a woman's 'poetic fire', how warm her fancy, how strong her ambition, how harmonious her numbers, how genuine her wit, if her work and her personal reputation did not measure up to current standards of morality and feminine behaviour, she could not be deemed a praiseworthy poet. Creating or reinforcing the image of the respectable woman author meant not only emphasizing the irreproachable nature of her behaviour and her work, but representing her as a woman who never actively sought fame. She had to be perceived as a woman of the 'tenderest moral sense' and depicted as one who felt a real 'indifference to glory'. Theophilus Rowe said of his sister-in-law:

> As she seemed to shun fame by concealing herself, during almost the whole of her life, in an obscure solitude, so she practised no arts to promote her reputation. She wrote no preface to any of her works to prepossess the public in their favour, nor suffered them to be accompanied with the panegyrics of her friends. She would not, indeed, so much as allow her name to be prefixed to any of them, except for some few poems in the earlier part of her life. (Rowe, I, p. lxix)

A poem by Cockburn published in the same year as Rowe's *Works* shows that for women 'fame', that is, a public name, can be as fearful as 'infamy'. As Behn had done years before, Cockburn addresses the problem of combining femaleness and fame, while revealing attitudinal and rhetorical changes that took place in women's writing after Aphra:

> Learning deny'd us, we at random tread
> Unbeaten paths, that late to knowledge lead;
> By secret steps break thro' th' obstructed way,
> Nor dare acquirements gain'd by stealth display.
> If some advent'rous genius rare arise,
> Who on exalted themes her talent tries,
> She fears to give the work (tho' prais'd) a name,
> And flies not more from infamy, than fame.[57]

In Cockburn's later years, women no longer described themselves as 'storming' and contending as they did in their late seventeenth-century poems, but as wandering 'at random'. They depicted themselves as thwarted in their intellectual aspirations; oppressed by secrecy and fear, they moved stealthily like escaped criminals or slaves through 'unbeaten paths'. Rather than confronting the opposition head on, the women in this poem follow Piers's recommended path of 'insinuation' and indirection, and they are not singular cases. Cockburn's hypothetical 'advent'rous genius rare' who dares not reach too high, echoes the Countess of Winchilsea's 'Introduction'. The Countess, who finds women to be 'Education's, more than Nature's fools, / Debarr'd from all improvements of the mind', draws a similar picture of suppressed female creativity: 'And if someone, wou'd Soar above the rest, / With warmer fancy, and ambition press't; / So strong, th' opposing faction still appears, / The hopes to thrive, can ne're out weigh the fears'.[58]

In an immediate response to Behn's death, the author of her elegy indicated that women were 'withheld by Impotence or Fear' from attempting to take her place. Cockburn and Winchilsea explained that there were good reasons for the trepidation that 'out weighs' hope and moves an author to anonymity. As Behn had done before them, they pointed to powerful societal pressures that deprived women of an education and equated 'fame' with 'infamy'. The women who came after Aphra could not claim to 'value fame' in Behn's heroic and outspoken fashion, though their persistence in writing, publishing, and formulating ways to render their names acceptable to a later age is proof that they valued enduring fame over heroic notoriety. Their manner of representing the lot of women in general and themselves as women writers in particular was the natural legacy of the 'Inglorious Revolution', which replaced the brave inheritance bequeathed them by Behn.

'The Native Liberty . . . of the Subject'

Configurations of gender and authority in the works of
Mary Chudleigh, Sarah Fyge Egerton, and Mary Astell

Carol Barash

In his *History of the Reign of Queen Anne* (1703), Abel Boyer describes
Queen Anne's triumphant entrance into the city of Bath shortly after her
coronation in 1702. The queen was welcomed

> by a fine Company of the Citizens, all clad like Grenadiers, and about 200
> Virgins richly attired, many of them like *Amazons*, with Bows and Arrows,
> and others with gild Scepters, and other Ensigns of the *Regalia* in their
> Hands.[1]

In this lavish spectacle we see dramatized a number of patterns that
derive from Anne's situation as a female monarch. The presence of
citizens 'clad like Grenadiers' suggests that Anne is a martial leader, the
symbolic head of the British military. At the same time, Anne's reign
evokes myths of particularly female – and potentially transgressive –
physical force, embodied in the '200 Virgins richly attired . . . like
Amazons', with their bows and arrows poised ready to fight on the
queen's behalf.[2]

In writings by women between 1702 and 1708, Queen Anne often
appears as the leader of Amazons. The depiction of Anne as the leader of
warrior women is an aspect of the larger representation of her as a figure
of female authority. In constructing Anne as a model of both female and
martial authority, writers – especially women writers – often compare
her to Elizabeth I. In the dedication to *The Platonick Lady* (1707), for
example, Susanna Centlivre asks:

> What cannot *England* boast from Women? The mighty *Romans* felt the Power
> of *Boadicea*'s Arm; *Eliza* made *Spain* tremble; but *ANN*, the greatest of the
> Three, has shook the Man that aim'd at Universal Sway.[3]

Again, in a manuscript poem by Sarah Fyge Egerton, Anne is said to outshine Elizabeth: 'all the Glory Eliza did obtain / Will be Eclipse'd by Anna's brighter Reign'.[4] Comparing Anne to Elizabeth often underscores Anne's military triumphs over King Louis XIV of France, 'the Man that aim'd at Universal Sway'. In contrast to the threat they see embodied in Louis XIV, women writers frequently claim to find protection in the 'security' provided by Anne's reign. In the dedication to her 1708 translation of Madeleine de Scudéry's *Essay on Glory*, Elizabeth Elstob claims that if Scudéry had been English, her successes would have been even greater:

> [H]ad this excellent Lady lived in our Nation, under a sovereign of her own Sex . . . with what justice and sincerity might she have ascribed those Perfections to her Majesty, which she does not but with an ill address, and not without some kind of Flattery, to that King [Louis XIV].

Because Anne only engages in just wars, Elstob continues, God supports her:

> Such is the tender and compassionate Nature of our Pious Queen, that she is not only a Safe Retreat to those Private Families which have fled out of the land of oppression . . . but her Generosity is yet more extensive and Magnificent in Restoring Kingdoms and protecting Empires and States.[5]

In this passage, Anne is represented as an Augustan monarch whose military actions are justified by their ends of 'restoring' and 'protecting' not only national, but international peace.[6]

Elstob's dedicatory verses to Scudéry bring to the surface a pattern implicit in many writings by women in the early eighteenth century: Queen Anne's presence on the throne of England emboldened women not only to write, but to defend their works as women. 'A *Sappho* should for *Anna* tune her lyre', wrote Catharine Trotter, 'And *Anna* may with nobler verse inspire'.[7] In Trotter's prologue to *The Revolution of Sweden* (1706), Anne's military triumph over Louis XIV places the woman author in a position to instruct men:

> Nor can the vainest haughtiest, Man disdain
> A Woman's Precepts in Great ANNA's Reign;
> If by a Woman you tonight are taught,
> Think on that Source from whence th'Instruction's brought.[8]

Repeatedly, we find a metonymic overlap between women writers' defences of Anne's political legitimacy and their defences of their own legitimacy as authors. For women writers, Anne is both leader and comrade in a battle – against men – for the authority to write as women and in defence of women's political demands. Women writers' apparent identification with Anne, the wager of a 'just' war against France, their sense of their own moral supremacy and their right to enforce obedience, continues after the death of Anne's husband, Prince George of Denmark, in 1708, breaking down finally as a result of Anne's seeming isolation from her Tory ministers after 1709.[9]

Coining the phrase 'Tory feminism' to suggest the ways in which late seventeenth- and early eighteenth-century women writers construct their relationship to monarchic authority, Catherine Gallagher argues that 'Toryism and feminism converge because the ideology of absolute monarchy provides . . . a transition to an ideology of the absolute self'.[10] All the writers discussed here rely on a notion of the queen as absolute monarch; they do so, however, not as individual subjects (and not always as Tories), but as part of a community of women symbolically authorized by the queen to speak on women's behalf.[11] While their authority to write and publish is upheld by their obedience to the female virtue and order they see epitomized in Anne's reign, their identification with the queen becomes most problematic when the queen enters their writings as woman as well as monarch. Often, as in Astell (below), we can see major changes in the construction of gender, monarchy and linguistic authority even in one woman's career.[12] And Gallagher's 'Tory feminism' actually breaks down altogether with the Tory victory in the elections of 1709.

Of the numerous women who wrote in praise of Anne in the early years of her reign, the works of Mary Chudleigh, Sarah Fyge Egerton and Mary Astell are linked by their use of Anne to sanction what we might call 'feminist imperialism', that is, the woman writer's movement into emotional and intellectual domains previously considered men's. If there seems to be, early in Anne's reign, something that looks like 'Tory feminism', it not merely upholds the individual woman author's reason with monarchic authority as Gallagher would have it, but likens women's virtue to the triumphs of English militarism in order to command others' obedience.

Paradoxically, these writers justify their claims of moral supremacy by drawing on an ideology of political submission and filial obedience.[13] Just as Anne's polemicists represented her as both guiding mother and dutiful daughter of the Church of England, Chudleigh, Egerton and Astell used this ideology of obedience to support Anne's authority and to urge the obedience of others to a range of demands, particularly education for women and women's intellectual and spiritual freedom within marriage. Appropriating writings by these women to the origins of English 'feminism' has tended to minimize the essentially contradictory positions they take in relation to problems of gender and authority.[14] In contrast, I have attempted to emphasize the ways in which women writers struggled with the conflicting political and symbolic strategies made possible by Anne's rule.

The years between the coronation of William and Mary in 1688 and the death of Anne in 1714 were characterized by fierce public debates about the relationship between gender and political authority.[15] The death of Anne's sister, Mary II, in 1694 and the lapse of the last of the Licensing Acts in 1695 inaugurated one of several moments in seventeenth-century England in which political, religious and sexual controversies flourished in print.[16] In the years between Mary's death and Anne's coronation, we find heightened attention to women's political and social status – debates about marriage, divorce and women's education – as well as a marked rise in the number of women signing their works, in various ways, as women.[17] For women writers, Anne seems to have represented an ideal 'female monarch' before she was actually crowned queen in 1702. Anne's political supporters argued that she – rather than her cousin and brother-in-law, William III – should be monarch now that Mary was dead.[18] If Anne was an ideal (because primarily mythic) 'female monarch' before she was actually queen, her symbolic presence seems to have encouraged women to produce their most aggressive writings in the first few years after she was crowned.

Whereas William and Mary's propagandists had emphasized Mary's wifely obedience, Anne's supporters and opponents alike portrayed her rule as materially and maternally female.[19] Although Anne had no living children at the time of her coronation (her only child to live beyond infancy, William Henry, Duke of Gloucester, died in 1701), the coronation sermon was based on *Isaiah* 49.23, and it drew on a maternal theme: 'Kings shall be thy nursing Fathers, and Queens thy nursing Mothers'. Anne's speeches, many of which she either wrote or substantially altered herself,[20] discuss political events as if to replace hereditary and familial ties with sympathetic bonds between ruler and people. Tory journalist Delarivier Manley writes, 'the Queen values herself upon nothing so much as being a Common Mother to all her Subjects'.[21] Often, as in the description of the union with Scotland as a fecund marriage, Anne and her propagandists use childbirth metaphorically in response to political opposition.[22]

Just as Anne draws on her symbolic position as mother of the Anglican Church to soften her government's assaults on its political opposition, Chudleigh, Egerton and Astell use their 'zeal' for the queen to triumph over their opponents. Both Chudleigh and Egerton began their writing careers – before Anne was crowned – with 'defences' of women that

responded to anti-feminist satire by men.[23] In contrast, in volumes of
poetry published during Anne's reign they write not in response to men's
satire but as women who claim to know what is in other women's best
interest. Astell, similarly, makes her boldest claims for women in works
dedicated to Anne. Of course, none of these writers is able, unproblematically, to erect her authority as poet on the model of the queen's
disembodied political authority. Their implicitly polemical offensives,
while symbolically authorized by the heroically martial queen, are
nevertheless couched as defences of obedience and order. Entwined in the
paradoxes of the queen's 'two bodies' – Anne is both disembodied,
atemporal 'prince' and all too physical, married and pregnant woman –
women often alternate between asserting a spiritual authority that
derives from the female monarch and attacking their own works as if they
were female reproductive bodies.[24]

Chudleigh's ideal 'reason' searches for, but cannot attain, a female
body from which to assert its claim to equality and Egerton undermines
the intellectual authority she elsewhere demands for women by attacking
her own texts as if they were women. In moving from the second part of
Astell's *Serious Proposal* (1697) to the third edition of *Reflections upon
Marriage* (1706), we see most clearly the consequences of the obedience
and aggression women defended on Anne's behalf. Astell argues in
Reflections upon Marriage that women's spiritual authority allows them
to triumph over the worldly power men hold over them, but only by
displacing their authority from this world to the next.

Both Chudleigh's and Egerton's 1703 volumes include poems to Anne
and dedicatory material that discusses women's relationship to language
in terms of Anne's position as female monarch. Chudleigh's *Poems, Upon
Several Occasions* begins with a poem addressed to the queen as a woman
who has just lost her son; the volume ends with a portrait of the
triumphant queen as abstract, disembodied, defeminized – if not quite
masculine – 'prince'. Shifting frequently between these two extremes,
Chudleigh's poems and prefatory material reveal that her self-authoriza-
tion as poet and social critic is intertwined with the paradoxes of Anne's
position as woman and queen. Beginning with the obeisance and
humility we frequently see in women poets' writings about Anne,
Chudleigh's dedication, 'To the Queen's Most Excellent Majesty', goes
on to defend her writing by situating it within Anne's political domain:

Madam,
   Tis not without awful Thoughts and a trembling Hand that these poems are
laid at your Royal Feet. The address has too much Confidence; the Ambition
is too aspiring; But to whom should a Woman unknown to the World, and

who has not Merit enough to defend her from the Censure of Criticks, fly for Protection, but to your *Majesty?* The Greatest, the Best, and the most Illustrious Person of your Sex and Age.[25]

Just as French Protestants flee from Louis and fly to Anne in Elstob's account, Chudleigh here flees masculine censure and flies to the queen for protection as woman and as writer. She thanks the queen for accepting her 'Ode on Your Happy Accession to the Crown', and uses the queen's symbolic protection to justify additional efforts in verse. Expanding and elaborating the female community she establishes between the female poet and the female monarch in the dedication, Chudleigh's preface goes on to use the woman poet's reason as the basis of her social criticism.

The preface begins by dramatizing the restoration of reason as monarch of the poet's troubled mind:

Ladies, for whom [these poems] are chiefly design'd . . . [will] find a Picture of my Mind, My Sentiments all laid open to their view; they'll . . . see me struggling with my Passions, blaming my self, endeavoring to pay a homage to my Reason, and . . . with a decent calmness, an unshaken Constancy, and a resigning Temper, to support all the Troubles, all the uneasinesses of Life, and then by unexpected Emergencies, unforeseen Disappointments, sudden and surprizing Turns of Fortune, discompos'd, and shock'd, till I have rallied my scatter'd Forces, got new Strength, and by making an unweary'd Resistance, gain'd the better of my Afflictions, and restor'd my Mind to its former Tranquility.

Just as she used the trope of patronage quite literally to have the queen protect her writings from male censure, Chudleigh here uses the Restoration, as trope, to link the authority of her own 'reason' to Anne's authority as monarch:

'Tis impossible to be happy without making Reason the Standard of all our Thoughts, Words and Actions, and firmly resolving to yield a constant, ready, and cheerful Obedience to its Dictates. Those who are goven'd by Opinion, inslav'd by Custom, and Vassals to their Humours, are Objects of Pity . . . . They act by no steady Principles, are always restless, disturb'd and uneasie.

The 'shock[s]' caused by these 'Afflictions' and the speaker's 'unweary'd Resistance' to them are repeatedly emphasized not only throughout the preface, but throughout Chudleigh's poems as well. Reason proves as embattled as the late Stuarts, and particularly Anne. Chudleigh's elaborate defence of reason, quoted below, sounds in fact very much like contemporary justifications of the queen's authority:

The Way to be truly easie, to be always serene, to have our Passions under a due Government . . . and not to have it in the Power of . . . Things foreign to us to ruffle and disturb our Thoughts, is to retire to our Selves . . . to be pleas'd with nothing but what, strictly speaking, we may justly pretend a Right to.

Just as Anne's military forwardness is figured as liberating England from the threat of France, in Chudleigh's account the 'due Government' of reason frees the female speaker of the preface from enslavement to 'Things foreign', and allows her to control those things she 'may justly pretend a Right to'. In her elegy on the death of the queen's son, Chudleigh's identification with the queen's uncontrolled grief allows the female poet, like an Augustan monarch herself, to 'restore' the queen's emotional 'peace' through verse (*Poems*, p. 42).

The choice of a virtuous life allows Chudleigh's speaker to harbour an aggressive sense of pride, which ultimately gives her power over others:

> There is a noble Disdain, a becoming and allowable Pride; 'tis commendable to scorn to be below others in Things that are essentially Praise-worthy, and they may be permitted to put a true Value on themselves, when instead of exciting them to Vanity . . . it tends only to the raising them above those mean despicable Things, those contemptible Accomplishments of which the most are proud.

She 'beg[s] others Pardon for presuming so freely to advise' them, attributing her forwardness to the 'Zeal' she has for their interest. Like Anne's professed 'Zeal for the Church of England', which was used to justify laws limiting dissenters' rights to gather and protest, Chudleigh's 'Zeal' for virtue puts her in the position of determining which acts are in fact virtuous, and which are only 'wrong Notions of Perfection, false Ideas of [one's] own Merits'.[26] Like Katherine Philips and Jane Barker, Chudleigh argues that the 'virtue' attained in her humble private life leads her to righteous, religious zeal, and ultimately to virtuous – and public – female action.[27]

Chudleigh's two poems to Anne, one in the middle and one at the end of *Poems, Upon Several Occasions*, trace the same path as her defence of reason in the preface.[28] In the first poem to Anne, Chudleigh's speaker again reverences the queen:

> Permit me at your Royal Feet to lay
> This humble off'ring of a trembling Muse;
>   Permit me there to pay
> This Tribute to transcendent Merit due;
> To that transcendent Merit which conspicuous is in You.
> Bold is th'Address, and the Presumption high
> But she all meaner Objects does refuse.

Like an incipient rebellion, her muse grows 'impetuous', becoming 'much too strong to be supprest'. She begs the queen's pardon for her muse's transgressions of the bounds of humble and self-effacing female conduct:

On you she gazes with admiring Eyes,
And ev'ry lower Object does despise:
Pardon her Transports, since from Zeal they spring,
And give her leave of You to sing. (*Poems*, p. 41)

As in her preface, Chudleigh's professed 'Zeal' for the queen justifies her writing's ambitious entrance into the marketplace. She is only following the queen's example in upsetting old rules about masculine dominion. In Chudleigh's poem, Anne's 'Glory' is said to 'entail a lasting Fame' on her sex. That is, the queen's radiance creates a new economy of 'entail', and she passes her fame symbolically to heirs female rather than male. The poem, in fact, demonstrates the effect of the queen's making female poets her heirs when the speaker fuses with the female monarch, in the first-person plural possessive 'our', to defend England from France: 'Long may You reign, long fill the *British* Throne, / And make the haughty *Gallick* Foe our *English* valor own' (*Poems*, p. 42).[29]

Chudleigh imagines a fictional community around the queen, a community which allows her to place her own 'valor' beside the queen's. She goes on to prophesy that Anne will triumph over the Salic Law which prevents women from ascending the French throne, and that she will inspire obedience in men:

If poets may to Prophesie pretend,
   If they're allow'd to pry
Into the hidden Secrets of Futurity,
They dare presage, You will your Pow'r extend,
And spite of *Salic* Laws, the *Gallick* Throne ascend . . . .
Go on great Heroin, and exalt your Name,
Go fearless on in the bright Tracks of Fame:
When Beauty leads, and Virtue shows the Way,
The Men will soon with joyful hast obey. (*Poems*, p. 43)

The first poem to Anne ends with the speaker's return to her resignation and duty: 'Secure within, [the Furies] Shock I dare sustain, / My Souls impassive and can feel no Pain' (*Poems*, p. 45). In the next two poems, however, 'The Resolution' and 'A Pindarick Ode', she must again wage battle with the enemies of reason.

Chudleigh's volume returns repeatedly to this conflict between a disembodied but emphatically male 'reason', upon which the female speaker can never fully rely, and the power of a markedly physical and female resignation.[30] This conflict is resolved in the volume's second poem to Queen Anne by projecting Anne back onto Elizabeth I, who seems nostalgically to Chudleigh to have inhabited more easily the mythical (male) body of the prince. Because she was neither married nor bearing children, Elizabeth could be identified with an ideal of chaste, virgin power embodied in the figure of Astrea:

> When Heav'n designs some wondrous Prince to raise,
> Deserving Empire and eternal Praise;
> It chuses one of an illustrious Line,
> In whom Hereditary Graces shine. (*Poems*, p. 121)

> Such was that Virgin Glory of our Isle,
> On whom *Apollo* long was pleas'd to smile:
> Who was with Wisdom, and with Science bless'd,
> By ev'ry Muse, and ev'ry Grace caress'd. (*Poems*, p. 123)

A happy resolution is created once again as Anne's 'becoming Pride' stems 'the dang'rous swelling Tide' of opposition and is 'with joyful Acclamations crown'd' (*Poems*, p. 123).[31] Chudleigh returns to the vantage point of her preface – the pride which allows one to look with pity on others' failures – but this time virtue and passion are united in the bodies of Anne's soldiers: 'Her Troops descend with noble Ardor fir'd, / By Heav'n, and their Heroick Queen inspir'd'. The volume ends with the speaker's wish to die at Anne's feet: 'O that I cou'd the best of Queens attend; / Cou'd at your Feet my coming Moments end' (*Poems*, p. 124).

Although Sarah Fyge Egerton uses fewer gestures of ritual obedience in placing her poetry as a female body before the queen, her poetry moves towards the same end as Chudleigh's, demanding male compliance as she enacts a woman poet's obedience to the queen. Where Chudleigh begins with Katherine Philips's model of a female retreat from the demands of the literary marketplace, Egerton starts like Aphra Behn, flirting with and manipulating an audience she assumes to be predominantly male. But these two very different strategies for situating their writings in the public domain converge. Egerton dedicates *Poems on Several Occasions, Together with a Pastoral* to Charles, Lord Halifax, apologizing for her ambition but claiming that her 'Zeal' for Halifax has forced her poems into print.[32] She gives him the poems as if they were virgin flesh:

> These Poems . . . I offer to your Lordship with all their Pristine Bloom, unsully'd by a vulgar touch, not handed round the Town for Opinion and Amendments; but just snatcht from their Recluse in all their native Rudeness and Simplicity.[33]

Although in 1703 she pretends to set her poetry forth as a seductively unsullied female body, Egerton actually started her public writing career in 1686 with *The Female Advocate*, a response to Robert Gould's *Late Satire on the Female Sex* (1683).[34]

Whereas, in the 1680s, overt conflict between men and women was not only a viable but indeed a profitable mode, by 1703 direct conflicts between men and women have been replaced, in the bulk of writing by women, with a hierarchy that places the queen – and other women who praise and imitate her – at the top.[35] While Egerton ostensibly places Halifax at the head of her volume, he oversees the book in name only. The dedicatory poems, written by other women, set up an alternative community, one extending the collective female authorship of *The Nine Muses on the Death of John Dryden* (1700) and praising Egerton as 'Sappho', the leader and inspiration of other women writers.[36]

This constitution of female poetic community in the prefatory material is developed in the poems which follow. Egerton's poems repeatedly dramatize the connections between women's writing and women's relation to political authority. For instance, in 'The Extasy', Egerton's speaker begins by hoping to soar above the material world and its conflicts:

> Mount, Mount, my Soul on high,
> Cut thro' the spacious Sky;
> Scale the great Mountainous heaps that be
> Betwixt the upper World, and thee.
> Stop not, till thou the utmost Region know,
> Leave all the Glittering Worlds below. (*Poems*, p. 2)

The authority of this position at first leaves the speaker claiming to feel naked and disarmed:

> In vain my dazled Soul would gaze around,
> (The beatifick Glorys so confound)
> It must be quite disrob'ed, e'er tread this Holy Ground. (*Poems*, p. 3)

But as she pretends to narrow her vision to earthly conflicts, she in fact draws confidence and authority from 'our' – i.e., the Queen's – imperial projects:

> In this Amphibious Ball [earth] is vast variety . . . .
> Here finny Herds of th'smallest sort . . .
> Wanton I'th'Flood, with no more Danger then
>   The Pastimes of Leviathan.
>   Here does in Triumph Ride,
> The stately Trophies of *Britania*'s Pride:
> Her Ships which to the *Indies* Trade,
>   Such Noble Fabricks are made;
>   And so numerous appear,
> The frighted Natives do our Traffick fear,
>   And doubt we will invade. (*Poems*, p. 5)

As in Chudleigh's first poem to the queen, Egerton uses the first-person plural to link the authority of her poetic vision to the queen's political authority. In the poems which follow she repeatedly grounds her own poetic authority – her right to demand political equality for women – in the violence, militarism and symbolic masculinity of

Anne's political projects.

In her 'Satyr Against the Muses', Egerton inscribes not only the muses, but all the dangers of writing poetry, as female. She claims that in the past 'Spite and Rage' inflamed her feminist muse to supply her with verse. Lately she has switched from the 'calm Author of blest Poetry' to 'the black Succubus of Misery' (Poems, pp. 14–15). So many people have taken to writing poetry, 'That Wit like Morris-dancers must advance,/ With Bells at Feet, and in nice measures Dance'. As competition makes poetry déclassé, the desire to captivate her audience amidst this frenzy brings forth her doubts about herself as a woman writer.

Twice in this satire Egerton compares the impeded production of poetry to a flawed female reproductive body. First, she claims that as soon as 'pregnant Heads, but think of Poetry', they are made 'Captive' by the slavery of rhyme so they cannot bring forth 'the Brain-delivery'. She expands this metonymic overlap between poetic production and female reproduction by comparing the opening of Pandora's box to the grotesque birth of verse:

> . . . they are mistaken who have told
> Spightful *Pandora*'s pregnant Box did hold
> Plurality of Plague, She only hurl'd
> Out Verse alone, and that has damn'd the World. (Poems, p. 16)

When Egerton's speaker finally asks Fate to 'Rescue' her 'From trifling torturing wretched Poetry', she is metonymically asking to be rescued from the burden of the female reproductive body, a burden that has been constructed by the demands of the marketplace.

In the following poem, 'To the Queen', it is not Fate but Queen Anne who rescues Egerton's 'trembling Muse' from this predicament. As in Chudleigh's volume, the speaker's worship of the queen is used as a justification of the forwardness of her verse, allowing her to 'press' her way through the crowds that choked and silenced her poetry in 'Satyr against the Muses':

> My trembling Muse, with awful Duty press,
> Mong'st kneeling crouds, with thy unfeign'd Address;
> Since meanest Slaves, to Altars may repair,
> With sacred Rites, of Sacrifice and Prayer.
> Heaven takes the Incense, if it is sincere,
> Freely as if the Great, had offer'd there,
> Bless'd with such hopes, my Muse, with Prostrate Zeal,
> Dare at the Feet of her great Sovereign kneel. (Poems, p. 17)

Around the queen Egerton constructs a fictional female community much like Chudleigh's:

Your Subjects modest merits [you] regard,
Virtue, not Impudence, now finds Reward;
Goodness like yours so [awes] the Bolder sort,
As makes a Sanctuary of your Court.

A virtuous stance once again justifies violence as Egerton prays for the queen's military triumphs over France:

Heaven be propitious to my Monarch's Arms,
And make them as Victorious, as her Charms,
Revenge on your proud Foes, their *Salick* Law,
With your fair Hand, their boasted Greatness awe. (*Poems*, p. 18)

But while Chudleigh ends poems at places from which public judgment would be possible – claiming the right to judge, but not specifically judging her contemporaries – Egerton explicitly links her own fantastic visions to Anne's political authority and even her imperialism.

After dutifully asking heaven for the queen's triumphs, Egerton's speaker switches to the first person and boldly demands comparable victories for herself as poet:

I shall not tremble, at the Launce, or Sword,
Will strait turn *Amazon*, but speak the Word;
Scarce can I curb, my eager loyal Soul,
For you I'd fight, Mankind from Pole to Pole,
Till all the Kingdoms, in one Empire meet,
Then lay the Crown at your Imperial Feet.
They'd bless the Arms, which did their Realms subdue,
And hug the Chains, which made them Slaves to you.

Egerton's poem to the queen ends by praising the queen and demanding action on her behalf: 'May every Subject you protect; Profess / As much as I, and dare to act no less' (*Poems*, p. 19). The following poem, 'The Liberty', moves from national political demands to sexual political ones, beginning with a condemnation of women's lack of formal education. The speaker asserts that she will 'not be scar'd, from Innocent delight' and will 'never to the Idol Custom bow' (*Poems*, p. 20). The poem ends with a commitment to conquer those emotional domains previously off-limits to virtuous women:

My darling Pen, will bolder Sallies make,
And like my self, an uncheck'd freedom take;
Not chain'd to the nice Order of my Sex,
And with restraints my wishing Soul perplex:
I'll blush at Sin, and not what some call Shame,
Secure my Virtue, slight precarious Fame. (*Poems*, p. 21)

Although the middle of Egerton's volume retreats from this assertion of female self-determination to the 'safe obscurity' of pastoral, she returns to the problem of female authority once more, near the end of the volume, in 'The Emulation': 'We will our Rights in Learning's World maintain, / Wits Empire, now, shall know a Female Reign' (*Poems*, pp. 32; 109).[37] Just as Anne's charms allow her to seek 'revenge' for the Salic Law that prohibits women from succeeding to the French throne in Chudleigh's *Poems*, so Egerton claims that it is virtuous to forego obedience in this situation, and to demand freedom in relation to men.

In their most zealous moments, both Chudleigh and Egerton condemn the inequality of marriage, particularly the word 'obey' in the marriage ceremony, which enslaves married women for life.[38] Although each of them backs away from this gesture at the end of her volume – Chudleigh returning to the idea of the prince's body, Egerton asking her muse for the fire to praise the male poet laureate – each uses the figure of Queen Anne to render a political hierarchy with aggressive female virtue reigning over the chaos of male sexual and economic demands.[39]

In Mary Astell's *Reflections upon Marriage*, the boldest presumptions of Chudleigh's and Egerton's poems are justified theoretically and pushed to demand changes for women within marriage. In 1696, two years after the death of Mary II, Astell dedicated the expanded edition of *A Serious Proposal to the Ladies, for the Advancement of their True and Greatest Interest* to 'Her Royal Highness The Princess Ann of Denmark'.[40] Astell writes in the dedication that the good reception of her work among 'Ladies in General', plus 'the Addition of a Second Part', has emboldened her to:

> a more Particular Application to Her who is the Principal of them [i.e. women], and whose Countenance and Example may reduce to practice, what [her book] can only Advise and Wish.

Princess Anne represents the ideal Astell has attempted to 'Advise and Wish' for other women. Anne's symbolic presence both sanctions the female community described in the first part of *A Serious Proposal*, and generates more writing to defend that community's interests. Astell's dedication concludes by eliding obedience to Anne – as virtuous female monarch – and the service to God she professes throughout *A Serious Proposal*:

> Princes become truly Godlike . . . when they shine as lights in the World by an Eminent and Heroic Vertue. A Vertue as much above Commendation as it is above Detraction, which sits equally Silent and Compos'd when Opprest with Praises or Pursu'd with Calumnys . . . the Service of God, and the Resembling Him, being its only Aim, His Approbation in a soft and inward Whisper, is more than the loud Huzza's and Plaudits of ten thousand Worlds.

Although Anne was not yet reigning, Astell makes her 'Godlike', just as she claims that women, though still subject to men, could approach God's divinity through the strength of their spiritual lives. In her dedication to other women, Astell urges them to imitate her *Proposal* – as she herself claims to imitate Anne – arguing that this change in their conduct will

> heighten [their] Value, by suffering [them] no longer to be cheap and contemptible . . . . fix [their] Beauty . . . by transferring it from a Corruptible Body to an immortal Mind. (p. 4)

Astell's 'immortal Mind' sounds very much like Chudleigh's 'unassailable Reason': it represents a position from which Astell can use Anne's 'Heroic Vertue', quite aggressively in fact, to judge the conduct of other women and men.

Like the speakers of Chudleigh's and Egerton's poems, Astell's narrator moves frequently towards God's vantage point:

> the true end of all our Prayers and external Observances is to work our minds into a truly Christian temper, to obtain for us the Empire of our Passions, and to reduce all irregular inclinations, that so we may be as like GOD in Purity, Chastity, and all his imitable excellencies, as is consistent with the imperfection of a Creature. (pp. 38–9)

It is from this position that she outlines the specific details of her proposed retreat for women in the following pages. The devotions described in this retreat refer implicitly to Anne, as they attempt to reinforce women's 'strict conformity to all the Precepts of their holy Mother the *Church*' and their resultant position above the economic and sexual demands of the world around them (p. 60). A religious woman, in relation to her own soul and the souls of other women, is in the position of the Augustan monarch:

> her Heroick Soul is too great to ambition any Empire but that of her own Breast, or to regard any other Conquest than the rescuing poor unhappy Souls from the Slavery of Sin and Satan, those . . . unsupportable Tyrants. (p. 65)

Although Astell uses Princess Anne symbolically, at the beginning of the first part of *A Serious Proposal*, to enforce women's authority over their own spiritual lives, she claims ultimately that friendship is better than monarchy because it is more pure, less tainted with ambitious and competitive motives (pp. 90–91). In Part II, all women are encouraged to become like the princess in relation to Louis XIV, 'to be kept [no] longer under [men's] Tyranny in Ignorance and Folly, since it is in your Power to regain your Freedom'.[41]

Finally, in *Reflections Upon Marriage*, Astell uses the spiritual authority accruing to women's devotional lives to criticize the 'Private

Tyranny' men hold over women in marriage.[42] Although she implicitly inscribes the narrator of *Reflections* as a man in the 1700 edition, she comes forward as a female author in the 1706 preface written during Anne's reign.[43] She claims that she has written all of *Reflections* herself, without turning over

> Antient or Modern Authors . . . with an *English* Spirit and Genius . . . meaning no hurt to anybody, nor designing any thing but the Publick Good, and to retrieve, if possible, the Native Liberty, the Rights and Privileges of the Subject. (sig. 2v)

The authority of Anne as female monarch allows Astell to challenge the belief that men are naturally superior to women:

> For if by the Natural Superiority of their Sex, they mean that every man is by Nature superior to every woman . . . it would be a sin in any woman to have Dominion over any man, and the greatest Queen ought not to command but to obey her Footman, because no Municipal Laws can supercede or change the Law of Nature. (sig. A1)

Just as Queen Anne claims a natural right to govern men, women who praise her are empowered to enter intellectual worlds formerly colonized by men:

> To all the great things that Women might perform, Inspir'd by her Example, Encourag'd by her Smiles, and supported by her Power! To their Discovery of New Worlds, for the Exercise of her Goodness, New Sciences to publish her Fame, and reducing Nature itself to a Subjection to her Empire! To their destroying those worst of Tyrants Impiety and Immorality, which dare to stalk about even in her own Dominions, and to devour Souls almost within view of her Throne, leaving a stench behind them scarce to be corrected even by the Incense of her Devotions! (sig. b4)

The images of cannibalism and burning flesh with which this passage ends suggest the fierce identification at work between Astell and her warrior queen – or, more precisely, the fantasy by which women writers imagined themselves fighting against their opponents on the queen's behalf. When a disembodied, disinterested 'Reason' fails to vanquish the opponents of women's virtue – because that reason was, time and again, a dominion possessed by men – Chudleigh, Egerton and Astell arm virtue in the garb of the female monarch and use her, symbolically, to sanction women's political and linguistic forwardness.

WRITING

True state within

Women's elegy 1640–1700

Kate Lilley

I

Elegy engages persistently with the figuration of desire under the aspect of lack, or interdiction, and the quest for a sufficiently reparative language. This generic problematic offers rich and suggestive material for an analysis of the relations between gender and genre. What positions are available to a woman as writing subject? What is her relation and access to strategies of consolation? What are the possibilities and impossibilities, at once formal and ideological, of inscribing herself within a specific historical formation, and a specific literary practice? Elegy makes up a conspicuous part of women's poetic production in the seventeenth century, and would command attention on quantitative terms alone; but it is also an unusually mobile genre, which upsets the putative divisions between high and low culture, literary and non-literary women, private and public, occasional and non-occasional writing.[1] What follows is an effort to recuperate women in seventeenth-century elegy from phantasmic objects to desiring, mourning, writing subjects, for, as Ann Rosalind Jones has recently argued, 'there is a difference between being the subject *of* discourse and being a subject *in* discourse'.[2] Equally, as subjects in discourse, women must negotiate gender ideology and the dominant tropes of feminine representation in their own writing, but in doing so they are neither entirely powerless and automatized, nor entirely free and powerful. I shall be concerned with those gendered processes of negotiation in the field of seventeenth-century women's elegy, as they are registered formally, at the level of genre and trope.

The canonical version of elegy is emphatically masculine – 'Astrophel',

'Lycidas', Gray's 'Elegy in a Country Churchyard', *Adonais, In Memoriam,* 'Thyrsis' – and this masculinity is compounded by, and encoded in, a persistent concern with vocation, the creation of heroic genealogies and lines of apostolic succession. Such narratives of succession are, in turn, linked to the rhetorical defence of patriarchal privilege against feminine incursions and monstrous seductions: the threat of the woman-as-subject. In Cowley's 'On the Death of Mrs. Katherine Philips', for instance, apparently decorous praise for, and sympathy with, the serenely isolated female elegized generates a gender-specific anxiety and envy on the part of the male elegist:

> The trade of glory manag'd by the pen
> Though great it be, and everywhere is found,
> Does bring in but small profit to us men;
> 'Tis by the number of the sharers drown'd,
> Orinda in the female coasts of fame
> Engrosses all the goods of a poetic name,
> She does no partner with her see;
> Does all the business there alone which we
> Are forc'd to carry on by a whole company.[3]

'Orinda' is praised and limited as an exotic maverick, not only disconnected from any fruitful tradition, past or future, but privileged to be so cut adrift: 'Of female Poets who had names of old, / Nothing is shown but only told, / And all we hear of them, perhaps may be / Male flattery only, and male Poetry' (III, lines 49–52). Such a commendatory trope, with its 'perhaps may be', breeds suspicion: Cowley's own 'male Poetry', if not another instance of 'Male flattery only', remains a highly ambiguous and defensive memorial. The elegy's economic imagery realizes the quasi-sexual threat of the 'engrossing', trespassing, writing woman whose 'circulation' and productivity endangers the masculine 'trade of glory'. As Cowley writes in the more explicitly sexualized context of 'Upon Mrs. Philips her Poems':

> So easily they from thee come,
>   And there is so much room,
> In the unexhausted and unfathom'd womb;
> That, like the Holland Countess, thou might'st bear
> A child for ev'ry day of all the fertile year.
> Thou dost my wonder, wouldst my envy raise,
> If to be prais'd I lov'd more than to praise. (lines 39–45)

Male elegists tend to honour or challenge their nominated 'fathers', from whom they inherit the mantle of authority, while women prominent in their own right are less likely to be elegized than are the mothers of great men, in a line descended from the Virgin Mary. On the whole, women as elegized are recuperated for heroic masculine genealogies, as facilitating muses (for instance, Jonson's 'Elegy on My Muse, the Truly Honoured, the Lady Venetia Digby . . .') or, more crudely, literal receptacles, as in this 1655 broadside elegy for Elizabeth Cromwell:

> Renowned mother of our Lord
> Great OLIVER Protector,
> Thou noble Root that didst afford
> *Great Britain's* Weal's Affector!
> Like *Helen*, sometime honoured
> For Great *Constantine's* Mother;
> So thou for Us hast born and bred
> One truely such another.[4]

Women appear as themselves books of virtue: Donne writes of Elizabeth Drury in the *Second Anniversary*, 'she tooke, / (Taking her selfe) our best, and worthiest booke' (lines 319–20). In the handful of elegies by men for Anne Bradstreet, Katherine Philips, Aphra Behn, Margaret Cavendish and Anne Killigrew, their uniqueness is stressed, thus minimizing their threat, and the fact of their writing tends to be subsumed under a more general praise of feminine accomplishment and virtue.[5]

What is perhaps more telling than these masculine representations and elisions of women as elegized is that, amongst the 150-odd women's elegies I have found, the only poem by a woman mourning another woman writer is the anonymous 1689 broadside 'An Elegy Upon The Death of Mrs. A. Behn; The Incomparable Astrea. By a Young Lady of Quality'. While linking Behn and Philips, this elegy expressly laments the impossibility of constructing or sustaining a female tradition:

> IV
> Who now, of all the inspired Race,
> Shall take *Orinda's* Place?
>   Or who the Hero's fame shall raise?
>   Who now shall fill the Vacant Throne?
>   The bright *Astrea's* gone . . .
> VI
> Let all our Hopes despair and dye,
> Our Sex for ever shall neglected lye;
> Aspiring Man has now regain'd the Sway,
> To them we've lost the Dismal Day:
>   *Astrea* an equal Ballance held,
>   (Tho' she deserv'd it all;)
>   But now the rich Inheritance must fall;
>   To them with Grief we yeild [*sic*]
>   The Glorious envy'd Field.
> Of her own Sex, not one is found
>   Who dares her Laurel wear,

Withheld by Impotence or Fear;
With her it withers on the Ground,
Untouch'd, and cold as she,
And Reverenc'd to that degree,
That none will dare to save
The Sacred Relick from the Grave;
Intomb'd with her, and never to return,
Fills up the narrow Urn,
Which more Presumption, or more Courage has than we.
(lines 68–72; 89–108)[6]

There are, however, some 15 elegies by women for male writers, most of these for Dryden in the two collections of 1700. *Luctus Britannici* contains an elegy each by Elizabeth Thomas (who corresponded with Dryden) and Sarah Fyge Egerton, amongst the contributions of 'the gentleman of the two Universities'. *The Nine Muses, or, Poems Written by Nine Severall Ladies Upon the Death of the Late Famous John Dryden, Esq.*, written in fact by six women at the instigation of Delarivier Manley, includes three elegies by Fyge, two by Manley, and one each by Mary Pix, Catharine Trotter, Sarah, Lady Piers and Susanna Centlivre. This is the only avowedly collective poetic text by women in the century, and a striking generic intervention in a particularly male territory: the public memorial volume. In terms of generic convention, the direct conflation of female elegists with female muses shows an even more startling rhetorical daring. By occupying the site of the muses, these women trope themselves not only as the source of their own power and voice, but as the source of all poetic power.[7]

Dryden seems an appropriate choice for Manley's venture in several ways: playwright, poet laureate, and a prominent elegist of both men and women, author of the ode on Killigrew (1686) and 'Eleonora' (1692), as well as elegies for Cromwell, Charles II and Oldham. He was also known as sympathetic to women writers, and as a friend to Aphra Behn. Most of the authors of *The Nine Muses* wrote for the stage (Manley, Pix and Trotter had been fairly recently satirized in *The Female Wits*, 1696–7); all could be loosely described as followers of Behn; and Catharine Trotter, at least, like Dryden and probably Behn, was a Catholic convert. Manley had claimed Dryden as a dramatic model in the preface to her play *The Royal Mischief* (1696), and in the elegy by her which opens *The Nine Muses*, she laments Dryden's loss as the chief elegist of his time, and particularly as an elegist of women, in the character of Melpomene, 'the Tragick Muse':

For who like him can e'er invoke me now
Who sang fair *Killigrew's* untimely fall,

And more than *Roman* made her Funeral.
Inspir'd *by Me*, for me, he cou'd Command,
Bright *Abingdon's* rich Monument shall stand
For evermore, the Wonder of the Land. (lines 10–15)

Between 1640 and Dryden's death in 1700, elegies by women for male
writers are scarce. Anne Bradstreet's 1650 collection, *The Tenth Muse*,
included a very belated elegy on Philip Sidney, and another on Du Bartas;
Katherine Philips published a memorial poem for William Cartwright in
1651; and then there is a gap of over 30 years before the appearance in
print of elegies by Aphra Behn and Anne Wharton on Rochester, who had
died in 1680.[8] In 1688 Behn's 'On the Death of E. Waller, Esq.' was the
sole female contribution to the volume *Poems to the Memory of that
Incomparable Poet, Edmond Waller Esquire*; Wharton, who had
corresponded with Waller, died in 1685, or she might again have been
Behn's partner in elegy.

The elegy by Wharton, who was Rochester's first cousin once removed,
was the best known and most often reprinted (after her death) of a number
of poems which stress his notorious death-bed recantation. She claims
him as the tutor of her 'Infant Muse' and, lamenting that 'this matchless
Pattern went astray', reclaims him as the model of 'a Penitence so fixt, so
true, / A greater Penitence, no Saint e're knew'. Behn's semi-satirical
Spenserian elegy, 'On the Death of the late Earl of Rochester', stands alone
in celebrating the unreformed Rochester as a model for writing and for
living, and in privileging the erotics of pastoral. In rejecting the sanitized
Rochester, she also offers a formal critique of the sanitized pastoral elegies
occasioned by his death: Oldham's 'Bion, A Pastoral, in Imitation of the
Greek of Moschus', Flatman's 'On the Death of My Lord Rochester:
Pastoral', and Samuel Woodford's 'An Ode to the Memory of the Right
Honourable John Lord Wilmot Earl of Rochester'. She mourns the loss of
his 'piercing, pointed' promiscuity ('freely he bestow'd, / And like a God,
dealt to the wond'ring Crowd') and, equally, his 'sharp Pen' and
'chastising stroke': 'That dear instructing Rage is now allay'd'.

A heroic, erotic figure of interdependent intellectual, verbal and sexual
energy, in Behn's text Rochester the libertine is also subordinated to
feminine desire and sexual potency. She figures him as a sacrificial slave
to women, his death as detumescence, scandalously rewriting the trope of
virgin vigil, usually associated with virgins protecting virgins, a charmed
circle guarding and venerating a now eternal chastity:

Mourn, all ye Beauties, put your *Cyprus* on,
The truest Swain that e're Ador'd you's gone . . .
Bring Garlands all of never-dying Flow'rs,

Bedew'd with everlasting Show'rs;
Fix your fair eyes upon your victim'd Slave,
Sent Gay and Young to his untimely Grave . . . .
So early Roses fade, so over all
They cast their fragrant scents, then softly fall,
While all the scatter'd perfum'd leaves declare,
How lovely 'twas when whole, how sweet, how fair.

Aligning 'Strephon' with Ovid, against the pious renovation of Wharton and other elegists, Behn, who was commonly linked with Sappho, tacitly twins herself with him. Anne Wharton responded equivocally, combining admiration with barely veiled censure in 'To Mrs. A. Behn on what she writ of the Earl of Rochester':

> May yours excel the Matchless *Sappho's* Name;
> May you have all her Wit, without her Shame . . .
> Scorn meaner Theams, declining low desire,
> And bid your Muse maintain a Vestal Fire. (lines 16–17, 22–3)

In Wharton's putative compliment poem, a merely implicit criticism of Behn's celebration of Rochester as libertine hero is subsumed by an explicitly gender-specific warning. Behn replies with a more deliberately blasphemous and defiantly erotic vision of her own election as Rochester's successor, figuring her texts as the fruit of this unholy poetic coupling:

> When lo the Mighty Spirit appear'd,
> All Gay, all Charming to my sight;
> My Drooping Soul it Rais'd and Cheer'd,
> And cast about a Dazling Light.
> In every part there did appear,
> The Great, the God-like *Rochester*,
> His Softness all, his Sweetness everywhere.
> It did advance, and with a Generous Look,
> To me Addrest, to worthless me it spoke:
> With the same wonted Grace my Muse it prais'd,
> With the same Goodness did my Faults correct;
> And careful of the Fame himself first rais'd,
> Obligingly it School'd my loose Neglect.
> The soft, the moving Accents soon I knew
> The gentle Voice made up of Harmony;
> Through the Known paths of my glad Soul it flew;
> I knew it straight, it could no others be,
> 'Twas not Alied but very very he.
> So the All-Ravisht Swain that hears
> The wondrous Musick of the Sphears,
> For ever does the grateful Sound retain . . . .
> So Gods of old sometimes laid by
> Their Awful trains of Majesty,

And chang'd ev'n Heav'n a while for Groves and Plains,
And to their Fellow-Gods preferr'd the lowly Swains.
(lines 26–46; 61–4)

Ann Rosalind Jones warns, 'It is important not to overestimate the room
for maneuver available to women', given 'the absolute centrality of men
as writers and as readers':

> Every woman poet recognized the necessity of winning men over to her side as
> mentors and as critics . . . And although women poets occasionally open or
> close their collections with appeals to women readers, it is very rare to find
> them acknowledging or taking encouragement from other women poets.
> (Jones, p. 80)

We can find here some explanation for the existence of women's elegies
for male but not for female writers, for although seventeenth-century
women did write commendatory poems for other women poets, they do
not seem to have written (and certainly did not publish) elegies. Elegy and
commendation imply a different order of speaking for, and different
claims for the value and longevity of the work, rather than the life. A
woman writer is not an unproblematically available subject position, not
the guarantee of what Jones calls a 'self-enclosed oeuvre' (p. 91): her texts
do not belong to posterity; they are temporary, evanescent, maverick. An
affirmative chorus is therefore desirable for a woman's solo publication
at the moment of its becoming public. There, it is appropriate and
decorous to gesture towards the collectivity of a group text. Sarah Fyge's
Poems on Several Occasions (1703), for instance, includes four commendatory verses, at least two of which are by women ('M.P.', i.e., Mary Pix,
'J.H.' (John Heydon?), 'S.C.', i.e., Susanna Centlivre, and 'E.C .').
Centlivre proclaims her as 'Thou Champion for our Sex', to whom
'Sappho the Great . . . / Would yield her Laurels were she living now', but
when Fyge died in 1723, no elegies were forthcoming.

This sense of a possible sorority, the parallelism of shared practices in
commendatory poems – as distinct from the alien heroism of vocation
and succession implied by literary elegies – has an analogue, I suggest, in
the preponderance of what I will call *proxy elegies* in the writing of
women. These are elegies addressed to and focused on the bereaved
rather than the elegized, encompassing what would usually be thought of
as distinct categories of elegy – private as well as public, familial as well as
non-familial – such as Katherine Philips's 'To my dearest friend Mrs. A.
Owen on her greatest Loss' and 'To Mrs. Wogan on the Death of her
Husband, a Good Man' (*Poems*, 1664), Jane Barker's 'To my Dear
Cousin Mrs. M.T. after the Death of her Husband and Son' (*Poetical
Recreations*, 1688), Aphra Behn's *A Poem Humbly Dedicated To the*

*Great Patern of Piety and Virtue Catherine Queen Dowager. On the
Death Of Her Dear Lord and Husband King Charles II* (1685), and
Margaret Cavendish's linked pair, 'On a Mother dyed for griefe of her
only daughter which dyed' and 'On a beautifull young maid dyed
daughter to the grieved Mother' (*Poems and Fancies*, 1653).[9]

Such elegies focus on the profoundly mediated character of women's
lives, women's texts, and the social, economic and legal consequences for
women of bereavement (the shift, for instance, from wife to widow;
mother to non-mother). In doing so they also engage questions of
inheritance, hierarchies of grief, and women's responsibilities towards
each other, both in a directly familial context, and with respect to the
feminized culture of mourning, as in these lines by Jane Barker:

Dear Coz. I hope by this time you have dry'd,
At least set bounds to th'almost boundless tide
Of flowing *Tears*: I'm sure my wish is so,
Which Love and Int'rest does oblige me to;
For you can bear no Sufferings alone,
All yours are mine by *participation*;

And doubtless all your *Friends*, in some degree,
Must bear a share, if they can love like me . . .
But after all that can be said on this,
I am not ignorant how hard it is
To conquer Passions, and our selves subdue;
Though advis'd by *Friends*, and assisted too
By the prevailing Powers of *Grace* from *Heav'n*,
Still *Counsel's* harder to be took than giv'n:
Not that I thought your Griefs profuse, but knew
Much to a *Son*, more to a *Husband's* due . . . .
(Jane Barker, 'To my Dear Cousin Mrs. M.T. . . .')[10]

If we look for elegies by women for more unequivocally public women
than writers, particularly queens, they too are very scarce – Anne
Bradstreet on Elizabeth I, Katherine Philips on the exiled Queen of
Bohemia, and two anonymous elegies for Queen Mary.[11] As in the case of
elegies for writers, the number of elegies by women for kings and other
heroic men, though still not large, is far greater: Philips's on Charles I and
a number of other prominent royalists; 'An Epitaph on Gilbert Sheldon,
Arch-bishop of Canterbury' by 'Ephelia' (*Female Poems*, 1679); Behn's
elegy for Charles II, *A Pindarick on the Death of our Late Soverign*
(1685); Anne Finch's *On the Death of King James II* (1701) and 'Upon the
Death of Sir William Twisden'; and Sarah Fyge's 'On the Death of
William III, King of England'.

Bradstreet's very belated 'In Honour of that High and Mighty Princess

Queen Elizabeth of happy memory' (dated 1643, published in 1650) is unusually combative and also unusually dislocated from the context of death and public mourning – that is, unusually appropriative. In silent comparison with the 'present troubles' lamented in her 'A Dialogue between Old *England* and New' (1642), Bradstreet (daughter of the prominent Puritan, Thomas Dudley) celebrates the apotheosis of female rule in Elizabeth's Protestant diplomacy and statesmanship:

> Was ever people better rul'd than hers?
> Was ever Land more happy, freed from stirs?
> Did ever wealth in England so abound?

But Bradstreet's elegy is more engaged by gender than politics, though the two are intertwined. In mourning a woman of 'no fit parallel', she polemically equates her own lateness with a woman's sense of being out of place, 'out of date' (in 'Proem') and outnumbered:

> 'Mongst hundred Hecatombs of roaring Verse,
> Mine bleating stands before thy royall Herse . . .
> Her personall perfections, who would tell,
> Must dip his Pen i'th' Heliconian Well;
> Which I may not, my pride doth but aspire,
> To read what others write, and then admire.

In the lines which immediately follow, Bradstreet redeploys her lateness as a vindicating weapon against the timely, opportunistic 'Masculines', whose elegies for Elizabeth prove their treason to her sex:

> Now say, have women worth, or have they none?
> Or had they some, but with our Queen ist gone?
> Nay Masculines, you have thus tax'd us long,
> But she though dead, will vindicate our wrong.
> Let such, as say our sex is void of reason,
> Know 'tis a slander now, but once was treason.
> But happy *England*, which had such a Queen,
> O happy, happy, had those days still been . . . .

For the sake of her argument, Bradstreet makes Elizabeth a synecdoche for all women; and the Queen's male elegists a synecdoche for all men: but the knowledge that these connections are flawed and finally rhetorical leaves the anomalous female elegist poised between nostalgia and the deferred consolation of the kingdom to come. As Ivy Schweitzer argues, Bradstreet's elegy eventually 'locates Elizabeth, the physical and symbolic center of the Renaissance, outside of her historical and literary context in the higher sphere of Puritan millennialism'.[12]

The precursor of Bradstreet's poem is another golden age elegy, Diana Primrose's even more fully polemical, anti-papist and anti-masculine *A*

Chaine of Pearle. Or a memoriall of queene Elizabeth. Published in 1630, 27 years after the death of Elizabeth, it justifies its own occasion. The elegist offers her 'lines so black and impolite' to 'all Noble Ladies and Gentle-Women', stressing elegy as permission rather than interdiction, generically sanctioning a woman's access to the rhetoric of blame as well as praise, breaching only gender decorum. Decrying her own 'ill-composed Pearly-Rowes', the elegist celebrates the lost Queen as the recuperable, enabling emblem of public chastity and powerful feminine voice who, by never 'yeelding to Mens Syren-blandishments,/Which are attended with so foule Events', was able to 'drowne a World of men' with 'Oratory-ravishments'.

What hierarchy governs the decorum – or indecorum – of a woman's mourning, a woman's text? That women participated at all in formal public elegy might seem surprising, given our assumptions of the privacy, domesticity and circumscription of women's poetry in the early modern period (and even beyond). The literature of public, polemical elegy, both high and low, was extremely copious in the latter half of the seventeenth century, but women's participation, though not negligible, accounts for only a small proportion of elegies known to be by women in this period.[13] These texts do, however, occupy an interesting place in the history of women's publication, not only because of their public character, but because they often mark the first and sometimes only publication of the woman concerned. *A Chaine of Pearle* is the only known text by Diana Primrose. Katherine Philips's 'In Memory of Mr. Cartwright', included in *Comedies, Tragi-Comedies, With Other Poems, By Mr William Cartwright, late Student of Christ-church* . . . (1651) was her first published poem. Whether or not the 'Elegy Upon The Death of Mrs. A. Behn' is by Manley, the author claims that it is the compulsion to elegize which has propelled her 'sullen Muse, that ne're before/The sacred Title wore' (lines 28–9) into print. Elizabeth Thomas's anonymous contribution to *Luctus Britannici* was her first appearance in print (though, on her own account, she was first moved to write by the death of female friends). *On the Death of King James II. By a Lady* (1701) was Anne Finch's second anonymous, solo publication (a broadside, *The Prerogatives of Love*, was issued in 1695, *The Spleen* in 1709, and her *Miscellany Poems* in 1713). There were also a number of women who did not regard themselves as writers at all, or at least not writers of poetry, who contributed elegies, usually brief and in very simple verse forms, to collections of Quaker testimonies, like those for Anne Whitehead in *Piety Promoted by Faithfulness* (1686).[14]

So, although some women did engage in expressly political memorials

– sometimes for immediate publication (for instance, Primrose, Behn and Finch) and sometimes not (Philips on Charles I)[15] – and some looked to writing for at least part of their income, most wrote within a domestic-erotic-familial space, privatized but by no means entirely discrete, personal but not at all cut adrift from politics. In fact, a number of their elegies expressly mourn the impossibility of any clear division between the private and the public, the familial and the political, as in Anne Killigrew's 'On my Aunt Mrs A.K. Drown'd under London-bridge, in the Queens Bardge, Anno 1641':

> When angry Heav'n extinguisht her fair Light,
> It seem'd to say, *Nought's Precious in my sight*;
> *As I in Waves this Paragon have drown'd,*
> *The Nation next, and King I will confound.*[16]

Elegy provided a framework for figuring the unstable relations and shifting boundaries of inside and outside, self and other, family and nation, the private body and the body politic. Anne Killigrew's long and graphic 'The Miseries of Man', for instance, turns out to be largely concerned with the attendant, mediated miseries of the non-combatants, women and children, as well as a lament for the injuries sustained on both sides, on and off the field, visible and invisible:

> And who can say, when Thousands are betray'd,
> To Widdowhood, Orphants or Childless made.
> Whither the Day does draw more Tears or Blood,
> A greater Chrystal, or a Crimson Floud.
> The faithful Wife, who late her Lord did Arm,
> And hop'd to shield, by holy Vows, from Harm . . .
> May now go seek him, lying 'mong the Slain:
> Low on the Earth she'l find his lofty Crest,
> And those refulgent Arms which late his Breast
> Did guard, by rough Encounters broke and tore,
> His Face and Hair, with Brains all clotted ore.
> And Warlike Weeds besmeer'd with Dust and Gore . . . .
> So that on each Event if we reflect,
> The Joys and Sufferings of both sides collect,
> We cannot say where lies the greatest Pain,
> In the fond Pursuit, Loss, or Empty Gain.[17]

Nor is this model of the problematics of the genre true only for aristocratic, royalist women. It applies equally (though differently) to a woman such as the Quaker, Mary Southworth Mollineux (1651–95), whose single 'Elegy' for her parents, dated 1682, ruminates on gender, love and authority. Giving almost equal space to father and mother (seven not entirely uncritical stanzas to him, six eulogizing her), she offers complementary models of parents' 'natural Affection': 'Affliction

and Chastisement be / Undoubted Characters of Father's Love' (stanza
1); 'those, who knew her well, might learn, / By her Example, to become
more mild' (Stanza 18). As a corollary, Mollineux insists on a daughter's
right (indeed 'filial Duty') to elegize, even as she questions both her own
ability to write and the decorum and efficacy of the genre itself:

> Well, though both he and she be gone to Rest,
>   And cannot with our Sorrows now be mov'd,
> Nor with the Frownings of this World oppress'd,
>   Wherewith some may as yet be further prov'd,
>   Their Names engraved in our Hearts, may not
>   Be raz'd, or cancel'd, or in Time forgot.
>
> Nor shall we study high Hyperboles,
>   So to perpetuate their Memory,
> Or raise a Monument of common Praise,
>   Which cannot add to their Felicity;
>   For they were what this insufficient Pen,
>   Cannot describe unto surviving Men.[18]

A critical engagement with questions of decorum and hierarchy looms
large in the consciously marginalized discourse of women's elegy. As
Mary Mollineux marks her poem as the daughter's elegy, so Behn's *A
Poem Humbly Dedicated to Catherine Queen Dowager*, and Finch's *On
the Death of King James II*, in the act of writing public elegy, assert the
priority of private grief, even at the highest level: the daughter-subject's
duty to elegize (offered as a specifically disinterested feminine loyalty)
defers to the bereaved Queen as chief mourner. Similarly, in the context
of familial elegy, Jane Barker's 'On the Death of my Brother' calls for and
dramatizes a public and professional mourning, whilst privileging a
sister's grief over that of 'the *Apollo's* of thy noble Art, /(Who seem'd to
grudge me in their grief a part)'. Barker's fear of masculine, public
usurpation of a woman's private grief is mooted and contained in the
repeated exercise of her right to elegize (she wrote four poems on the
death of her physician brother). It is also rhetorically resolved by
introducing as reported speech a public, professional endorsement of her
own familial priority as the authentic origin of mourning:

> But I, as if the Fountain of this Source,
> With Handkerchiefs strove to retard the course;
> But all in vain, my real loss was great,
> As many thought, whose Words I here repeat:
> 'I cannot blame you for lamenting so,
> 'Since better friend no friend did e'er forgo;
> 'A publick Sorrow for this loss is due,
> 'The Nation surely, Madam, mourns with you'.

II

Familial elegy accounts for the greatest concentration of elegies by women in the seventeenth century.[19] Amongst them are poems from daughters to parents, mothers to children, sisters to siblings and wives to husbands, but by far the greater number mourn the loss of one or more male relatives, a brother, father, husband or son. Many of them are proxy elegies, written on behalf of a bereaved friend or relative. Centering on a discussion of Katherine Philips, the most prolific woman elegist of the century, I want to trace some of the implications of a woman's discourse of familial relationship, in relation to narratives of women's fate, for an understanding of the negotiations between textuality and sexuality, gender and genre in this period.[20]

By seventeenth-century standards Philips herself did not suffer unusually from bereavement, but her textualizations of the relations, constraints and contradictory loyalties of a woman's life are deeply elegiac.[21] She places her own history as one among many parallel narratives of a woman's fate, of desire reined in by the conservative and feminine virtues of submission and conformity to hierarchy and order, to ideals of virtue and chastity. The experience and the expectation of loss, the sense of lack as structural and impersonal, are crucial to her literary production and to her figuring of a woman's relation to writing.

The necessity and constancy of Philips's discourse of mourning pivots on the early death of her only son, Hector, in 1655, and the failure of succession it threatens:

> Seaven years Childless Marriage past,
> A Son, a Son is born at last;
> So exactly limm'd and Fair,
> Full of good Spirits, Meen, and Aire,
> As a long life promised;
> Yet, in less than six weeks, dead . . . .
> So the Subtle Alchymist,
> Can't with Hermes-seal resist
> The Powerful Spirit's subtler flight,
> But 'twill bid him long good night.
> ('Epitaph. On her Son H.P. at St. Syth's Church where her body also lies
> Interred', lines 5–10; 15–18)[22]

In the last year of her life, 1664, Philips wrote of another only son and heir, Lord Rich (son of Lady Mary Rich): 'For since such expectations brittle prove,/What can we safely either hope or love?' ('On the Death of my Lord Rich').

Katherine Philips wrote an elegy and an epitaph on Hector in the year of his death, and the related 'Song: 'Tis true our life is but a long disease',

which ends: 'Our hopes are crost, / Or else the object lost, / Ere we can
call it ours'. A year later Katherine had a daughter to mitigate the loss of
her 'first and dearest childe', but in 1660 Katherine's step-daughter,
Francis Philips, also died: they had lived as mother and daughter for 12
years and since at the time of Katherine's marriage in 1648 Francis was
not yet one, their intimacy was all the greater. In direct contrast to the
poems for Hector, her 'lovely boy', Katherine's elegy for Francis, 'In
Memory of F.P.', never at any point specifies the gender of the elegized
encrypted in the title's initials, maintaining an intimate but gender-
neutral I/thou relation. She adopts a maternal subject position which
embraces the children of her own flesh and those consigned to her
protection 'through dearest ties and highest trust' (line 79), assimilating
the death of Francis to a mother's 'lost estate', where yield does not
guarantee an increase (in her case, $1 + 1-1 + 1-1 = 1$) and the accumulation
of grief leads only to an increased awareness of rhetorical inadequacy:

> If I could ever write a lasting verse,
> It should be laid, dear Saint, upon thy hearse.
> But Sorrow is no Muse, and does confess,
> That it least can, what it would most express.
> Yet that I may some bounds to Grief allow,
> I'll try if I can weep in numbers now. (lines 1–6)[23]

The poet-as-mother's desire for 'a lasting verse' to deck the hearse of her
unlasting child yields a discourse on the blighted fruits of elegy, mourning
women's productivity and care as inherently flawed, and women's
impoverished relation to language.

The occasion of elegy always marks the recognition of desire as lack
and the confession of a structural inadequacy – 'Sorrow . . . least can,
what it would most express' – but the syntax of this opening inscribes a
particularly acute engagement with the processes of resisting and
representing elegy's negative knowledge, refusing silence: 'If I could ever
. . . but . . . yet . . . I'll try'. A woman's difficulty in troping the self as text is
doubled with a mother's resistance to the reification of her lost child (the
opposite of 'Ben Jonson his best piece of poetry'). In the lines that follow,
she conducts a self-conscious trial of her ability to rehearse the
conventional gestures of elegy, the high rhetoric of apostrophe and
questioning, and finds them ill-fitting, 'in vain':

> Ah, beauteous blossom, too untimely dead!
> Whither, ah, whither is thy sweetness fled?
> Where are the charms that always did arise
> From the prevailing language of thy eyes?
> Where is thy beauteous and lovely mien,
> And all the wonders that in thee were seen?

> Alas! in vain, in vain on thee I rave;
> There is no pity in the stupid grave. (lines 7–14)

Figuring herself as like the 'bankrupt' who 'Begs for his lost estate', the elegist points to the difference of woman's 'estate', a maternal, domestic, affective, erotic economy where debts pile up as a consequence of the failure to limit 'injurious tears' (line 76) and 'Affection's sad excess' (line 78). A woman's 'ruin' is located in the double bind of her affective surplus (it is required of her and she is punished for it) and, more fundamentally, in the insecurity and contingency of a woman's labour and a woman's name; her problematic relation to language, law, publication and literary history. As Anne Bradstreet writes in the 'Prologue' to *The Tenth Muse*:

> My foolish, broken, blemish'd Muse so sings;
> And this to mend, alas, no Art is able,
> 'Cause Nature made it so irreparable.

A woman's productivity is troped as inherently flawed, even before she begins to elegize her particular history of loss. In Philips's elegy for 'F.P.', woman as cultivator and nurturer is likened to the swain who 'beholds his ripen'd corn/By some rough wind without a sickle torn' (lines 65–6). Men sow and women reap, but the harvest is bitter, invisibly decimated; when the crop fails her profit turns to deficit, and she is left to mourn her vanished 'fortune': 'Such fools are we, so fatally we choose,/That what we most would keep, we soonest lose' (lines 55–6).

'Fortune' and 'fate' are the talismanic words which echo throughout seventeenth-century women's elegy, often privileged in poetic titles: 'Ephelia' and Anne Wharton both wrote poems called 'My Fate'; Sarah Fyge called one 'The Fatality'. They are the bearers of a sense of women's biocultural destiny: that 'fate' which inheres in the 'fatality' of her body; the inherent instability and treachery of the subject positions available to a woman as mother, daughter, sister, lover, friend, virgin, wife, widow. In 'My Fate', 'Ephelia' laments this perpetual sliding and mediation, her text modulating from parental to love elegy:

> Oh cruel Fate, when wilt thou weary be?
> When satisfied with tormenting me?
> What have I e're design'd, but thou hast crost?
> All that I wisht to gain by Thee, I've lost:
> From my first Infancy, thy Spight thou'st shown,
> And from my Cradle, I've thy Malice known;
> Thou snatch'st my Parents in their tender Age,
> Made me a Victim to the furious Rage
> Of cruel Fortune, as severe as thee;
> Yet I resolv'd to brave my Destiny,
> And did, with more than female Constancy.

Not all thy Malice cou'd extort a Tear,
Nor all thy Rage cou'd ever teach me Fear:
Still as thy Pow'r diminisht my Estate,
My Fortitude did my Desires abate;
In every state I thought my Mind content,
And wisely did thy cross Designs prevent:
Seeing thy Plots did unsuccessful prove,
As a sure Torment next, thou taught'st me Love . . .
Of all her Plagues, this was the weightiest Stroke,
This Blow my resolv'd Heart hath almost broke:
Yet, spight of Fate, this Comfort I've in store,
She's no room left for any ill thing more.[24]

Masculine, canonical elegy is dominated by the drive towards succession and self-placing, and the construction of heroic genealogies. Its central narratives concern desire deferred, the reification or elision of the elegized, and strategies of textual possession and inscription.[25] Women's elegy, at least in the seventeenth century, seems to partake of a logic of renunciation and cancellation, expressly refusing the reification of the elegized. The woman elegist tropes writing as immaterial – invisible ink – at her own expense. Again and again women's elegies refuse the consolations we associate with elegy, to close either by announcing the death of their writing:

An Off'ring too for thy sad Tomb I have,
Too just a tribute to thy early Herse,
Receive these gasping numbers to thy grave,
The last of thy unhappy Mothers Verse
(Philips, 'On the death of my first and dearest childe', V)

or, as in the elegy for 'F.P.', their own desire to die:

But I'll resign, and follow thee as fast
As my unhappy minutes will make haste . . . .
For such a loss as this (bright Soul!) is not
Ever to be repaired, or forgot. (lines 83–4; 87–8)

In all her writing, Philips dreams of a charmed, inviolate circle, an inner sanctum within the safety of which texts circulate 'freely'. Her 'Society of Friendship' as an ideological model celebrates a closed, chiefly feminine world of writing and reading, while her poems addressed to public figures, like her letters to 'Poliarchus' (Charles Cotterell, the Master of Ceremonies at the court of Charles II), idealize the elite culture of the court as a class sanctuary from 'the rabble', and the horror of uncontrolled publication as 'exposure'. To Cotterell, on learning of the pirated edition of her poems in 1664, she wrote:

[I] who never writ any line in my life with an intention to have it printed . . . to
entertain all the rabble . . . to be the sport of some that can, and some that
cannot read a verse. This is a most cruel accident . . . really it hath cost me a
sharp fit of sickness . . . I am so innocent of that wretched artifice of a secret
consent . . . I am so little concerned for the reputation of writing sense, that
provided the world would believe me innocent of any manner of knowledge,
much less connivance at this publication, I shall willingly compound never to
trouble them with the true copies.[26]

But this tightly controlled and limited model of a dialogic, literary chain
of poems and letters is always threatened – never a closed system,
hermetically sealed, but susceptible to rupture and 'cruel accident'. A
woman stands to lose all of those signs and ties through which her
identity is constructed: her name, her property, her children, her
husband, her texts. None of the circles can be adequately sealed:

Her life was chequer'd with afflictive years,
And even her comfort season'd in her tears.
Scarce for a husband's loss her eyes were dried,
And that loss by her children half supplied,
When Heav'n was pleas'd not these dear props t'afford,
But tore most off by sickness or by sword.
She, who in them could still their father boast,
Was a fresh widow every son she lost.
Litigious hands did her of right deprive,
That after all 'twas penance to survive.
(Philips, 'In memory of that excellent Person Mrs. Mary Lloyd . . . 1656', lines
53–62)

In some 20 published elegies, Philips mourned not only her own losses, but
their repetitions and analogues in the lives of her female friends and their
families, and in the history of the nation. Her alliances are often contradictory, proposing an uneasy continuum between the private and the
public, the personal and the political. Her familial elegies are shot through
with political material, and vice versa: for example, 'On the death of the
Queen of Bohemia' records, 'With how much glory she had ever been / A
daughter, sister, mother, wife, and Queen'. Philips as royalist, in defiance
of her Presbyterian family and parliamentarian husband, responds to the
horror of 'usurpation' by asserting the virtue of control in the
metonymically related arenas of private family and public government:

And if well-order'd Commonwealths must be
Patterns for every private family,
Her house, rul'd by her hand and by her eye,
Might be a pattern for a Monarchy . . . .
Happy were they that knew her and her end,
More happy they that did from her descend . . . .
('In Memory of Mrs. Mary Lloyd', lines 37–40; 97–8)

Hedged around with disclaimers of ideological investments, Philips tropes politics as the ritual stage of moral fable: a masque of betrayal and usurpation, where familial treason is epitomized.

> I think not on the State, nor am concern'd
> Which way soever the great helm is turn'd:
> But as that son whose Father's danger nigh
> Did force his native dumbness, and untie
> The fetter'd organs; so this is a cause
> That will excuse the breach of Nature's laws,
> Silence were now a sin, nay passion now
> Wise men themselves for merit would allow . . . .
> Tombs have been sanctuaries; Thieves lie there
> Secure from all their penalty and fear.
> Great Charles his double misery was this,
> Unfaithful friends, ignoble enemies . . . .
> And what shall then become of thee and I?
> ('Upon the double Murther of King Charles I', lines 1–8; 13–16; 22)

Aligning herself with the son's right to defend his father, Philips is clearly figuring, through displacement, women's thwarted and interdicted relation to language – 'native dumbness', 'fetter'd organs', 'nature's laws' – and justifying a woman's intervention in the masculine hegemony of public discourse, her right of reply: 'Silence were now a sin'. 'Upon the double Murther of Charles I' covertly engages the relations between politics and sexual politics, language and gender. Even in her most public, expressly political elegies, Philips founds a discourse of mourning on a negative figure of woman's subjection in language: that striking image of internal bondage, the internalization of disempowering ideology, 'fetter'd organs'.

In the letter to Charles Cotterell quoted earlier, Philips describes her traumatic precipitation into the transgression of a fully public and vulnerable discourse as in some sense a woman's just and inevitable punishment for the act and enjoyment of writing, however private. The guilt associated with the act of writing, the horror and 'sickness' generated by its subsequent unauthorized publication, is highly sexualized, implicitly equating the desire for self-expression, textualization, with a clandestine and interdicted autoeroticism: writing is 'fugitive', 'above my reach and unfit for my sex', 'incorrigible inclination', 'folly' that is both externally and internally interdicted. The exposure of a woman's writing to public slander and regard calls into question her innocence – writing presupposes knowledge – and bears a relation to the potent tropes of sexual and maternal guilt. Philips consistently figures maternity under the sign of bereavement: 'reckon children 'mong those passing joys,/Which one hour gives, and the next hour destroys' ('Elegy on F.P.'). Maternal severence may be healed only by death – and not by elegy. Frequently, in maternal elegies, the mother chastises herself for her involuntary expulsion of the child from the protection and integrity of her own body, and for 'selflove', as in this elegy by Gertrude Thimelby, dating from the 1650s (unpublished until 1813), for an only child, a son:

Deare infant, 'twas thy mother's fault
So soone inclos'd thee in a vault:
And fathers good, that in such hast
Has my sweet child in heaven plac'd.
I'le weepe the first as my offence,
Then ioy that he made recompence:
Yet must confess my frailty such
My ioy by griefe's exceeded much:
Though I, in reason, knowe thy blisse,
Can not be wish'd more then it is,
Yet this selflove orerules me soe,
I'de have thee here, or with thee goe.
But since that now neyther can be,
A vertue of necessitie
I yet may make, now all my pelf
Content for thee, though not myselfe.[27]

Women's elegies play out conflicting narratives: a woman's impossible desire to bury her children, her writing, her voice, within the integrity of her own body, as another 'fetter'd organ', but self-subjected; and the conflict of this desire with her troubled being-in-the-world, her will-to-voice and to knowledge. Closure, stasis, equilibrium – these are the professed and confessedly unrealizable goals of Philips's life and writing, in her royalist politics and in her formal and generic alliances, privileging the rituals and decorums of occasional, epideictic writing, the poetry of retirement, the letter and verse epistle with its nominated other, and the self-sufficient couplet. These containing strategies are matched, however, by the constancy of Philips's mourning for 'no middle state' ('The World'). Not only within the memorial poems, but in her many eroticized lyrics of parting, absence and farewell addressed to women friends (which might be thought of as love elegies), and in elegiac meditations like 'Submission' and 'The World', Philips laments that 'extremes are still contiguous' ('The World'). It is the inability to protect, exclude, seal off, to which her writing recurs, and the impossibility of perfect repair. These goals are figured as unrealizable and phantasmic, except in death. In elegy after elegy, death as telos is equated with coherence, perfectibility, fullness; the recuperation of innocence, sanctity, virginity:

Here we but crawl and grovel, play and cry;
Are first our own, then others' enemy:
But there shall be defac'd both stain and score,
For Time, and Death, and Sin shall be no more.

('The World', lines 93–6)

Philips's many elegies for women friends construct conservative models of the limited heroic potential of the subject positions available to women, privileging 'free obedience' and 'majestic serenity': 'She kept true state within, and could not buy/Her satisfaction with her Charity' ('In Memory of Mrs. Owen', lines 39–40). A conservative women's heroism – and this seems especially true for aristocratic women – is located in (and can afford to be located in) embracing submission: 'virtue of necessity', stoicism and duty in the face of the accumulations of 'afflictive accident'. The closest analogue of masculine, heroic, public elegy in women's writing is the muted heroism of friendship elegy, of which Philips was a most prolific exponent, where the stoicism of the female elegist is mirrored in the female elegized. Such poems elegize and eulogize the modest, private, retired, accomplished, well-born woman, and point to the properly circumscribed, domestic character of a woman's life (and death), idealizing virtue, quietism, good name and service, as in the progressive Bathsua Makin's 'Upon the much lamented death of the Right Honourable, the Lady Elizabeth Langham' (1664):

To that nobility her birth had given
A second added was, derived from heaven;
Thence her habitual goodness, solid worth,
Her piety; her virtues blazon forth;
Her for a pattern unto after ages,
To be admired by all, expressed by sages,
Who when they write of her, will sadly sorrow
That she did not survive to see their morrow.
So good in all relations, so sweet
A daughter, such a loving wife, discreet
A mother; though not hers, not partial
She loved, as if they had been natural.
To th'Earl and Ladies she a sister rare,
A friend, where she professed, beyond compare. (lines 11–24)[28]

A woman's chance for satisfaction is located in multiple service roles, and in the decorous idealizations and recuperations of memorial writing and 'successive imitation':

Thy even mind, which made thee good and great,
Was to thee both a shelter and retreat.
Of all the tumults which this World do fill,
Thou wert an unconcern'd spectator still:

And, were thy duty punctually supplied,
Indifferent to all the World beside.
Thou wert made up within resolv'd and fix'd,
And wouldst not with a base allay be mix'd;
Above the World, couldst equally despise
Both its temptations and its injuries . . .
'Tis sin then to lament thy fate, but we
Should help thee to a new eternity;
And by successive imitation strive,
Till time shall die, to keep thee still alive;
And (by thy great example furnish'd) be
More apt to live than write thy Elogy [sic].
('In Memory of Mrs. E.H.', lines 17–26; 45–50)

These saintly, chaste, disembodied female models emblematize the desire for a gendered closure in the writing of Philips and many other seventeenth-century women writers, particularly those committed to the Royalist cause. But a woman's desire to cancel desire, to seal off the potentially transgressive irruptions of grief, self-fashioning and worldly affairs, to perfect renunciation and self-discipline, is never entirely efficient. It is precisely this failure which engenders writing, and then guarantees the centrality and copiousness of her mourning discourse, its repetitions and resurgence, despite – or even because of – her 'resolve never to versifie more':

Hard Fate; that choice we eagerly pursue,
Is, or to be undone, or to undo.[29]

Seizing the means of seduction

Fiction and feminine identity in Aphra Behn and
Delarivier Manley

Ros Ballaster

In 1978 Elaine Showalter asserted that eighteenth-century women writers
'refused to deal with a professional role, or had a negative orientation
toward it . . . Moreover, they did not see their writing as an aspect of their
female experience, or as an expression of it'.[1] Recent research into this
period hitherto neglected by feminist criticism has disproved Showalter's
claim, revealing large numbers of women writers who were openly
professional, even cynical, about their literary endeavours.[2] How, then,
did the woman writer 'figure' her entry into the literary market? This
essay considers the work of two of the best-known female writers of
amatory prose in the late seventeenth and early eighteenth centuries in
the light of their deployment of fictionalized (auto)biography as a means
of 'figuring' the female writer as eroticized heroine of her own text. Far
from seeking to conceal their professional status behind a modest veil of
amateurism, it contends, they exploited their new visibility to produce a
specifically female, erotic form.

For the feminist critic to lay claim to uncovering a definitive 'origin' for
a tradition of women's writing is, as the case of Showalter demonstrates,
not without risks. If Aphra Behn and Delarivier Manley were not in fact
the 'first' women writers to publish narrative prose on a professional
basis, their ignorance of any English tradition in women's fiction on
which to draw, and the attendant perception of their position as 'novel',
produces a new attitude toward the status of the woman writer in the
years following the Restoration. Without an indigenous tradition with
which to identify, these women turned to France for their generic models
– to the French romance, the *nouvelle*, the *chronique scandaleuse* and
the letter novel – all forms which women had adopted to considerable

profit across the channel.[3] Behn and Manley's prose fictions simultaneously assume a knowledge of these forms on the part of their reading
audience and stress their difference from their continental 'sisters'.
The famous preface, either written or translated by Manley, to the
scandal narrative of *Queen Zarah* (1705) argues that British readers have
tired of the lengthy French romance and warmed to the new 'little
history':

> These little pieces which have banished *Romances* are much more agreeable
> to the Brisk and Impetuous Humour of the *English*, who have naturally no
> Taste for long-winded Performances, for they no sooner begin a book but they
> desire to see the end of it.[4]

This preface, with its emphasis on the reader's pleasure in amatory
narrative, demonstrates a hard-headed attitude to the exigencies of the
marketplace, equally typical of Manley's predecessor, Aphra Behn.
Behn's *Love-Letters Between a Nobleman and his Sister* (1684–7) was one
of the best-selling epistolary fictions of her day, running into more than
ten editions before 1740. In its dedication, as elsewhere, Behn makes an
explicit link between sexual and economic exchange. In a compliment to
her dedicatee, Thomas Condon, she comments that 'commodity . . .
rarely fails in the trade of love, though never was so low a Market for
beauty in both Sexes, yet he that's fortified and stor'd like happy you,
may never fear to find his price'.[5]

Behn turned to fiction in the 1680s at a point when the London theatre
was in political crisis and economic decline and her own drama had
incurred royal disfavour as the result of an unfortunate attack on the
Duke of Monmouth in her prologue to a fellow playwright's work,
Romulus and Hersilia (1682). Her comment on 'commodity', then, might
well be applied to her own situation as a woman who supported herself
by her pen. Amatory novels were not a lucrative source of income when
measured next to the drama, but the trade in narratives of sexual intrigue
was enough to secure her a decent livelihood.[6]

Behn and Manley both represent themselves as trafficking in love,
unperturbed by the hostility their 'improper' ventures into the world of
publishing might generate. Both lay claim to the status of 'hero', the
advantages of literary 'fame' outweighing the loss of their 'fame' as
women (the reputation of chastity), which was the inevitable effect of a
woman publishing for profit. In her preface to *The Lucky Chance*,
performed at the Theatre Royal in 1687, Behn declares, 'I value Fame as
much as if I had been born a *Hero*', while in 1709 Manley responded to
the success of the first volume of her *New Atalantis* with the comment

that she, 'like a Hero, who has gain'd an impossible Victory, [can] scarce believe the Conquest'.[7] However, the assertion of heroism is not here employed as a means of disguising or concealing the sex of the author. Like those women who, with the restoration of Charles II to the English throne, were for the first time allowed to earn money by appearing on the stage, this new generation of female writers wilfully made its sex visible. Femaleness, and even more explicitly, female sexuality, was now a commodity to be turned to profit by women. Self-consciously professional, transforming her personal and often scandalous 'history' into fiction, the female writer of amatory prose ultimately sought neither to vindicate herself nor to convert others. Along with her male counterparts, she exploited the image of the seduced and violated female body to enter the world of exchange.

Yet the assertion of the profit motive may itself have been a 'cover' for an even more daring venture into the public sphere. Behn and Manley were first and foremost Tory propagandists: the main object of their fiction was thus ideological. The amatory structure of these novels might, then, be viewed as a thin veil behind which lay a directly political engagement. Thus the story of the seduction of a young Tory heiress by her Whig brother-in-law that makes up Behn's *Love-Letters Between a Nobleman and his Sister* is a fictionalized presentation of a contemporary scandal (the elopement in 1682 of Lady Henrietta Berkeley with Lord Grey of Warke, a notorious co-conspirator in the Rye House Plot and Monmouth rebellions), which Behn deploys in order to represent the Whig rebellions led by the Duke of Monmouth against his father and uncle as an equivalent crime against nature and proper (Tory) order and values. Manley's 'key' novels employ the seduction-and-betrayal structure of the conventional amatory plot to expose the political 'plots' of leading Whig politicians in the troubled Junto years (1705–10) of Queen Anne's reign. The sordid sexual misdemeanours of prominent Whig figures were to be taken as proof of their unscrupulous and corrupt methods in government.

The sphere of 'love' was indeed considered the 'proper' realm of the woman writer, but the exploitation of love for the sake of 'interest' constituted a breach of gender boundaries. Under these circumstances, economic 'interest' seems to have served as a more acceptable explanation for women's literary production than political 'interest'. Thus, when Manley's autobiographical persona, Rivella, is prosecuted by the government for libel as a result of her scandalous writings, she seeks to ridicule her questioners on the grounds that they have mistaken love fiction for political propaganda. Rivella asks:

Whether the Persons in Power were ashamed to bring a Woman to her Trial for writing a few amorous Trifles purely for her own Amusement, or that our Laws are defective, as most Persons conceiv'd, because she had serv'd her self with Romantick Names and a feign'd Scene of Action? (*Novels*, II, p. 850)

Whether Behn and Manley were using amatory fiction for economic or party political gains, they were clearly aware of the subversive nature of their enterprise. Their encroachment on the rights of men lay in their turning of the depiction of the seduced female body to the advantage of another woman. Their texts repeatedly inscribe a certain interpretative battle between men and women over the scene of seduction, seeking to appropriate the power of representation and fiction-making for the female writer. The metaphor of the female body as voluble text to be interpreted or 'mastered' by the reader or author was, of course, by no means an original one. Patricia Parker has ably demonstrated its centrality to early and mid-seventeenth-century 'romance' discourse.[8] However, the deployment of this metaphor by women in fiction frequently addressed to women was, precisely, 'novel'. The conventional heterosexual love plot, in which the innocent woman is deceived by the amatory 'fictions' that the libertine man spins her, and then abandoned for a new love-object, is here exercised in an exchange between women. The female writer 'seduces' her female reader by her amatory plots, substituting her fiction for the 'real' world of masculinist control over representation.

Both Behn and Manley are makers and breakers of genre, drawing on formal devices from a range of available prose structures (in Manley's case satire and the romance, in Behn's epistolary fiction and the 'little history'). Generic transformation, as other critics have argued, is one means of questioning received notions of gender identity. Jacques Derrida has suggested that:

> The question of the literary genre is not a formal one: it covers the motif of the law in general, of generation in the natural and symbolic senses, of the generation difference, sexual difference between the feminine and masculine genre/gender, of the hymen between the two, of an identity and difference between the feminine and masculine.[9]

The 'mixing' of genres, manipulation of generic conventions and boundaries may, then, release a meditation on the nature of the (gendered) writing self. At a historical moment when the generic boundaries of the novel were in process, Behn and Manley employed generic ambiguity to address the instability of gender identity.[10]

This essay will look in more detail at two forms of prose fiction at which Behn and Manley were particularly adept, in order to demonstrate the means by which both writers implement generic disturbance to unsettle the conventional subject positions of the romance plot – that is, to disturb the opposition of masculine seducer/fiction-monger and feminine victim/reader. From this subversion of generic expectation and attendant challenge to fixities of subject position and gender identity, Behn and Manley seek to generate a newly empowered speaking position for the female writer, resistant to the impositions of form on the part of the 'masculine' critic or reader upon the female text/body.

I Aphra Behn and the letter: righting the female self

From the 1670s onwards in Britain, epistolary fiction was a highly popular form of narrative prose and, moreover, a form that was consistently identified with women. The letter was generally assumed to be a private form, written to lover, friend or member of the family, rather than directed towards a public. Thus, the female letter-writer could experiment with literary expression without appearing to disturb the division of private and public spheres. The anonymous 'Portuguese letters' of a nun to her French lover and the scandal travelogues in letter form of Marie, Countess d'Aulnoy, were French imports which enjoyed enormous popular success in Britain in the late seventeenth century. Thus the association between women's writing and an 'artless' mode of epistolary production was already well established by the time Aphra Behn turned to fiction in the 1680s.

Behn began her career in fiction-writing with an epistolary narrative, publishing the first part of her *Love-Letters Between a Nobleman and his Sister* in 1684. These letters both imitate and challenge the conventions of the Portuguese letters, first translated into English by Roger L'Estrange as *Five Love-Letters from a Nun to a Cavalier* in 1678. The *Five Love-Letters* establish a firm dichotomy between the deceived woman and the duplicitous male lover. The nun, Mariana, represents herself as victim of her lover's fiction-making capacities:

> 'Tis now a Clear Case that your whole Address to me was only an Artificial disguise . . . Yours was a deliberate desire to fool me; your business was to make a Conquest, not a friend; and to triumph over my Heart, without ever engaging or hazarding your own.[11]

Against her lover's artifice, Mariana sets her own innocence and spontaneity, manifested in her prose style. In her own *Love-Letters*, Behn is reiterating a commonplace when she comments that 'true' love in the letter is 'all unthinking artless speaking, incorrect disorder, and without method, as 'tis without bounds or rules'.[12] The Portuguese style has, then superseded the amatory rhetoric of the French romance: Cupids, darts, tempests and mythological deities are displaced by parentheses, hiatuses, naturalistic imagery and impassioned imperatives and interrogatives.

The imitations spawned by the *Five Love-Letters* in Britain and France continue in this vein to the point of parody. Thus the 'Woman of the World' who anatomizes her passion in the *Seven Portuguese Letters* (1681) informs her lover that 'he may be able to judge what disorder [her] mind is in, by the irregularity of this letter'.[13] Truth, it appears, is the property of the woman, but, paradoxically, it is only signified by the adoption of a particular rhetorical style, which in this case 'artificially' calls attention to itself. The unstable signifier is invested with the capacity of demonstrating the truth of a voice.

Behn's *Love-Letters* progress, part by part, away from the Portuguese style into a more 'mixed' use of narrative voice. The first part (of 1684) substantially consists of letters between the lovers, Sylvia and Philander, both of whom indulge in 'Portuguese' linguistic excess. The second part (of 1685), set after their elopement to Holland, introduces a third-person narrator and a series of other correspondents, including Octavio, a young prince of the House of Orange who falls in love with Sylvia. The third part (of 1687) almost entirely abandons the epistolary mode, providing the reader with summaries of letters and revealing the previously uncharacterized third-person narrator to be female and, by implication, Aphra Behn herself. As the lovers move out of the mirroring dyadic exchange that marked their courtship, authorial control over their 'voices' is made more and more explicit. At the same time, the interest of the romance plot is increasingly overtaken by the concerns of the political plot. The subplot of the failed rebellions led by Cesario (Monmouth) against the French (British) monarchy has, by the middle of the third part, virtually substituted as the novel's 'centre'.

If, as Peggy Kamuf has suggested in her *Fictions of Feminine Desire*, the story of Mariana the nun is the drama of a woman learning through renarration of the scene of her seduction to speak her own illicit active desire in order to escape hysterical enclosure signified by the convent, the story of Sylvia is that of the education of a woman out of her deluded belief in the very possibility of any such authentic 'discourse of desire'. Sylvia progresses through the course of the narrative from the position of victim of the seductive rhetoric of love into that of an arch-manipulator of that same rhetoric. In brief, Sylvia learns the tricks of the professional woman writer of amatory fiction, presenting to her various readers/ lovers a series of personae designed to gratify their erotic fantasy and her own 'interest' in social and political control. Mariana's letters, in contrast, might be seen as the struggles of the amateur woman writer to come to terms with her own sexual desires through the operation of 'speaking' them in relation to an absent and silent lover. The *Five Love-Letters*, Kamuf argues, constitute 'a written account of [a woman's] passage out of a closed hysterical silence' with 'the interlocutor as the silent pole through which passes the invention of the writing subject'.[14] Here, the absent lover functions as a silent 'other' through which the woman passes her narrative in order to 'cure' herself of the physical symptoms of hysteria.

However, Sylvia's passage out of the hysteria born of the tedious cycle of seduction and betrayal is effected by learning to mimic the masculine seducer's facility with romantic language. The three parts of the *Love-Letters* narrate three of Sylvia's sexual affairs. The first sees Sylvia the victim of Philander's seductive rhetoric, deceived by her belief in the absolute correspondence between word and emotion, signifier and signified. The letter, for Sylvia, is the mediator of passion between lovers, the token of an *a priori* desire: 'to him I venture to say any thing', she writes, 'whose kind and soft imaginations can supply all my wants in the description of the soul' (*Love-Letters*, p. 31). The second part of the novel narrates Philander's desertion of his mistress when he develops an amatory interest in Calista, sister to Octavio. Discovering his infidelity, Sylvia is at first in despair, but quickly turns to 'managing' her new lover, Octavio, in order to engineer her revenge upon Philander. Behn shows us her heroine preparing to seduce Octavio to her 'interest' by deploying the rhetorical artillery of the outmoded French romance: 'she lay expecting her coming lover on a repose of rich embroidery of gold on blue satin, hung within-side with little amorous pictures' of classical tales of seduction such as Venus and Adonis and Armida disarming her warrior lover (p. 281). Sylvia leans on her pillows pretending to read a book of 'amours' and Behn comments that 'she verily believed, that acting and feigning the lover possessed her with a tenderness against her knowledge and will' (p. 281). Here, then, amatory representation is no longer at the service of desire, but the generating ground of it.

At this stage, Sylvia's experiments with amatory representation are unsophisticated, relying on the worn-out clichés and conventions of the romance. Luckily in Octavio she has found a lover who willingly blinds himself to the 'truth' behind her representations – in the scene above, for instance, that his love for Sylvia will entail the sacrifice of his 'heroism' or honour. When he receives a letter from her that struggles to conceal her anger at his treatment of her as a common prostitute, we are told, 'however calm it was, and however designed, he found, or at least he thought he found the charming jilt all over', but 'all he fears is, that she will not put so neat a cheat upon him, but that he shall be able to see through it, and still be obliged to retain his ill opinion of her' (p. 249).

By the third part of the novel, however, we find Sylvia, now separated from Octavio, reaching new heights of sophistication in her adoption of amorous identities as both letter-writer and agent in her own history. In order to gain money from Octavio, who has retired into a monastery, she writes to him, 'as a humble penitent would write to a ghostly Father' (p. 349), mimicking the style of the popular *Letters of Abelard and Heloise* (first published in France in 1616). Meanwhile, she pursues a young Spanish rake under three different disguises, one male and two female. Finally, she reveals her identity to him in a series of dazzling quick changes at her lodgings, ensuring his fidelity through her facility to offer him an entirely new object of desire when or if his interest in those already on display should wane:

> He sees, he hears, this is the same lovely youth, who lay in bed with him at the village *cabaret*; and then no longer thinks her woman: he hears and sees it is the same face, and voice, and hands he saw on the *Tour* and in the park, and then believes her woman. (p. 441)

Sylvia's theatrical display here invokes another of Behn's heroines, the precocious Hellena of *The Rover* (1677), who secures the wandering affections of the rake, Willmore, through her facility with male and female disguise. Once again, the role of the 'actress' is a potent metaphor for the woman writer, a median point between the naked economism of the prostitute and the self-immolation of the 'pure' woman.

Is Sylvia's performative strategy, however, merely a reversal of sexual roles, whereby the seduced virgin is transformed into the female equivalent of a male rake? The metaphor of the actress would suggest otherwise. Sylvia is presented as developing a specifically feminine use of amorous representation. She gains sexual and economic power by a tantalizing process of narcissistic display and identity concealment, moving between genders at the boundaries of difference, exploiting myths of seduction to her own ends. Like Behn herself, she provides her reader/lover with a series of feigned identities, withholding her 'true' self, or rather putting the 'truth' of selfhood into question.

It is significant that Behn's only appearance as a 'character' in her own novel takes place at the point where another inversion of traditional gendered subject positions is acted out. She appears as one of the audience to Octavio's initiation into a closed religious order – in other words, she appears as a specularizer of the seduced and betrayed *man*, retreating into hysterical enclosure as a result of his mistress's faithlessness. Behn subtly combines erotic and spiritual elements in her description of the ritual that accompanies Octavio's entry into the Order of St Bernard. Octavio is shorn, stripped and reclothed in front of an audience of desirous women:

> he looked methought, as if the gods of love had met in council to dress him up that day for everlasting conquest; for to his usual beauties he seemed to have the addition of a thousand more; he bore new lustre in his face and eyes, smiles on his cheeks, and dimples on his lips . . . ten thousand sighs, from all sides, were sent him, as he passed along . . . . (pp. 398–9)

Here Behn offers to her readers for consumption the eroticized figure of the betrayed lover. It is now the female writer who indulges her readers' voyeuristic fantasies through the objectification of the male body. Thus, through her heroine's progress towards control of the affective powers of the letter, along with the introduction of a walk-on part for herself as female voyeur, Behn challenges the 'integrity' of the Portuguese style, insisting upon the fictional status of amorous forms and, by extension, the gendered subject positions by which they operate.

A less well-known experiment in epistolary form on the part of Aphra Behn is her *Love-Letters to a Gentleman*, first printed as an appendix to the 'Memoirs on the Life of Mrs. Behn. Written by a Gentlewoman of her Acquaintance', in the posthumous *Histories and Novels of the Late Ingenious Mrs. Behn* (1696).[15] Earlier in the same year, Charles Gildon had published 'An Account of the Life of the Incomparable Mrs. Behn' along with his bowdlerized edition of her play *The Younger Brother*: the claim to female authorship in the 'Memoirs' appears to have been a response to his comment in the 'Account' that 'to draw her to the Life, one must write like her, that is with all the softness of her Sex, and all the fire of ours'.[16] These accounts and the publication of a third edition of the *Histories and Novels* with an expanded version of the 'Memoirs' suggest that Behn had succeeded in instilling a certain amount of curiosity about her personal history in the reading public.

The *Letters to a Gentleman* are in keeping with Behn's strategy of self-eroticization outlined with respect to the *Love-Letters Between a Nobleman and his Sister*, and common to much of her writing. In her history of *Oroonoko: or, the Royal Slave* (1688), Behn portrays herself as the 'Great Mistress' who 'seduces' the rebellious black slave prince and his beautiful wife into passivity on behalf of the white male colonists by weaving stories to the former of classical Rome and to the latter of nuns.[17] Behn's concern in the *Letters to a Gentleman*, as in *Oroonoko*, is to win power through language over her reader/lover. The seven letters, close imitations of the Portuguese style, dramatize the female writer's struggle to 'effect' her male reader, seduce him into submission and resist his wilful misinterpretations:

> [T]hough I scorn to guard my Tongue, as hoping 'twill never offend willingly, yet I can, with much adoe, hold it, when I have a great mind to say a Thousand things, I know will be taken in an ill sense. Possibly you will wonder what compells me to write, what moves me to send where I find so little Welcome; nay, where I meet with such returns it may be I wonder too.... (Letter 3, p. 405)

The entire correspondence is dominated by a metaphor of exchange. Behn describes herself as 'a young Gamester', who, in expending her words on the silent lover, only 'rook[s] in [her] Heart . . . to make it venture its last Stake', while her lover 'like a Miser wou'd distribute nothing' (p. 406). She 'will be purchas'd with Softness, and dear Words, and kind Expressions, sweet Eyes, and a low Voice' (p. 408). While the letters appear to imitate the style of Mariana, the deployment of these images of economic exchange, the insistent search for a fictional voice that will succeed in generating desire in the lover – make her writing *profitable* and secure a *return* – seems to undermine the notion of authenticity that underpins the Portuguese style. This is the language of the professional woman writer, turning the discourse of sexual desire to profit, employing it to undermine rather than express or explore the notion of the proper female 'self'.

Behn's *Letters to a Gentleman* stand ambiguously between the classifications of fiction and autobiography. They were not published during her lifetime and appear to be personal writings for the eyes of a single lover, possibly the notorious John Hoyle whom she addresses in her love poetry as 'Lycidus'.[18] However, their debt to the Portuguese letters, and their formal organization into a short narrative, suggest they are a fictional experiment rather than a personal document. It is this inscription of the female writer's personal 'history' as 'fiction' that Manley was to go on to exploit in her scandal fiction. Behn's experimentation in her letter fiction with the figure of the female writer as an erotic enigma, withholding her identity from the reader in order to maintain the latter's erotic attention, sets a precedent upon which Manley was to enlarge.

II Delarivier Manley and the scandal chronicle: fictionalizing female autobiography

Delarivier Manley knew Behn's work and seems consciously to have invoked her as a model. Her prefatory poem of 1696 to Catharine

Trotter's dramatic version of a Behn novel, *Agnes de Castro*, locates Trotter as part of a more widespread female challenge to male dominance in the arts:

> *Orinda*, and the Fair *Astrea* gone,
> Not one was found to fill the Vacant Throne;
> Aspiring Man had quite regain'd the Sway,
> Again had taught us humbly to Obey;
> Till you (Nature's third start, in favour of our Kind)
> With stronger Arms, their Empire had disjoyn'd.[19]

The first character introduced in Manley's major scandal novel, *The New Atalantis* (1709), is Astrea, the goddess of Justice, who has descended to earth in order to acquire a knowledge of sexual and political mores amongst mortals for the better training of her charge, a young prince (the future George II). Astrea the goddess and Astrea/Aphra here double as precedents for Manley's entry into the male-dominated world of satirical prose.

Like Behn's *Love-Letters*, Manley's fiction presents amatory plots and tropes as a means towards and a cover for the satirical representation of contemporary party politics from a Tory perspective. Here too, then, there is a complex play between discourses that are ostensibly radically disjunct – the personal 'intrigue' substitutes for the political 'intrigue'. Sexual perversity is employed as a metaphor for political corruption. Manley's major precedent for the genre of scandal fiction was not, however, Behn, but the well known French spy and traveller, Marie, Countess d'Aulnoy. D'Aulnoy's *Memoirs of the Court of England* were published in translation in England in 1707 along with a collection of letters by Manley herself entitled *The Lady's Pacquet Broke Open*.[20]

Manley, as Behn had done with the Portuguese letters, imitated, parodied and challenged her model. Marie d'Aulnoy presents herself as a disinterested observer of the peculiarities of other countries and customs in order to satisfy the curiosity of a female correspondent, her cousin, back in France. Introducing the *Memoirs of the Court of England*, she explains: '[t]he Acquaintance of so many Persons of Distinction gave me opportunity of knowing a thousand diverting Stories, of which I have composed these *Memoirs*, and, according to your Desire, put them into as regular a Method as I could'.[21] D'Aulnoy's personal history is rarely discussed, nor does it intertwine with the events she narrates. It is, indeed, her very lack of involvement or 'interest' that guarantees the authenticity of her narrative. In contrast, Manley provides her scandal novels with complex and involved pseudo-origins as ancient manuscripts many times translated, discovered in obscure Eastern libraries. Countering the simple frame of d'Aulnoy's claim to 'write nothing but what I have seen or heard from Persons of unquestionable Credit',[22] Manley constructs an elaborate system of narration and counter-narration from multiple sources. Evidently, the two women were in very different positions as political correspondents or commentators. Manley was no traveller: she sought to stir up moral outrage against leading Whig figures and encourage Tory political loyalty among a disaffected public. Moreover, she needed to protect herself from the severity of libel, or even treason, laws and to drive her political point home. Where d'Aulnoy presents herself as the peripatetic source of a series of stable and indisputable texts/testimonies, Manley inverts the order, depicting herself as a sedentary editor toiling in libraries to secure some kind of stable meaning or utterance from a mass of competing and corrupted sources from the four corners of the globe.

Manley herself figures as literary character rather than narrator in this morass of fiction-making. Indeed, twice in her literary career she fictionalized her own scandalous history, that of a bigamous marriage to her cousin, the Whig lawyer and politician, John Manley. The first version is offered in the second volume of *The New Atalantis* (1709) (*Novels*, I, pp. 712–26). Here, Astrea and her companions eavesdrop as the abused Delia narrates her sad history to a priest. The story is presented as an intimate 'confession', exploiting the feminine writer's supposed purchase on authenticity and truth-telling. Delia/Manley informs her confessor that 'the *Native* Love I have for *Truth*, as well as due Respect to the Person I am entertaining . . . shall make me carefully consider nothing so much, in the Relation I am going to give you' (p. 713). Manley proceeds to present herself through Delia as the iconic suffering heroine of amatory convention, led astray by the male rake's potent persuasive force. Delia excuses the sin of continuing to live with her husband for three years after he had disclosed his bigamy, on the grounds that she was 'young, unacquainted with the World, had never seen the Necessities of it, knew no Arts, had not been expos'd to any Hardships' (p. 721).

This same story is, however, given a wholly different slant in *The Adventures of Rivella* of 1714, Manley's one purely autobiographical novel. Here, Delia is transformed from the innocent victim of masculine fiction-mongering into the sexually knowing and emancipated female writer, Rivella. Jane Spencer comments, of the discrepancy between these two representations, that Delia and Rivella enact

> a meeting-ground for two conceptions of womanhood: one of the passionate, sexual being as often depicted in Restoration drama, the other of the innocent,

passionless, easily deceived creature gaining ascendancy in the early eighteenth century. (*The Rise of the Woman Novelist*, p. 58)

However, we might interpret the division between Delia and Rivella as being less a split between differing conceptions of the feminine, than a dramatization of the opposition between masculine and feminine reading positions, or interpretative strategies, in fiction. In order to elaborate this argument, we need to take a closer look at the action of *Rivella*, and the complexities of its publishing history.

The story of Rivella is narrated by a man to a man. Rivella's long-standing friend, Sir Charles Lovemore, who has known her since childhood, responds to the young chevalier d'Aumont's request to 'introduce' him to the popular authoress by telling him her history. The text itself is ostensibly a translation from the chevalier's French transcription of the tale as told to him by Lovemore. It is significant that the names of both men associate them with the 'business' of amatory fiction, that of love, since Lovemore's story is marked throughout by an attempt to impose a definitive amatory 'form' upon Rivella's literary and personal activities. The history of Rivella is indeed that of an attempt on the part of a male arbiter of taste to stamp the mark of 'more love' upon the too manl(e)y writing of a woman. Lovemore struggles throughout the story to contain Rivella's writing activities within the private sphere. Her charms, he tells us, are best appreciated in private: 'Few who have only beheld her in Publick, could be brought to like her' (*Novels*, II, p. 744). He admires her facility with the letter form, traditionally associated with the private, domestic and 'proper' feminine. Her letters are 'so natural, so spiritous, so sprightly, so well turned', he asserts, 'that from the first to the last, I must and ever will maintain, that all her other Productions however successful they have been, come short of her Talent in writing letters' (p. 753).

Yet Rivella continues to resist Lovemore's attempts to lead her into the paths of virtue and a literary career in sentiment. He comments in despair: 'I still preach'd, and she still went on in her own Way, without any Regard to my own Doctrine, till Experience gave her enough of her Indiscretion' (p. 781). Once Rivella has been imprisoned and tried for the publication of a 'party' novel (as Manley herself was in October 1709 for the publication of the first volume of *The New Atalantis*), Lovemore triumphs. He persuades her 'to be asham'd of her Writings' and extracts a promise that she will 'entertain her Readers with more gentle and pleasing Theams' (p. 852). There is, of course, a significant inaccuracy here in that Manley went on to publish another party novel, the *Memoirs of Europe*, only a year after her trial and was not to abandon party writing until after the death of Queen Anne. Rivella's story then is one of *ostensible* victory on the part of the male critic in imposing a particular form, that of amatory narrative, upon the female writer.

Appropriately, *Rivella* concludes with the reader's eye firmly fixed not upon the woman writer's fictional forms, her books, but on the outline of her material physical form obligingly conjured up by her male narrator. Lovemore describes for d'Aumont an imaginary encounter with the authoress herself:

> I should have brought you to her Table well furnish'd and well serv'd . . . . From thence carried you (in the Heat of Summer after Dinner) within the Nymphs Alcove, to a Bed nicely sheeted and strow'd with *Roses, Jessamins* or *Orange-Flowers*, suited to the variety of the Season; her Pillows neatly trim'd with Lace or Muslin, stuck round with *Jonquils*, or other natural Garden Sweets, for she uses no Perfumes, and there have given you leave to fancy your self the happy Man, with whom she chose to repose her self, during the Heat of the Day, in a state of Sweetness and Tranquility: From thence conducted you towards the cool of the Evening, either upon the *Water*, or to the *Park* for Air, with a Conversation always new, and which never cloys . . . . (pp. 855-6)

Lennard Davis has described this scene as a 'colossal autoerotic reverie the likes of which had probably never occurred so directly between author and reader in the history of narrative up to this point' (*Factual Fictions*, p. 119). Yet the most striking aspect of Lovemore's fantasy is surely its indirectness. All he can offer his reader, d'Aumont, is an imprint in a bed, the perfume of flowers, the echo of the woman writer's voice in conversation. Manley's texts may be available for the male gaze, but the equation of her text with her body is, it transpires, precisely a male fiction. 'Proper' femininity amounts to little more than the appropriation of an image of the woman by masculine desire in her absence. What Lovemore 'pimps' is his own fantasy of the absent author who is, ironically, in reality *his* author. While the man appears to have authored the perfect female object, it is she in fact who has authored him. It is, after all, Lovemore who is the fiction, not Manley.

The publishing history of *Rivella* bears out the attribution of irony to Manley's autobiographical text.[23] It was, indeed, not a text initiated or at first 'authored' by Manley herself. Early in 1714 she received word that Charles Gildon (initiator of the chain of 'memoirs' connected with Behn) had started work on a scandalous biography of her life under the title *Adventures of Rivella*, the first two pages of which had already come off the press. The publisher, Edmund Curll, himself infamous for scandalous monographs, set up a meeting between Gildon and Manley which resulted in a promise from the latter to produce her own manuscript. In March 1714 Curll received the work with instructions to publish it anonymously. It seems more than fortuitous, then, that Manley should have constructed her text as a dialogue between two men, seeking to disclose the 'truth' behind the authoress's fictions. Gildon and Curll, like their counterparts, Lovemore and d'Aumont, were seeking to 'pimp' the female writer to her audience, offering an answer to the all-important question posed by d'Aumont at the beginning of the novel, 'Do her Eyes love as well as her Pen?' (*Novels*, II, p. 744).

Seen in this light, *Rivella* is a brisk riposte rather than an autoerotic reverie, which operates by a teasing withholding of writerly identity similar to Behn's 'self'-representation in her novels. *Rivella* emerges as a covert form of resistance to the imposition of 'form' upon the female writer, whether literary (Lovemore's conviction that the woman writer's 'business' is with romance fiction alone) or physical (his attempts to describe the physical characteristics of the female writer as an indulgence of male scopophilia). Manley successfully transforms autobiography into fiction; the 'truth' that autobiography is expected to expose is revealed to be nothing more than the projection of gendered fantasy on the part of the (male) reader into the fictional text.

It appears, then, that Behn and Manley's experimentation with amatory form in the late seventeenth and early eighteenth centuries consistently allegorizes the female writer's relation to romance, attempting to mark out a specifically feminine position in the business of fiction-making. The very 'novelty' of the novel, its low status as a literary form at this period and the fluidity of its generic boundaries, provides a small number of women writers the opportunity to explore and challenge gender boundaries.

In *The New Atalantis*, Manley produces a fantasy of a separatist women's community known as the Cabal. The members of the Cabal are sworn to secrecy and fidelity: '[i]n this little *Commonwealth*', Manley tell us, 'is no *Property* . . . they have no reserve; mutual *Love* bestows all things in *Common*' (*Novels*, I, p. 589). Some of the Cabal's members are cross-dressers and most are aspiring writers and artists. Manley makes it clear that it is their envy of the power to 'represent', or the power of art, that motivates the women's cross-dressing activity, rather than the desire to be men: '[t]hey do not in reality love *Men*; but doat of the Representation of *Men* in *Women*' (p. 739). The Cabal's differential model of exchange and its cross-dressing practices provide an admirable metaphor for both Behn's and Manley's engagement with the question of the female writer's relation to literary form. Both women sought to enter the literary market as women without being relegated to the margins of fiction. If amatory fiction was the only profitable genre for women writers, then they would enter the market in 'disguise'. Thus they adopt a series of fictional identities, masquerading as the archetypically 'feminine' woman, the seductress, the whore, the male rake. Behn and Manley offer their male and female readers travesties of gender, passing between the dichotomous poles of the private and the public, sexual and party politics, masculine and feminine. Ultimately, Behn's and Manley's fiction 'plots' its way out of the repetitive cycle of seduction and betrayal, which habitually structures amatory fiction, by invoking the heroic activities of the female writer, neither subjected to, nor subject of, the patriarchal plot, but rather writing her own, differently.

De-ciphering women and de-scribing authority

The writings of Mary Astell

Catherine Sharrock

Mary Astell perceived the women of her society to be mere 'Cyphers in the World' but she was not prepared to acquiesce with this definition of them.[1] Her texts embark upon the de-ciphering of the social codes that authorize the marginalization of the female subject. This de-ciphering moves towards a revision of the 'cyphered' female identity, by disrupting the patriarchal discourse through which it is articulated. As the language that defines a woman's containment is destabilized, the female is less bound by masculine author-ity (the interplay between textual and socio-political constructions) and is potentially subject, instead, only to her own prescription. In this way, Astell's writings suggest that a woman may inscribe herself beyond, rather than be inscribed (or de-scribed) by, the dominant discourse – the 'Cypher' acquires her own authorizing signature. However, such a manoeuvre becomes highly problematic and raises the questions of whether it is possible to write one's way out of ideology.

The act of writing is a projection of the person who writes into the public domain of discourse. This translates the person, as subject of ideology, into a text that, by necessity, expresses the writer's relation to the ideological framework within which she/he writes. Discourse both defines and is defined by ideology. One can never write from a position outside ideology, but only negotiate with it from within its confines. However, as a symbolic activity, the entrance into print may signify a transgression of ideological codes. During Astell's time, a woman's writing assumed precisely this status. It betokened a textual revision of her politically prescribed role as silent subject of the language of patriarchy. What happened when a woman writer addressed the ideological implications of her symbolic position? Anne Finch writes:

> Alas! a woman that attempts the pen,
> Such an intruder on the rights of men,
> Such a presumptious Creature, is esteem'd,
> The fault, can by no vertue be redeem'd.[2]

By invoking her critical reception, Finch undercuts a male evaluation of her writing as being, by its very existence, 'unladylike'. Yet one might ask whether that invocation also discloses, in part, her ambivalent attitude to the 'intrusion'. The implicit dialogue with an absent party might be read as an expression of her continuing dialogue with the dominant ideology, even whilst she apparently defies it.[3] The phrase 'attempts the pen', perhaps suggestive of a desire to seduce the masculine 'pen', also betrays her lack of confidence in wielding that 'masculine' implement and hints at her internalized sense of female inadequacy.

Such internalized notions of gender difference seem to occur again in Aphra Behn's description of her writing self as 'my Masculine Part, the Poet in me . . .'[4] However, Behn's splitting of her gendered identity, through which she implies that her 'feminine part' is cut off from the practice of writing, reads more like a conscious manipulation of social codes than an unconscious inability to escape them. In her plays, women are not the passive puppets of male direction, but active agents of their own plots. The dramatist locates herself within the perimeters of propriety and then exploits that positioning by mocking those very terms of politeness. Androgyny may serve as a convenient evasion of a woman's transgression of gender boundaries, by presenting the writer as one operating in accordance with the pregiven concepts of masculinity and femininity. Simultaneously, the idea of an androgynous writer also renders the sexual identity of writing more flexible. It does so by allowing a dual gender to infiltrate the unisex and 'masculine' nature of writing. As a consequence, the partial conformity of textual (female) androgyny may query the equation of masculinity and textuality.

Bathsua Makin perhaps works against this equation when she adopts a masculine persona. She proclaims in *An Essay to Revive the Antient Education of Gentlewomen* (1673), 'I am a Man my self': a literal, strategic dissociation from her female self.[5] In assuming a male guise, she is able to put forward her argument with an air of disinterested authority that would be unavailable to her if she were to confess to her gender. By being able to present herself as an educated man, her text symbolically foreshadows its own objective: the lessening of the educational gulf between men and women. Here androgyny articulates its own sexual challenge.

Yet, we may ask, how can the androgynous (female) text question the male monopoly over words and knowledge when it wraps both *its* words and *its* knowledge in 'masculine' clothing? How can a woman validate her right to be an author when the only author-ity to which she lays claim is masculine: an author-ity which excludes her? So the androgynous (female) text has to be reread here as one which undermines its own attempt to alter the status quo, by conceding to the male author-ity by which that status quo is supported. There is, then, hardly any hope of change. But one should note that Makin, at least, is not asking for radical change. She does not demand equality, but only a discreet reupholstering of inequality: 'My intention is not to equalize Women to Men, much less to make them superior. They are the weaker Sex, yet capable of impressions of great things, something like to the best of Men' (p. 29). Her manipulation of androgyny, I would argue, echoes the continued allegiance to patriarchal values that she expresses here. Just as she writes as a woman only from within the protective covering of 'masculinity', so she requests only a female education that could be contained by the systems of patriarchy. For the 'impressions of great things' that a woman might receive are the imprints of the male mind. The woman remains a cipher to the signifying author-ity of the man.

Astell, on the other hand, is acutely aware of some of the problems inherent in a female writer's engagement with author-ity. Early in her career this manifests itself in the form of bashfulness, which seems at once to be sincere and yet somewhat disingenuous. For example, in her dedication of a collection of poems to Archbishop William Sancroft in 1689, she denigrates her poetry as 'but a few trifles, which even themselves stand in need of an excuse'. Then, plumbing the depths of 'Humility', she asks that he might 'pass a favourable censure upon the failures of a Womans pen, who would very thankfully be informed of her errours and amend them . . . .'[6] The pliant pupil succumbs to the preachings of the pedagogue. His authority, as a man, erases her author-ity as a poet. Yet one should not overlook the fact that she both wrote these poems and then presumed to dedicate them to him: acts which, in themselves, suggest a more confident attitude to her writing than she was prepared to own. She may bow her head, abashed, but, curiously, the pen keeps moving.

By 1694 a marked change in attitude has taken place. In *A Serious Proposal to the Ladies*, Part I (1694), she is prepared to banish any male reader who would not humble himself to her: 'But I will not pretend to correct [those men's] Errors, who either are, or at least *think* themselves too wise to receive Instruction from a Womans pen' (*SP*, I, p. 12). A year later, as she opens an epistolary debate with John Norris, Astell is happy to dismiss stereotypical views of femininity in order to defend her right to be heard: 'Though some morose Gentlemen wou'd perhaps remit me to the Distaff or the Kitchin, or at least to the Glass and the Needle, the proper Employments as they fancy of a Womans Life', she expects 'better things' of her would-be correspondent. When she then requests that he might attend to 'the Impertinences of a Womans Pen', she does so from the position of having textually discredited the codes of propriety that could have silenced her.[7] The pedagogical roles have been reversed. She is now dictating the terms on which she wishes to write.

I am not suggesting that her work should be read as a gauge of her increasing personal confidence or, indeed, that her writings easily trace the path of such a liberating evolution. Such readings would overlook the complexities inherent in her positioning amidst a patriarchal society and the language within which its values are encoded. When, in *A Serious Proposal to the Ladies*, Astell offers a trenchant critique of many aspects of patriarchy, her boldness may, in part, be accounted for by the prescribed gender of her readership. Whilst she does not assume that the 'Ladies'' sympathy can be relied upon, she is not always having to negotiate directly with the degree of hostility that she considers inevitable from men, whose interests are being thwarted. Of course, the very fact that she demotes men to a secondary level both as textual subjects and as readers suggests that she is continuing to shift ideological ground. Still, here, as in her later *Reflections upon Marriage* (1706), where her frequent use of 'we' and 'us' indicates that her assumed readership is again female, Astell's occasional catering for a male audience is not insignificant. The idea – implicit within the optimistic trajectory of a developmental or evolutionary reading – that she might gradually be able to free herself from the restrictions of the dominant ideology is deeply qualified, even as she offers her most incisive alternative to masculine author-ity.

In trying to circumvent masculine author-ity, Astell has not also been contending for its feminization. The distinction, though fine, is crucial. It is in *Reflections Upon Marriage* that its significance emerges. Here she introduces herself as a writer who specifically rejects the title of 'Author' on the following grounds:

> We are all of us sufficiently Vain, and without doubt the Celebrated Name of *Author*, which most are so fond of, had not been avoided, but for very good Reasons: To name but one; *Who will care to pull upon themselves an Hornet's Nest?* 'Tis a very great Fault to regard rather who it is that Speaks, than what is Spoken; and either to submit to Authority, when we should only yield to Reason; or if Reason press too hard, to think to ward it off by Personal

Objections and Reflections. Bold Truths may pass while the Speaker is *Incognito*, but are not endur'd when he is known; few Minds being strong enough to bear what Contradicts their Principles and Practises without Recriminating when they can.[8]

The anonymity for which she opts thus acts as a protective shield against an antagonistic readership. Anonymity ensures a double autonomy for the text. By being released from its 'Author', the text is, simultaneously, freed from the prejudiced perceptions of a reader who responds only to the imagined personality of the writer. The depersonalized script produces a depersonalized reading. Here the idea of an objective reader aspires to the ideal of a discourse that is sexually and politically non-partisan. As I shall later explore more fully, this ideal is philosophically mirrored by Astell's Cartesianism. Now I wish to focus upon the interlinking of her philosophical and political goals, as she develops the model of an impersonal text to liberate herself, as well as her female subjects, from a pregiven political framework.

We must look again at the erasure of herself as an 'Author'. The previously quoted passage obliquely links the being an 'Author' with the concept of 'Authority'. If the reader were to refer to the 'Author', then 'he' would also be found to 'submit to Authority, when he should only yield to Reason . . .' Both the intrusion of an 'Author' and the now complementary 'Authority' deflect the reader's gaze away from what 'Reason' might endorse. Furthermore, that 'Reason' is to offer a new, because challenging, alternative to the findings of 'Authority', which are sanctioned only through reference to what is already established – the 'Principles and Practises'. If Astell had claimed to be an 'Author' she would, therefore, have implicated herself within the partisan perception of 'Authority'. As it is, her disavowal of the label may be read as her dissociation from the 'Authority' that clings stubbornly to an old regime.[9]

In the light of this, Astell's delineation of her literary project becomes particularly suggestive. Her 'Reflections', she writes, 'have no other Design than to Correct some Abuses, which are not the less because Power and Prescription seem to Authorize them' (*R* 'Preface', not paginated). Yet again she distances herself from 'Authority' by being about to write against what is 'Authorize[d]'. And when she later selects the title of 'Reflector', in preference to that of 'Author', she pursues her apparent disengagement from the notions of 'Power and Prescription' now seen to legitimize 'Authority' (*R* Preface, not paginated). Without such pregiven 'Authority', the Astell who only 'reflects', like the Astell of *A Serious Proposal to the Ladies* who only 'proposes', cuts herself off from author-ity and its dual significance. It is at this point that the dynamic exchange between an author who authorizes and an authority that commands, linguistically bonded in the text and context of author-ity, most evidently admit to their guilty partnership. Rather than feminizing author-ity, Astell presents the concept of author-ity as being detrimental to the interests of women.

The 'Power and Prescription' that legitimize 'Authority' become interchangeable with the 'Custom' that depicts as normal, and so supposedly 'Natural', the subjugation of women to men. What Astell is dealing with here are the workings of patriarchal ideology. By planning to 'Correct some Abuses' within the 'Authorize[d]' system, she thus implicitly identifies her text as one which is to counter parts of that ideology. When, as so often throughout her writings, she insists that women's inferiority is not the effect of 'Nature' but 'nurture', she leads us to a critique of what, in Althusser's terms, constitutes the 'illusory' fabric of ideology.[10] Most pertinent to this essay, however, is her illustration of the way in which men act as agents of production within that ideology, by taking to themselves the 'Authority' that is bolstered and perpetuated by 'Custom'.

Into her critique of this masculine framework she inserts the findings of 'Reason', the antagonist of 'Authority'. For her writing defines as irrational the premises upon which female identity is constructed within patriarchal society. In this way, she interprets a derogatory notion of 'femininity' as a contrivance of patriarchy and of the discourse through which it is articulated:

> Women are from their very Infancy debar'd those Advantages, with the want of which they are afterwards reproached, and nursed up in those Vices which will hereafter be upbraided to them. So partial are Men as to expect Brick where they afford no Straw; and so abundantly civil as to take care we [women] shou'd make good that obliging Epithet of *Ignorant*, which out of an excess of good Manners, they are pleas'd to bestow on us [women]!
> (*SP*, I, pp. 16–17)

Masculine speech 'author-izes' women's inferiority, by defining as '*Ignorant*' the intellectual level to which women have been reduced. The end echoes and is generated by the means. But Astell's own ironic speech uses that very irrational author-ity against men. For, as the subjects of *her* discourse, men become the disappointed victims of their own unreasonable expectations: 'So partial are Men as to expect Brick where they afford no Straw . . .' Ideological deviousness is ridiculed as the quaint stupidity of *male* 'Ignorance'.

In *Reflections Upon Marriage*, Astell's dissection of male duplicity uncovers how the would-be wife is the abused subject, created and confined by the male tongue:

> 'We who make the Idols, are the greater Deities; and as we set you up, so it is in our power to reduce you to your first obscurity, or to somewhat worse, to Contempt; you are therefore only on your good behaviour, and are like to be no more than what we please to make you.' This is the Flatterer's Language aside, this is the true sense of his heart, whatever his Grimace may be before the Company. (R, p. 24)

The woman, inscribed within patriarchal discourse, is susceptible to its dictates to the degree that she has already internalized its values. It is important to stress that Astell does not see women as being totally innocent puppets of patriarchy, as she regularly chastises them for behaving in a manner that befits the low esteem in which they are held. Only occasionally does she admit to her own complicity with them in behaving in this way herself. As I shall argue later in this essay, her attitude towards other women often teeters on the edge of the patronizing contempt that she identifies as a masculine trait.

At present, I wish to draw attention to her implicit assumption that she can extricate herself from the intellectual constraints of the dominant ideology. When Astell disrupts patriarchal discourse by decoding the 'Flatterer's Language', she also presumes that she can dismantle that discourse by exploiting its own vocabulary:

> 'Tis true, thro' Want of Learning, and of that Superior Genius which Men as Men lay claim to, she was ignorant of the *Natural Inferiority* of our Sex, which our Masters lay down as a Self-Evident and Fundamental Truth.
> (R Preface, not paginated)

Here the very 'ignorance' that is supposed to epitomize the female is claimed by Astell, only then to have its customary application inverted. Rather than confirming her 'Natural Inferiority', her 'ignorance' conveniently explains why she has not recognized her apparent inadequacy. Such intellectual pirouetting in itself challenges the idea of a woman's mental deficiency. As she thus wipes out the trace of her weakness, she also robs the masculine 'Truth' of the referential evidence that it actually requires for its verification. Astell, it would seem, has won her case.

But has she? In parodying the terms used in patriarchal discourse – 'Ignorant', 'Natural Inferiority' – she may have created an ironic disjunction between their conventional usage and her own interpretation of them, but parody can never acquire its own semantic autonomy. Margaret Rose, in her study of parody and fiction, defines parody itself as a meta-language.[11] Because it has to mimic the language upon which it comments, parody/meta-language can exist only in relation to that very language. When, as by Astell, it is the language of ideology that is being parodied, her words must, therefore, be seen to be functioning in conjunction with that semantic framework. Although she may try to revise the signification of that language, she can never fully erase it. Her parodic writing palimpsestically redisplays the very words that it had tried to efface, by allowing them to rewrite themselves over her own rewriting of them.

Moreover, irony, itself such a recurrent feature of Astell's polemical writing, destabilizes any meaning that she might hope to infer. Just as one can never wrest any positive statement from irony, neither can one determine the exact position of the speaker within the ironic discourse. As a consequence, Astell not only situates herself in an ironic relation to the dominant ideology, but she also exists at an ironic distance from her own words. One could argue that, by disengaging herself from her text in this way, she furthers her exposé of the politics of authoring. The destabilization of meaning through irony complements Astell's goal of resisting the 'Power and Prescription' embedded within author-ity. If language can be seen merely to dally with the idea of reference, then patriarchal discourse may be deprived of its power to define its textual/political subjects. However, emerging from this is an understanding of irony as merely a play between words. Barthes's perception of irony as 'nothing other than the question which language puts to language' becomes particularly apposite.[12] In Astell's writings, the question that remains in play is whether patriarchal 'Authority' can be revised simply by discrediting it as an intellectual concept. Can the subject of ideology escape its frame of reference?

Astell's response to the poverty of women's socio-political circumstances is to try to change women's terms of reference. This assumes, almost exclusively, a theoretical stance. For she does not propose that maltreated wives should leave their husbands or that women should try to wrestle their way into positions of political power. In fact, she very pointedly argues against any such ideas. Even the retreat that she devises for the more privileged women of her society rechannels its inhabitants back into some of the stereotypical roles allocated to them by the patriarchal society.[13] Her main aim is to try to change women's ways of perceiving what is available to them and, in this conceptual manner, to lift them beyond the confines of their present existence. By insisting upon the primacy of the intellect and its non-gendered nature, Astell philosophically opens the way for this particular transformation (SP, I, pp. 47–8).

'*Thinking*', she contends, 'is a Stock that no Rational Creature can want' (*L*, p. 2), by which she means that women, as well as men, have all the mental apparatus that they require. This intellectual capacity is to direct women away from the patterns of behaviour by which they are bound within the patriarchal structure. Astell asks her female readers to examine where their real interests lie:

> This is a Matter infinitely more worthy your Debates, than what Colours are most agreeable, or what's the Dress becomes you best. Your *Glass* will not do you half so much service as a serious reflection on your own Minds, which will discover Irregularities more worthy your Correction, and keep you from being either too much elated or depress'd by the Representations of the other. (*SP*, I, p. 6)

The 'Representations of the other', now such a tantalizing phrase for any feminist critic, offers both a literal and a symbolic reading here. The mirror that reflects the woman's image deflects her attention away from the more substantial musings of introspection. And the 'other' thus refers to the 'Glass' that depicts her appearance as it is received by her own eyes. But as the 'Glass' outlines only the woman's appearance, so it also frames her in the stereotypical pose of vacuity. As already noted, the ciphered female identity relies, for its significance, upon the imprints of the man. A woman's expression of 'femininity' betokens her conformity to the figure of the woman sculpted by masculine desire. In this way, the phrase 'the Representations of the other' evokes the male imaging of women, with the 'Glass' then reflecting her image only as it is formed by the gaze that fashions her the 'other' – the gaze of the man. When she urges women to move away from the mirror and into themselves Astell, therefore, turns self-reflexivity into a symbolic release from the trappings of patriarchy.

It is by 'paying too great a deference to other Peoples Judgments, and too little to [their] own' that women remain mere pawns of patriarchal power.[14] Self-reflexivity, with the aid of reason, thus facilitates an individually undertaken reassessment of the terms governing a woman's life. By denying herself an ideologically prescriptive agency as an 'Author', Astell has opened up a potentially egalitarian space in which female writer and female reader might together explore the issues of patriarchy. Just as Astell only 'reflects' (or 'proposes'), the female reader is invited to 'reflect' inwardly upon her own circumstances. (Barthes's identification of the death of the author with the birth of the reader is graphically illustrated here).[15] Into this posited intellectual autonomy Astell introduces the concept of self-worth. Again she seeks to undercut any dependence upon men: 'We value [men] too much, and our *selves* too little, if we place any part of our desert in their Opinion, and don't think our selves capable of Nobler Things than the pitiful Conquest of a worthless heart' (*SP*, I, p. 10). Here we have the matrix of Astell's idealist vision. She does not court an actual revolution, but she does aspire towards a notion of difference, which predicates itself upon a woman's intellectual and spiritual aloofness from the evaluative schemes and behavioural codes of the dominant ideology.

The mental autonomy sought through the non-gendered intellect is complemented by the non-gendered soul's disengagement from temporal affairs (*SP*, I, pp. 47–8). This Cartesian partnership is supposed to generate for women the alternative terms of reference mentioned earlier, by privileging the spiritual above the material. Astell, in fact, fully inverts a secular mode of perception by proposing that women should have 'a true Notion of the Nothingness of Material things and of the reality and substantialness of immaterial . . .' (*SP*, II. p. 22). However, it is at this point that one begins to encounter the problems inherent in Astell's idealism, as the very words she uses to define a woman's alterity query the extent to which she has herself moved beyond the existent ideology. So, when addressing her female reader, 'We will therefore enquire what it is that stops your flight, that keeps you groveling here below, like *Domitian* catching Flies, when you should be busied in obtaining Empires' (*SP*, I, p. 14). Her contempt for women's earthly existence is unmistakable, but it is debatable whether the transcendence of this, which she advocates, can be achieved. The imperialist terminology evokes the 'Masculine Empire' in which women are colonized subjects, '*Slaves*' to both the despotic authority of the state and the 'Private Tyranny' of the husband (*R*, Preface, not paginated, p. 27). Of course, one could read her appropriation of 'Empires' as the feminization of imperialism. In this way, the enslaved female breaks free of her 'Yoke' by dismantling the linguistic ties that bind her to an oppressive regime (*R*, p. 27).[16] Yet, immediately, such an idea becomes at best precarious, given the association of the concept of an 'Empire' with the abuse of power so fundamental to colonialism. In order for a female 'Empire' to avoid aping its masculine counterpart it is not enough to assume the innocence of the term once the gender of its user has been changed. As she tries to render 'Empires' female, Astell bequeaths both to herself and to women the problem of neutralizing the issue of power whilst still retaining its political rhetoric.

However, she seems to be unaware of such a problem, for her transference of 'Empires' from a temporal to a spiritual setting would suggest that, for her, the secular implications of imperialism can, in this way, become obsolete. In her poem 'Ambition', the empires courted by those who value earthly 'Fame' are denigrated in order to privilege the 'higher Mansion' of 'Immortality' that is supposed to put one outside of the temporal schema. She aspires towards a heavenly 'Crown of Glory' which fashions the 'imperial Law' of ambition (about which she is at first uneasy) serviceable to her becoming 'Great in Humilitie'. So the empowered subject of 'imperial Law' is metamorphosed into the humble subject of God.[17] By casting ambition as spiritual, she sublimates its goal and disowns its temporal significance. Similarly, in *Reflections Upon Marriage*, she tries to turn ambition into a positive female characteristic by refocusing its activity. Of spiritual women she writes:

> She will freely leave [men] the quiet Dominion of this World, whose Thoughts and Expectations are plac'd on the next. A Prospect of Heaven, and that only, will cure that Ambition which all Generous Minds are fill'd with; not by taking it away, but by placing it on a right Object. (*R*, p. 84)

Ambition's 'cure' renders it immune to the 'infectious' breath of earthly ambition, from which she recoils in her poem.

In both cases her relation to ambition and to the imperialist framework within which it is expressed remains ambiguous. She sets up a scenario in which earthly and heavenly ambition may still be seen to be complementary by dint of their both pursuing some mode of transcendence. Thus she informs women: 'You may be as ambitious as you please, so you aspire to the best things, and contend with your Neighbours as much as you can, that they may not out do you in any commendable Quality' (*SP*, I, p. 7). It is an excess of virtue that enables a woman to shine amidst her neighbours. Although ambition then becomes ethereal as a concept, its competitive nature realigns it with its jostling earthly counterpart. Perhaps the most important aspect of this latest shift is Astell's seeming obliviousness to its having taken place. For the 'Empire o'er my self', which she seeks in her poem (and through which the inner and spiritual sublimation becomes operative), would seem to exclude any colonized subjects from its imperial sway. Catherine Gallagher reads this self-monarchy as a positive emblem of a woman's inner freedom, with female subjectivity tracing a figurative path towards women's political equality with men, but she does not take into account the role of ambition within imperialist rhetoric, which has now turned the once potentially liberating concept of self-reflexivity (as a movement away from the 'other'-reflecting 'Glass') into a covert imitation of imperialist patriarchy.[18] Rather than being neutralized, the politics of imperialism are merely displaced into a hierarchical play of virtue. In this way, Astell's 'Empire' doubly overlooks her subjugated colony of less virtuous women.

Furthermore, this hierarchy of virtue assumes a specifically political significance by being woven into the fabric of class differences. As Regina Janes observes, Astell only refers to the lower classes (the precapitalist working class) in order to emphasize the advantages of the upper classes.[19] Astell does not then go on to lament the inequalities, but endorses their conformity to a God-given plan. The questioning of class differences becomes an act of impiety: 'For unless we have very strange Notions of the Divine Wisdom we must needs allow that every one is placed in such a Station as they are fitted for' (*SP*, II, p. 206). It is, she implies, also people's religious duty both to accept their positioning and to make use of whatever opportunities this affords them:

> For since GOD has plac'd Different Ranks in the World, put some in a higher and some in a lower Station, for Order and Beauty's sake, and for many good Reasons, tho' it is both our Wisdom and Duty not only to submit with Patience, but to be Thankful and well-satisfied when by his Providence we are brought low; yet there is no manner of Reason for us to Degrade our selves; on the contrary, much why we ought not. The better our Lot in this World and the more we have of it, the greater is our leisure to prepare for the next; we have the more opportunity to exercise that God-like Quality, to tast that Divine Pleasure, Doing Good to the Bodies and Souls of those beneath us.
> (*R*, pp. 38–9)

Most revealing here is Astell's translation of a 'Providential' social ranking into a system of benefactors and beneficiaries. In part this is a pragmatic response to the actual differences in circumstances, with only those women with 'leisure' having the scope to 'exercise that God-like Quality', while, by necessity, lower-class women are not able to participate actively within this charitable scheme. The more privileged woman's beneficence might then compensate for the poverty of those 'beneath' her and, in this way, pay homage to the harmonious 'Order and Beauty' of the divine structure. Social inequality becomes subservient to the pleasing aesthetics of asymmetry.

Such a manipulation of the facts of class differences is heightened by Astell's inserting into beneficence the 'God-like Quality' that elevates it as an activity. By 'Doing Good' the upper classes are then able to place themselves in a position of greater proximity to the Godhead than their social inferiors. Instead of minimizing the effects of inequality, charity thus reproduces temporal disparity in a spiritual context, by moulding into the external trappings of class the internal hierarchy of virtue. In recommending charity, Astell writes: 'Ladies of Quality wou'd be able to distinguish themselves from their Inferiors, by the blessings they communicated and the good they did' (*SP*, I, p. 89). The social construction of 'Ladies of Quality' is here reinforced by Astell's insistence upon their essential superiority.

This qualitative difference is also marked out in an intellectual framework, for Astell prescribes that the 'Children of Persons of Quality' be 'instructed in lesser Matters by meaner Persons deputed to that Office, but the forming of their minds shall be the particular care of those of their own Rank . . .' (SP, I, p. 91). Again this is a realistic reaction, in part, given the lack of a formal education then available to the lower classes; nevertheless her use of the term 'meaner Persons' in conjunction with 'Rank' betrays more than a practical insight. She superimposes upon a social reality the evaluative assessment that had fashioned the lower classes unfit for education in the first place. In essence, the education of 'Ladies', for which she so forcefully contends, acts as a means of reaffirming the boundaries of class, for it would 'Raise [them] above the Vulgar by something more truly illustrious, than a sounding Title or a great Estate' (SP, I, p. 4). And here we return again to the sublimated ambition explored earlier in her poem, where the 'Titles' and 'Land' denoting temporal success are dismissed in deference to their other-worldly echoes.

Therefore, when touching upon class issues, Astell not only accepts the epithets and demarcations of the dominant ideology, but actually reiterates them. This would seem, at first, to be particularly ironic given that her reading of gender stereotyping entails a critique of the artificially produced limitations of 'femininity'. Recognizing as ideology the social figuration of the woman within the terms of sexual difference, she still fails to detect the link, encoded within her own writing, between this and the political marginalization of the lower classes.[20] Because she assumes class distinction to be God-given, it is construed by her as being natural and so supposedly free from the taints of ideology. Yet, by dividing women into ethical and intellectual categories, she in fact participates in its construction.

Bathsua Makin's writing exactly echoes this shifting away from and back into the dominant ideology. With Astell she rejects, as the distorting effects of 'custom', the idea that women are by 'Nature' incapable of benefiting from education. Similarly, she then goes on to use the fact of upper-class women's 'leisure' to exacerbate social division, by sectioning off the privileged as those most able to devote their time to education. She also, though more explicitly than Astell, argues that knowledge should be restricted to those whom God 'hath blessed with the things of this World, that hath competent natural Parts . . . .' She charts this out:

$$\text{Women are of two sorts}\begin{cases} \text{RICH,} \\ \text{POOR,} \end{cases}\begin{cases} \text{\textit{Of good natural Parts.}} \\ \text{\textit{Of low Parts.}} \end{cases}$$

(*An Essay to Revive the Antient Education of Gentlewomen*, pp. 3, 22, 31)

Economic inequality and its concomitant social ranking are justified, as if by natural selection. Not even graced with the title of 'natural', the 'low Parts' of the poor are made to generate an unnatural aberration, crippled by poverty.

We are not facing here what some critics have interpreted as either the problematic or complementary exchange between Astell's Tory and proto-feminist positions, but rather the interplay between conservative values and the delimitation of a proto-feminist agenda.[21] Even so, I would contend that, in Astell's writings, the movement between these two becomes most revealing not within an easily classifiable political domain, but in the more amorphous area seen by her as being beyond ideology – the internal and spiritual. It is within these spheres that her apparently contradictory attitudes towards class and gender coalesce. For she does conceive of there being a more flexible movement between the classes, even whilst still clinging to the political structure that polarizes them.

However, this fluidity is to be realized only through her disavowal of the importance of temporal life. In this way, the social hierarchy can apparently be questioned and, she assumes, invalidated by an alternative spiritual order of the conscience:

> . . . when a Superior does a Mean and unjust Thing . . . and yet this does not provoke his Inferiors to refuse that Observance which their Stations in the World require, they cannot but have an inward Sense of their real Superiority, the other having no pretence to it, at the same time that they pay him an outward Respect and Deference, which is such a flagrant Testimony of their sincerest Love of Order as proves their Souls to be of the highest and noblest Rank. (R, pp. 49–50)

The 'inward Sense of their real Superiority' thus distinguishes, as being more 'real', the 'Rank' of virtuous souls above the differentiations of social 'Stations'. Temporal hierarchies may then be conceptually inverted, by allowing the social 'Inferiors' to usurp the place of their now falsely conceived 'Superiors'. Catherine Belsey's reading of this reversal as an exposé of the contradictions inherent in society's evaluative system is pertinent only up to a point.[22] Astell's writing does not support its own revolutionary insights. The spiritual 'otherness', upon which this theoretical transformation relies, is, ironically, denied by God's authority. It is only by showing an 'outward Respect' for the social demarcations of superiority and inferiority that lower-class people can prove their souls to be of 'the highest and noblest Rank', by thus demonstrating their 'Love of Order'. And that 'Order' is the God-given, 'natural' selection of class. As a foreshadowing of heavenly humility, this may be plausible and point towards an other-worldly reassessment of human differences. However, within the temporal scheme, the spiritual sublimation, which was supposed to soar beyond ideology, may again be found to fall back within the guidelines of a conservative political terrain.

It is this conflict between ideal aspirations and material manifestations that links Astell's handling of class and gender issues. In relation to both class and gender she only credits the idea of suffering when it impinges upon a person's spiritual experience. The privileged classes, she contends, are racked by inner torment because of the exacting demands of their duties. On the other hand, those 'in Subjection' are actually basking in the delights of temporal ease, as they do not have any duties to fulfil (R, p. 46). Human life thus becomes burdened only for those in a position of responsibility, and that responsibility entails 'Doing Good'. So we are back again within the displaced social hierarchy, for even as Astell insists that a person be esteemed, not according to where he or she stands in the world, 'but as he is more Wise and Good', she reinvokes the politically divisive orders of intellect and beneficence (R, p. 49). And the temporal disadvantaging of women succumbs to the same contradictory treatment.

With respect to the abuse suffered by women in marriage, Astell tries to transform earthly pain into a spiritual bonus:

> ... never truly a Happy Woman till she came in the Eye of the World to be reckon'd Miserable.
> Thus the Husband's Vices may become an occasion of the Wife's Vertues, and his Neglect do her a more real Good than his Kindness could. (R, p. 17)

We have encountered this sublimated notion of what is 'real' before. Here a stoical acceptance of 'misery' places the wife, with the lower classes, in a humble submission to divine authority. For marriage itself is construed in heavenly terms – 'Sacred', an 'Institution of Heaven', a 'blessed State' – and its mode of operation reflects the providential order (R, pp. 8, 11). However, it does not then follow that God should be blamed for a bad marriage, as Astell attributes the latter only to the corruptions of human practice. Instead, divine inscription is to be traced within the authority that the husband commands – the 'Law of the Father' is bequeathed to his 'Sons'. Yet it is because the husband's authority is not innate, but bestowed on him by God, that Astell then suggests that a wife's obedience be reinterpreted in terms of her submission only for 'GOD's sake' (R, p. 83). 'Obedience', she argues, can only be lastingly exacted and respected in accordance with 'the Reasonableness of the Command' and 'the Conscience of Duty' (R, p. 83). In this way, although a woman can never choose to disobey, she can at least salvage her self-respect by exercising her right to reflect upon the propriety (or impropriety) of her husband's commands. Exactly what this might lead to in the end is unclear. However, the inner satisfaction of awaiting her reward in heaven and the righteous awareness of her own piety are deemed sufficient compensations for whatever injustice a woman might meet at the hands of her husband. Yet even the very rational and ethical codes, to which the wife refers for her eventual salvation, actually legitimize her oppression. In material terms, the escape route afforded through a deference to God becomes a blind alley. The 'Passive-Obedience' that Astell has sought to transform within the marital sphere becomes, after all, a wife's only fate (R, p. 27). Once more Astell comes up against her own boundaries, as her unquestioning submission to God's authority impedes her revision of patriarchal politics.

Astell's writings suggest a utopian vision of difference that is an echo of the dystopic reality. This vision culminates in the following sublimation, as she muses upon the deferred gratification that women are to receive: 'She will discern a time when her Sex shall be no Bar to the best Employments, the highest Honour; a Time when that distinction, now so much us'd to her Prejudice, shall be no more . . .' (R, pp. 84–5). The disadvantaging of a woman because of her gender will be rectified only when her gender – her 'distinction' – is erased in heaven.

In the end, the revolutionary potentials of the non-gendered intellect and soul collapse, even for the socially privileged woman. For Astell unwittingly affirms that women are unable to inscribe themselves, *as* women, within either a temporal or spiritual system. In tracing the textual path that moves Astell from an aspiration beyond the existent ideology to a reinscription within it, we find that her writing author-izes more than she is prepared, or able, to claim. Conditioned by her own internalized values, Astell's texts write themselves out of her conscious control and into the hands of patriarchy.

HISTORY

Women's history?
Writings by English nuns

Isobel Grundy

Women's history before the nineteenth century – history written about, or by, or for women – is generally assumed to be non-existent, a classic absence or silence. Examination, however, shows that the presumed absence is merely an absence of what we have mistakenly expected to find. Fully-fledged female writers of mainstream, national political history emerged late: Catherine Macaulay in Britain, 1763, and Mercy Otis Warren in the USA, 1805. The differences of these women from their male peers (though they exist and merit attention) are less immediately striking than their likenesses. Their great works fall under the stricture of Jane Austen's Catherine Morland about history writing: 'the men all so good for nothing, and hardly any women at all'.[1]

But to scrutinize the presumed absence preceding Macaulay and Warren reveals a wealth of forgotten historical writings by women. Women used, modified or originated such genres as epic or fictionalized history, like (probably) Elizabeth Cary, Lady Falkland;[2] biography, like Lady Falkland's daughter (either Anne or Mary Cary) and Margaret, Duchess of Newcastle; scandalous court memoirs, like Delarivier Manley; and family history, like Lady Anne Clifford and Cassandra Willoughby, later Duchess of Chandos.[3] Lady Falkland's daughter-biographer wrote in a Benedictine convent in Cambrai, one of a number of English nuns in Continental Europe writing – in biography, autobiography and chronicles of their communities – a history of a whole female culture. Together they make up one of those barely explored sub-genres which are now emerging in such numbers among works written by women.

Their generic relationships are not, like Macaulay's or Warren's, with classical forebears like Thucydides, Julius Caesar, or Tacitus, but with kinds of writing that are familiar and vital to modern historical researchers: personal records, memoirs, topical pamphlets and annals. They have a marked, perhaps surprising, affinity with the work of female Quakers and other sectarians, both in spiritual autobiography and in theological and political polemic. But whereas the typical Quaker narrative traces a journey towards a religious community marked by gender equality, the life stories of nuns go further, recording a quest for a specifically female community. One of Lady Falkland's sons, the poet Patrick Cary, 'erased several passages' from his sister's life of their mother, 'which he considered too feminine'; whatever he shared with her as sibling or writer, gender evidently marked out a stylistic barrier between them. It seems at least highly likely that the literary qualities he condemned as feminine were the same ones (warmth of human feeling, non-reverence, domestic detail, humour and 'a certain dry intelligence that puts to shame the effusive contemporary masculine biographers') that in this century arouse informed admiration.[4]

English writing nuns were outsiders several times over: they transgressed national imperatives in adhering to a proscribed religion, gender imperatives of fertility and helpmeet status in choosing enclosure (which also meant almost certain exile),[5] and an additional gender taboo in writing. (Though most wrote with the approval or even at the behest of male spiritual advisers, they nevertheless reflect an unease at breaking the silence traditionally enjoined on women.) The marginal status of Catholics being an effect of history, they were acutely aware of the impact of historical events on their own lives, familiar both with the concept of the personal as political and with the need for revised versions of texts authorized by others. Seventeenth-century nuns knew far more about their heroic foremothers during the Counter-Reformation period – Margaret Roper, Margaret Giggs and others – than their opposite numbers in the radical sects knew about, for instance, Anne Askew or Katharine Parr.

Nuns and nunneries were much depicted by those outside the convent walls, from Restoration dramatists and fiction-writers[6] to sentimental novelists and romantic poets, all according to chiefly anti-Catholic and sexist stereotypes, and according to an ahistorical viewpoint, which conflates or confuses the contemporary with the often distant past. Women entering nunneries in these fictions are objects of sometimes prurient pity; the enclosed female world awaiting them is either a weapon of patriarchy (cruel father forces daughter to forego for this the fulfilment of marriage) or at best a second choice (girl crossed in love prefers *even* a convent to the enforced infidelity of marriage to the wrong man); older nuns are harsh and frustrated if not actively sadistic (with predatory lesbianism often part of the package); younger nuns tend to long for escape, generally by means of a male rescuer, back to an outside world which (no matter how indistinct its historical era) is the site of personal freedom and expressiveness. In the churning emotional uncertainties of Pope's *Eloisa to Abelard* (1717), convent life looks now like blessed relief from feeling and now like stony deprivation of it; in either mood it is an annihilation of the active, desiring self.

This composite story gained its currency at the expense of a wholly different version told by the women themselves. Their texts, in self-depicting historical genres, were written not for the world but for each other, stories of women for women to read. They share their piety with two genres their authors inherited: saints' lives and devotional works. Other defining characteristics not shared with these genres – those noted in the Cary daughter's biography – seem to have been fostered by the female community in which the works were written.

The first female biography of a natural mother was pre-dated by one of a spiritual mother: the life of Margaret Clement by Elizabeth Shirley (d. 1641, Augustinian at St Ursula's and St Monica's, Louvain), written about 1612. Having recorded the early history of her order in writing of Clement, Shirley in turn supplied, by her own life, matter for its later history, as continued by anonymous female chroniclers who took up the narrative one from another.[7] One of these, writing about 1660, may have been Winefrid Thimelby (1618–90), who also left personal writings which give depth and colour to the composite historical picture. If she did write an instalment of the St Monica's Chronicle as well as her revealing letters from the convent to her family, she exemplifies a joining of interests common in convent annalists and autobiographers. Catherine Holland (an Augustinian at Bruges – founded from St Monica's – writing c. 1664) and Catharine Burton, or Mother Mary Xaviera (a Teresian at Antwerp, writing c. 1697), both find meaning and structure for their narratives of their own lives by directing them towards an eventual merging with community history.

None of these works was published anywhere near the time of writing: Thimelby's letters were printed with other family papers in 1813; excerpts of Cary's life of Falkland appeared in 1857, the rest – except the lost 'feminine' bits – in 1861; Burton's autobiography was published in 1876; and Holland's (with 'a few omissions') in 1925;[8] the Chronicle of St Monica's, with excerpts from Shirley's life of Clement, appeared piecemeal in Morris and Hamilton in 1872, 1904 and 1906 – Hamilton claims to have omitted only 'a very few pages which the chronicler would never have wished to be made public', and regrets that later sections have been lost (I, p. xi). It is no wonder that such confusing, incomplete and unobtrusive appearances have registered no mark on the accepted picture of early English biography, autobiography, history or herstory.

The shared elements already mentioned should, however, modify the accepted picture. They come sharply into focus if briefly contrasted with writings by another nun who does not share them. Prayers and letters by Trevor, Lady Warner (1636–70), were used by a male contemporary as the basis of a life of her; they reflect quite a different type of spirituality and of relation to history from those of the women so far named. Lady Warner chose convent life as an opportunity for self-abnegation, for rejecting the body and human affection. She refused visits from her former husband (then also a religious, later eminent in the church) and shrank from physical contact with her bewildered small daughters. She symbolically negated her identity by destroying a miniature of herself which he had intended for one of them. Where other nuns expressed daughterly feelings towards their institutions (though some made more than one choice before finding the right one), she continued shifting from one order to another, seeking 'more scope for Mortification, to which she found herself very efficaciously moved'.[9] This type of religious sensibility can express itself in devotional but clearly not in historical writing.

The likeness is therefore more superficial than real between Trevor Warner and Catharine Burton, another self-tormentor. Burton's anguish led her not to erase herself but to explore herself and leave a verbal self-portrait. Born of Catholic parents, growing up 'wild and higher spirited than [her] brothers and sisters', a keen story-teller with a prize-winning memory, she plunged into spiritual turmoil after a smallpox attack at 16 (pp. 22–4). Dreams of hell, she says, were the source of her trouble. External reasons can be guessed at: the physical illness (often linked with piety in saints' lives) and a possible fear of marriage, especially as her mother had died of her tenth child at 34, when Catharine was eight; but she says nothing of parental pressure to marry, and three sisters also became nuns (p. 3). She describes suffering religious terrors, harsh self-imposed penances and a whole series of ailments (perhaps exacerbated by the penances), which lasted to the age of 25. Her vocation to become a nun began as a vow offered to God in hopes of a cure, and became a passionately grateful response to what she saw as a miracle (pp. 78, 83). (Neither she nor any other source makes mention of her ever being ill in the convent until a few years before her death.)

In her account, strong feelings do not cease with becoming a nun. The death of the sister who had been her mistress of novices causes 'a grief which I thought I could never outgrow', but no physical symptoms and no self-blame. (A male contemporary calls her love for this nun 'too great a tie'; she herself makes neither apology nor defence.) Nor is this her only focus of feeling: prayer sometimes brings a sensation of 'sweet carresses' from Christ (pp. 157, 121).

She does, however, relate a conflict during her convent years, even more severe than the earlier one with her illness: it is a conflict over the telling of her story, and she places it at the story's head. It begins when she is nearly 30, and just promoted to the responsible position of sub-prioress. (There are many parallels among female Quakers, who often found the call to the preaching ministry a severer test than the original call to conversion, and among nuns, like Magdalen Throckmorton who had to overcome 'great difficulty in speaking', especially in administering rebuke, before becoming a very successful prioress.) But, as before, Burton narrates the conflict as one between forces external to herself, leaving the reader to deduce her self-division. The call to 'write my life and the favours God had done me' comes as a command from St Xavier, delivered in a vision. She responds first with peace and joy, but then with 'great repugnance . . . having no talent in writing, nor time for it' (p. 14). Her predictable humility slides into a less predictable fear of conflict with the new job. She turns to her spiritual director in the hope, she says, of his countermanding the saint's call, but he endorses it.

Burton presents herself as making no choice, ready in religious obedience either to write or not to write; her director, meanwhile, swings like a demented pendulum between giving and retracting orders. Once she begins writing and finds it easy, he says his permission was only a trial of her obedience and she must burn her story. He also uses 'some very slighting expressions' about her work-in-progress, and adds insultingly 'that if every nun were to write her fancies, we should have pleasant volumes'. Burton, like patient Griselda, burns her work when commanded, starts again when commanded. Then – a strategy used by female writers of many sects, cf. p. 23 above – she finds a higher authority to appeal to, and claims to write not as originator but as ancillary to an unchallengeable power. St Xavier promises, in a dream, to dictate the work to her; she gets the whole thing finished in four months, without subtracting time from any other duty, cheerfully ignoring her superior's continued mixed messages of alternate praise and abuse (pp. 17–19). By the end of her narrative, she is well on the way to her future position as elected superior of the community (part of its history) and has successfully made her mark on it, challenging (by indirection) the male authority within it for the right to tell her own story up to the point of entry into the communal history.

Catherine Holland's narrative explicitly and joyously constructs herself as female subject enlisted in unequal battle between the sexes. Her meek and nervous Catholic mother soon dissociates herself from opposition to her 'earnest Protestant' father, 'whom I both loved and feared', who 'often told me he would break my Will, or my Heart'. As a child, Holland leans towards her mother's faith even before she knows what it contains, clearly from no other motive but defiance of her father (Durrant, pp. 273–4).

She paints her life in the world as more tumultuous, and as more distant from her eventual religious life, than Burton does. She contemplates suicide at ten, lives with 'ever craving' senses, and often steals away in her early twenties, 'to walk all alone in the Woods ruminating, and thus discoursing with my self: What am I? Why am I?' (pp. 276, 279) After this merely human or androgynous, wide-open moment she faces a strictly gendered path in life, 'courted for my Riches' by Protestant suitors (p. 283), longing to be a nun but despairing of success 'as long as my father lived' (p. 277). She tells how despair repeatedly drives her back to addictive but unsatisfying worldly pleasure; aversion to 'the Slavery of Marriage' (p. 304) drives her back to the struggle which implies willing her father's death. Her divided family heritage, and her upbringing in Holland during the English Civil War, give her a clear sense of the microcosmic relation of her personal struggle to the public historical one, each about legitimate rule. One of her provocations to revolt is reading Church history (p. 286). She uses the vocabulary of war; she 'longed for the Combat' and hastened 'into the Field' against an Anglican bishop (in her terms a 'pretended' one: pp. 293, 295). Her own mostly female allies are feeble: her mother, a marchioness and a Jesuit (both over-respectful of paternal authority); the prioress whom she aspires to join (distant, reachable only by letter); her maid; and the 'Conductress' of her flight (p. 302). She several times remarks that she is 'left all alone to fight this Battle' (p. 287).

Holland's is a singularly upbeat, triumphant text. When she briefly mentions the inner confusion typical of spiritual autobiography ('which Way soever I turned the Eye of my Mind, I saw nothing but a Labyrinth, Impossibilities, and Difficulties': p. 290), she does so to heighten the clarity of purpose which she sees in the religious life, just as the slavery of marriage and the loneliness of the world heighten the freedom and community of that life. 'Well if Man will not help me, I am sure God will.'

'At my going from my Father's House I did not shed a Tear.' 'I thought if there had been no ship to convey me over the Sea, I durst have ventured to have gone over in a Pair of Oars or a Cock-Boat' (pp. 299, 302). She denies an aspect of socialized femininity by denying physical cowardice, and denies her filial relation by adopting the Duke of Norfolk as father (he attends her ceremony of profession and shames her father into disgorging a dowry: p. 304). Not her father's death, but merely his defeat encompasses her desire. The emphasis on self-assertion and self-realization, though by no means uncommon in spiritual autobiography, is here unusually strong: this tale of strife closes with a triumph, as the narrator succeeds in crossing the battle lines and reaching her own headquarters.

Her convent's annals provide a context for Holland's autobiography, and contradict any expectation that this filial rebel might have problems with a strictly regulated community under the ultimate rule of a male anthropomorphic god and male human superiors. No longer embattled, Holland retains her energy: noted – and loved – for wit and merriment, she is quite often disciplined for carrying these propensities too far. At such times she habitually addresses herself as she goes to make her penance: 'Come Kate along with me' (p. 306). There is a sense here of autonomy and self-control which contrasts interestingly with her earlier picture of herself as 'all alone'. Her text, like Burton's, closes on the merging, but not the extinction, of individual history with that of the community.

The humour, tolerance and appreciation paid to Holland by herself, and also by the chronicler, are characteristic of attitudes of convent biographers from the earliest, Elizabeth Shirley. Margaret Clement, 'our good grandmother' (Durrant, p. 184), had been Shirley's prioress; in Clement's old age Shirley became prioress, the spiritual mother of her erstwhile spiritual mother. Shirley exploits this paradox to depict a loving renunciation of superiority one to the other. She enforces the parallel between the natural and the religious relationship by stressing shared domesticity (housekeeping details crop up in most accounts of convent life by women). Her relation to Clement as grandmother, like Cary's to Lady Falkland as mother, is neither submissive nor rebellious (like Burton's to her director or Holland's to her father), but affectionate, teasing, often ironical. These texts delight in subverting reader expectations, in revealing strength in apparent weakness and vice versa, in echoing Biblical paradoxes about the last being first, or the meek inheriting, or serpents and doves.

The life of Falkland by her daughter has elements of the traditional saint's life: before she joins the Catholic church the tale encompasses oppression, submissiveness to her husband and a Clarissa-like aiming at perfection; later it covers more oppression, loneliness, near-starvation, returning her husband good for evil, and so on.

Yet Cary handles each of these elements in a human, daughterly tone, avoiding the odour of sanctity. She depicts the future Lady Falkland as a child, acquiring learning and making a sensation in a lawcourt rather like the boy Jesus in the Temple. But the learning is marked by illicit reading at night and running up huge debts to the servants for candles: that is, in worldly terms, by prodigality and filial unruliness. And the vanquishing of injustice is achieved not by prayer or holiness but by sheer detective work: perceiving that a terrified old woman accused of witchcraft is confessing indiscriminately to whatever she is accused of, and engineering a confession so patently impossible that it discredits all the rest. This is a triumph of rationality rather than piety, an exposé of the corrupt court rather than a sanctification of the protagonist.

Cary gives a faintly comic tone to family life with Falkland throughout her career: her brilliance, her eccentricity, her sanctity, are rendered as highly inconvenient to those around her in their infringing of social norms. The life bears the same relation to a stock satire on learned ladies as Henry Fielding's Parson Adams does to a stock satire on pedants. Lady Falkland is portrayed as wholly lacking that sense of the absurd which her biographer abundantly demonstrates. She remains on her knees for long conversations with her mother (who is seated) despite an all-too-human weight problem: 'she was but an ill kneeler, and a worse riser'. Deprived of support by her husband, she survives partly because her one remaining, devoted young servant brings home food from the tables of others in a sort of doggy bag (pp. 22, 32).

The links which Cary constructs between sanctity and humdrum domesticity are not wholly unknown in male saints' lives: William Roper's life of Thomas More springs to mind. But More is depicted as having control of the domestic comedy in which he participates; the earthly struggle which parallels his spiritual struggle is one of national politics, whereas Lady Falkland's earthly struggle involves her in constant indignities of one kind or another. The model of saintly Catholic motherhood was a familiar one during the years of persecution: while husbands often outwardly conformed for the sake of the family property, wives went to prison for the sake of the family conscience. The domestic saint's life is well represented by a memoir which Herbert Aston wrote of his wife after her death in childbirth in 1658. He describes a Catholic, female spirituality grounded in family love, and makes the home – a mix of productive work, quiet order, piety and fun – sound very like the convents as their historians describe them. In her last moments, Katherine (Thimelby) Aston laughs and jokes about her eldest daughter being a better housewife than she is anyway. 'It is true, she said often she could not live, but I never took it for serious, she did it with that mirth in her countenance, such love in her lookes.'[10]

Kinds of love which are generally considered opposed, or at least distinct, often run together in this discourse. Katherine Aston, nicknamed Belamore or Good Love by her husband, elicited both from him and from his sister Constance letters of love whose hyperbolical and erotic diction draws on their reading of the metaphysical poets.[11] Related in turn to these are the letters sent from St Monica's convent, Louvain, to her family at home by Katherine's sister Winefrid Thimelby, who became prioress of and possibly a chronicler of St Monica's. Interpreting the convent to those outside, she reveals with surprising frankness the conflicting elements in her feelings: 'Doe not suppose me a well mortifyed nun dead to the world; for alas tis not so, I am alive, and as nearly concern'd for thos I love, as if I had never left them' (II, pp. 44–5). Two generations before Eloisa, she writes, 'I am no stone' (II, p. 65).

Yet her letters sound a frequent note of gaiety. She poises her discourse not, like Eloisa, between passion and renunciation but between yearning for the absent on one hand and non-pious high spirits on the other. Like Cary raising a smile at her mother's stoutness or absent-mindedness, she offers details of convent life for the amusement of those who will find them alien. Her hair, she writes, 'is too short to do any thing with', and grey; she has had her portrait painted by request: 'O the shame!' (II, pp. 8; 15). She deliberately lends a hint of worldly coquettishness to the austere, asexual image of a short-haired woman, and to the threat of passing time. Repeatedly she voices acceptance of her own fluid and multiple emotions.

Embedded in Thimelby's letters is the life story of a niece who came to the convent partly in response to her begging her sister and brother-in-law to 'give me a child' (II, p. 7). Kate arrives in time to be 'bridmayde' (II, pp. 30–31) at the marriage to Christ of another aunt, Gertrude (Aston) Thimelby, widow and poet. But she echoes and intensifies Winefrid's pattern of divided feelings. Winefrid interprets Kate's feelings with tender solicitude and with no reference at all to the rule of authority, either that of natural father or of convent superiors. She responds to Kate's death with two sentences which perfectly catch her capacity to balance conflicting feelings: 'She truly lives, and shall never dy. She laughs at our fond tears, for God has wyp'd her eyes' (II, p. 101). The word 'laughs' echoes the slightly disturbing high spirits with which Kate's mother was described as meeting her death and Burton and Holland as entering their convents.

The chronicle of St Monica's, a more fully historical text, gives comparable weight to the minutiae of personal relations. The families and the pre-convent lives of the nuns are as important as the life within the community. With frequent and strongly marked deaths, closure is avoided as membership, offices (and the chronicler's pen) pass from one individual to another. Editors differ as to when and where such handing-on occurred: Morris thinks there was a break in about 1631; Hamilton apparently thinks that the chronicler writing to about 1660 (who may or may not be Winefrid Thimelby) had carried the tale from the inception of St Monica's. With a brief to cover the first 50 years from the cloister's founding in 1609, she opens by casting back 50 years more to Edward VI's persecution of Catholics, providing a historical context for the actual foundation.[12]

She opens, therefore, on Elizabeth Shirley's life of Margaret Clement, whose dates make her an ideal focus for analysis of the situation when St Monica's was launched from its parent community, three years after Clement's jubilee or celebration of 50 years as a nun. The biography provides the chronicler's first heroine: Clement's mother Margaret Giggs, whose link with St Thomas More, and personal fame for heroic exploits, make her a thematically appropriate curtain-raiser. Her daughter Margaret Clement is cited together with 'Sister Anne Clitherow, daughter to Mrs Clitherow, the proto-martyr of her sex in England, who followed well her holy mother's virtuous steps' (Hamilton, I, p. 33).

The chronicler, who has Shirley's life of Clement at her fingertips and recommends it as further reading, thus sets the 'good grandmother' of an earlier writer in relation both to that grandmother's mother, and to an illustrious sister and *her* mother. As biographies traditionally begin with genealogy, so the history of St Monica's begins with female genealogy, a record of individuals both as mothers and as women (something that Luce Irigaray has recently called for).[13] And while nuns' autobiographies tend to picture dubious or cruel parenting, the chronicle depicts much admirable mothering, which strengthens and frees its daughters.

Clement and Clitherow are backed by a wide and heterogeneous network of mothers. An old beggar woman succeeds where Shirley's Catholic brother and various priests had failed, and converts her from Protestantism with a tale of the Virgin's miraculous rescue of a woman in childbirth (Hamilton, I, pp. 102-4). Another beggar woman (Irish this time) and another tale of the Virgin convert Jane Hatton, daughter of a leading local Protestant father and a mother already dead (I, pp. 116–17). A Catholic aunt brings up Ann Mortimer to hold her faith even after marriage to 'a heretic and a most fierce man' (I, p. 199). Agnes Tasburgh reaches the convent on money given by her grandmother, having held bravely to her mother's Catholic religion until her Protestant father 'said he would cut her tongue out of her head if she spoke one word more' and told her 'never to expect one penny from him, as though she were not his child' (I, pp. 255–6).

Reading the chronicle, we realize that Catherine Holland, preferring her mother's religion to her father's, was following a common pattern. First to defy her earthly father about her religious desires is Clement herself; she is also first to oppose the convent to marriage, as Holland does too. Shirley is another who 'never had any mind to marry' (I, p. 105). The chronicler says that God called Mary Worthington to religion at ten years old by showing her the miseries of marriage as felt by 'a gentlewoman, who had a very untoward husband' (II, p. 66). One would-be nun forced into marriage against her will treasures up the idea of religious vocation for one of her daughters (I, pp. 240–1). The only male relations mentioned as being in favour of convent life are those of a 'crooked' woman and an epileptic. An early – female – biographer of Mary Ward observes wryly how in such cases the convent is praised as 'beautiful, pure, pious, and peaceful', while if the would-be nun is 'considered promising by the world', the 'little song' is changed to one of a 'cursed land . . . which devours its inhabitants'.[14]

The chronicler of St Monica's assures her readers that she has founded her narrative where possible 'upon the relation of the persons them-selves', and that on completing each part she goes back to her original informants to check 'whether all was right written and nothing mistaken' (I, p. 24). She is in fact a conscientious scholar. Her substantiated account differs widely from the manipulative and sentimentalized 'little song' of peace and purity: instead of this it stresses humour, mundane administ-ration and domesticity, as well as constant struggle and heroinism.

Female heroism is sometimes measured against masculine norms. Shirley recorded that Clement's male director was 'confounded, she being a frail woman', at her 'great courage and magnanimity' (Durrant, p. 200). The chronicler notes that Mary Wiseman distinguished herself from a man facing martyrdom with her by choosing a particularly frightful death not adjudicated by a jury, who thus would not bear the guilt of it (Hamilton, I, pp. 82–3). Humour infuses struggle: the Copley sisters, interrogated at night, hide their Catholic books in bed with them, leaving Virgil out to be confiscated (I, pp. 114–15); a gentlewoman trying to influence Shirley against convent life turns out to have a vested interest in employing her as family help (I, p. 105).

Domesticity is central in these women's texts: when a vision comes to reassure Shirley in the anxious early days of the new house, it is of 'a glorious shining light, round like unto a pewter dish' (I, p. 76). The chronicler presents in loving detail the new community's dower of household stuff from its mother house, down to 'pots and pans, tubs, and such-like necessary things' (I, p. 67). She presents religious abstinence through the small indulgences which define it: nuns living on 'coarse rye' bread and 'exceeding small' beer enjoy a tiny weekly treat of 'common gingerbread' (I, p. 35). At the time of the move, a gift of 'two great tarts, the one of minced meat, made costly, the other of fruit, very good . . . . served our poor sisters for a whole week.' The nuns greet the gift with 'exuberant gaiety' which overflows in verse ('I leave you to guess our dear Mother's surprise / At finding a table well covered with pies') and in a 'comical little drawing' of them eating. The chronicler includes both verse and drawing in her manuscript; she stresses that this gaiety springs in the midst of trouble and effort. The prospect of one egg a week each and no salt 'made them good recreation among themselves, to see what a pretty shift they must make' (I, pp. 69–71). The narrative consistently interweaves such mock-heroic or throwaway detail of hardships within the community with the real persecutions suffered outside, which occur in flashback to individual experience when nuns are professed, or promoted, or die.

The nuns face floods, war and plague at intersections of the convent's history with the history of Europe.[15] But the chronicler does not privilege such events over those defined by the community: terms of office and holy deaths; the acquisition, care and development of buildings, land and household stuff; and the detail of personal lives. These elements are recurrent, as the community is self-renewing, with biography and autobiography flowing into its broader stream. The movement of the text is strongly cyclical: the present moment, constantly passing away and constantly renewed, is placed in sequential relation to a past of heroic action and a future of institutional continuity and hoped-for personal salvation.

The convent tradition secured our possession of one text which is better known than any I have yet mentioned: the narrative by Winifrede Maxwell, Countess of Nithsdale, of how she successfully sprang her Jacobite husband from the Tower of London on the eve of his intended execution, early in 1716. The tale has a cloak-and-dagger ambience which sounds far more modern than, say, the future Lady Falkland's brush with a witch trial, or the Copley sisters' visit from the law while in bed; but the heroism is of a similar flavour. Adventure is an exercise in gender solidarity: two female accomplices; a 'poor woman' who lends her house; the Welsh maid whose quick wit saves the day when a man panics. It is tinged with female exasperation at male behaviour: Lord Nithsdale has to be coaxed into women's clothes, even to save his life; 'However God Almighty helpt me in that also when the time came'.[16]

Lady Nithsdale did not write her story till some years after the event, in a letter to her sister Lady Lucy Herbert, a prioress of Augustinians at Bruges: 'This is the full relation of what you desired . . . which noe body but your selfe could have obtain'd from me'.[17] Lady Lucy's commissioning, preserving, and probable circulation of the letter (of which copies soon multiplied) brought an outgrowth of the convent historical tradition to the eyes of a secular readership, as a footnote to mainstream history. The ladies of Llangollen (a miniature female community) owned a copy; an editor of 1827 tried to appropriate it for a different signification by calling it 'illustrative of that self-devotion which women often evince when called upon to act in the cause of their husbands or of their children'.[18] Comparison with Catherine Holland or the St Monica's chronicler suggests that, on the contrary, Lady Nithsdale is relating an episode of exhilarating female intervention in the process of power, addressing an audience of nuns who were well versed in an early tradition of women's history-writing.

Producing the voice, consuming the body

Women prophets of the seventeenth century

Diane Purkiss

Anna Trapnel, the Fifth Monarchist prophet, had experienced visions and inspirations before her dramatic twelve-day trance at Whitehall in January 1654, but it was this sustained prophetic utterance which made her famous – or notorious – and drew her to the attention of a public outside the radical millenarian sects. Trapnel had been waiting at Whitehall with a group of Fifth Monarchists who had gathered to support one of their number, Vavasour Powell, who was being questioned by the Council of State. While sitting in a small side-room, warming herself by the fire, Trapnel suddenly fell into a prophetic trance: 'carried forth in a Spirit of Prayer from noon to night'.[1] She had many visitors at Whitehall, including several members of Barebone's Parliament, two women and ministers of various persuasions; four books by Trapnel or about her Whitehall prophecies were published the same year, suggesting the interest generated by her trance.[2]

'She delivered in that time many and various things, speaking every day three or four hours', wrote one commentator (*Strange*, p. 1). Not all Trapnel's Whitehall utterances were prognostications. For the radical sects in the seventeenth century, prophecy was any utterance produced by God through human agency. Hence the prophecies of women discussed in this essay include hymns, general moral exhortations, scriptural exegeses, prayers, spiritual autobiography and mystical revelations, as well as predictions.[3]

Anna Trapnel was one of many women prophets who spoke and wrote prophecy in public and in private in the seventeenth century.[4] But such public displays of prophetic power opened women prophets to surveillance by many different groups of interested parties. First, in Trapnel's case, the specific political content of her prophecies and their evident hostility to Cromwell's protectorate meant that Cromwell's agents kept watch on her activities. Their reports eventually led to her arrest in Cornwall and transportation to London to be imprisoned in Bridewell by the Council of State.[5] Secondly – and perhaps most importantly – acceptance of a woman prophet depended on the belief that her utterances were divinely inspired. As both Ann Kibbey and Phyllis Mack have shown, divine inspiration was uncomfortably similar to its supposed opposites: diabolic possession, witchcraft, and madness.[6] Though many accepted that Trapnel's prophetic statements and trances were the products of divine agency, others did not. Trapnel was arrested and charged with witchcraft on her tour of Cornwall, and in her own writings she registers anxiety about those who did not acknowledge the genuineness of her divine inspiration: 'England's rulers and clergy do judge the Lord's handmaid to be mad, and under the administration of evil angels, and witch' (Trapnel, *Report*, 'To the Reader').

Properly, surveillance is a term for a process of examination, or (over)looking, which has as its goal the acquisition of an empowering knowledge of the object of scrutiny. It was the visibility of women prophets which opened them to examination by church, state and public. In the case of women prophets like Trapnel, this visibility is not a mere metaphor for notoriety. Because Trapnel did not merely publish texts, but actually spoke them in public spaces, her body was necessarily on display. Mary Poovey has suggested that in the seventeenth and eighteenth centuries, the publication of texts by women served to mediate between the private(ized) female self and the public sphere; the text could enter 'the world', be known, scrutinized and exchanged in ways proscribed for the woman herself.[7] Women prophets' entry into the public sphere was direct and unmediated. Their writings were circulated, but they also 'made spectacles of themselves' by appearing and speaking.[8]

This bodily visibility was produced in and by radical Protestantism's discourses of the body. These discourses involved an unsettling saturation of the believer's body with iconic or semiotic significance. Iconoclasm was fuelled by the belief that the bodies of the godly were the truest icons, made by God Himself in his own image. This understanding was reflected and reproduced in many diverse bodily practices which used the believer's body as a sign for divine workings, from Eleanor Douglas's appropriation of the bishop's chair at Lichfield as a protest against episcopal rule to the valorization of the mutilated bodies of Prynne, Burton and Bastwick as signifiers for the sufferings of the godly.[9] Women's visibility, however, transgressed gender norms. First, the notion that the believer's body could be a sign for God or a site for the inscription of divine meanings depended on a perceived likeness between that body and the deity: man was made in God's image, and was therefore the truest image of Him. But woman was further removed from God than man; she was made not in God's image, but in man's. Her difference from man meant that she was not a true icon of God.[10] Second, in the seventeenth century women's bodies were consigned to privacy and enclosure. The privacy of the female body was a sign of female chastity; the public female body was a sign of unchastity, since it was exposed to the gaze of men other than husband or father.[11] Part of the unsettling power of women prophets came from this transgression of gender norms. But such practices also made them vulnerable to hostile scrutiny and male anxiety.

In this essay, I will discuss the bodily practices, narratives and metaphors which were an important part of women's prophetic utterances and performances, focusing particularly on illness, the practice of fasting, the metaphorization of food and feasting, and the troping of the reproductive female body. Throughout, it will be assumed that the body is not a stable constant, a 'natural' ahistorical fact against which the contingency of culture can be assessed. Rather, the body is always already caught up in cultural discourses and practices, and the bodily practices I discuss are produced in and by them. I will argue that the visibility of the woman prophet's body was a means by which she negotiated a space to speak within the constraints of seventeenth-century religious discourse, and hence a way for her to threaten established orders and hierarchies.

I

The relation between the female body of the woman prophet and the masculine voice which issued from it was always intrinsically unsettling. The spectacle of a woman prophet speaking cannot be equated with an unproblematic logocentrism which would validate her voice by displaying its point of origin. Rather, prophetic utterance necessarily involves a radical dislocation of the voice from the body, since in authentic prophecy the voice comes from God, while the body through which it speaks is a passive conduit. Jane Lead describes herself as an 'earthen and empty vessel'. One commentator on Trapnel's trance stressed the difference between her normal speaking voice and the prophetic voice, which spoke more swiftly and also more loudly.[12] Male prophets also foregrounded the split between voice and body, but my interest lies in the

way in which the necessary split between voice and body generated by
prophecy allowed women prophets to represent their own anomalous
position in relation to language. For some women, the demands of
prophecy did involve an entire effacement of the female speaking voice
which appears to represent a total disjunction of voice and body. Hester
Biddle, for example, writes:

> Wo to thee City of Oxford, thy wickedness surmounteth the wickedness of
> Sodome, therefore repent whil[e th]ou hast time, lest I consume thee with fire,
> as I have done it; therefore harden not your hearts, lest I cons[u]me you, and
> my wrath burn like fire, and I consume you in my fierce anger.[13]

Here, the 'I' who speaks is not a self-representation of Biddle, but is God.
Biddle's own voice is erased in the interests of representing the single,
unified divine utterance. But the textual spectacle of male power speaking
through a woman's body might signify not only female silence, but also a
disturbing – if vicarious – female empowerment. We might also want to
speculate about the pleasurable opportunities this kind of speaking
created for women: to speak authority, to speak anger, to speak strength
– but to speak them not as themselves, but as another, to become the
silent Other of their own speaking.

In Trapnel's writings, prophetic discourse generates opportunities to
represent the fissured subject position constructed for women in the
seventeenth century. Characteristically, woman was the object of
discourse, the ground of representation, or the unstable site which
offered the possibility of fixing meaning. However, women were also able
to speak, to say 'I'. Consequently they occupied a marginal position with
respect to language, neither speaking at its centre nor excluded from it
altogether. Some of Trapnel's prophetic utterances suggest that she is
using the conventions of prophecy to represent this marginal position:

> They will say the spirit of madness and distraction is upon her, and that it is
> immodesty; but thou knowest Lord, that it is thy spirit; for thou hast cast thy
> servant where she would not, and hast taken her contrary to all her thoughts
> . . . Oh thy servant knows it is from thy Spirit. (*Cry*, p. 67)

In this passage, the female subject is not entirely effaced, as in Hester
Biddle's writing. Nor is she allowed to be fully present. Instead, Trapnel
writes herself as the third person: 'thy servant', 'her', becoming the object
and not the subject of her own speaking. But the question, 'Who is
speaking here?' becomes insistent, since the direct address to God seems to
require that we understand Trapnel to be the subject, the one who speaks.
Trapnel becomes both the effaced subject *and* the object of her discourse,
replicating the problematic position of women within language.

This fractured speaking voice is, remarkably enough, given not only a divine father but an earthly mother in Trapnel's writings. Trapnel's prophetic powers are for her the result not of direct divine action, but of divine action compelled by the power of her mother's voice:

> My mother died nine years ago, the last words she uttered upon her death-bed, were these to the Lord for her daughter. Lord I Double thy spirit upon my child; these words she uttered with much eagerness three times, and spoke no more . . . . (*Cry*, p. 3)

This story, in explaining Trapnel's gifts as the product of her mother's prayer, associates Trapnel's mother with the power of words. Whereas Trapnel characteristically pleads with God from the third person, her mother is able to speak as an authoritative subject; her words, repeated three times, are not a prayer but an incantation, words of power. Trapnel's mother's dying speech represents the full subversive power of the woman prophet, for it inverts the most basic of all hierarchical relations, the relationship between God and the believer. The woman commands, and commands God. In imagining her mother's words as an efficacious act, Trapnel associates the power of words not with God but with woman in a manner she is not able to replicate in her self-representation. But her own more fractured utterances are subversively represented as the product of a woman's verbal power over God.

II

It is significant that this verbal empowerment occurs at the moment of the physical death of Trapnel's mother, the moment when subjectivity and voice are detached from the body. The vocal power of this woman can be read as a symbolic inversion of the kind inscribed in the *ars moriendi* tradition, in which the speaker's proximity to physical death licensed minor reversals of hierarchical relations, so that wives could give orders to husbands and children to parents.[14] Such inversions were themselves predicated on the liminal status of the dying person: suspended between earth and heaven, partaking of both. Such a position was also replicated in the trances of women prophets, states in which their spirits were in heaven or with God, their bodies on earth. Thus, the production of the prophetic voice is associated with physical weakness, illness or incapacity. For Trapnel, physical weakness seems always to function as a facilitator of the power of the speaking voice. Here she describes her first prophecy:

> Seven years ago, I being visited with a fever, given over by all for dead, the Lord then gave me faith to believe from Scripture, After two days I will revive thee, and thou shalt live in my sight. (*Cry*, p. 3)

Both Trapnel and her amanuensis insist upon her physical weakness during her prophetic outbursts. At Whitehall she is so weak that she takes to her bed; in Cornwall after a burst of singing and speaking, she announces 'weakly' that she must go to bed, 'for I am very weak'; in bed she has another vision (*Report*, pp. 20–1).

In the seventeenth century, illness and bodily weakness were feminized. Women were thought to be particularly prone to illness, and illness and weakness were in turn negative signs of femininity, underwriting woman's subordination.[15] In Trapnel's writings, this gender difference is at once reinforced and undermined: the attributes used in the dominant discourse to signify feminine inadequacy are privileged as facilitators of verbal empowerment. Illness and physical incapacity stage the body as the passive prey of external forces, hence an authentic site of divine intervention.

Similar devices were used by other seventeenth-century women prophets. In 1654 Elinor Channel's prophecies appeared under the title *A Message From God (By a Dumb Woman)*. Channel's amanuensis, the royalist Arise Evans, explains that he found her wandering the streets, anxious to find someone to write down her visions. She had walked to London from Surrey for this purpose; when her husband forbade the journey, Channel became dumb, and he relented. We could read Channel's dumbness as female resistance to her husband's patriarchal authority. Put into discourse by Arise Evans, however, it generates other meanings. The dramatic silencing of Channel seems to stage on her body the same erasure of female subjectivity as in Hester Biddle's texts. Evans reads Channel's dumbness as a sign of her prophetic trances:

> But as she said, when she is Dumb, all her sences are taken up, and the Matter which troubles her Mind, is dictated and made plain to her by the Spirit of God; so that when she comes to herself she has it by heart.[16]

Channel's bodily incapacity to speak guarantees the purity of the divine voice which issues from her.

Channel's dumbness is only one instance of the signs produced on the bodies of women prophets and extensively examined and read by their contemporaries. If we read such signs as produced by the women themselves, we might construe them as parodic or subversive reifications of the construction of women, which by their excess function to open a space for alternative constructions. But in arriving at such a reading, it is necessary to acknowledge that such somatological representation also turned women's bodies into signs which could be reread and appropriated to serve masculine agendas and discourses putting women firmly into the place assigned them. But such masculine co-optations were precisely what enabled women prophets to be heard.

The protracted fasts of some women prophets are another example of bodily weakness as a signifier for prophetic empowerment. Sarah Wight is said by Henry Jessey to have fasted for 75 days:

> It being now above 75 days since she did eat at all, and full 65 days since she did sip or drink two dayes together, her drink being only fair water for about twenty dayes: and since that, some small beer: and both these only at once in two, three or four dayes.[17]

Martha Hatfield took no food for over two months, according to James Fisher.[18] Anna Trapnel took no food for the entire period of her Whitehall stay; throughout her writings she associates inedia with her trances (Cry, pp. 5–6; Strange, p. 3). It might seem tempting to conflate fasts with illness, dumbness and mortality, especially since both the fasting women and their amanuenses sporadically insist that their inedia is imposed upon them rather than voluntary. I want to suggest, however, that it is anachronistic to associate such protracted fasts solely with weakness, and more problematic still to link them with an understanding of woman as victim, prey to self-destructive impulses.[19]

First, fasting in Puritan discourse represented not just an act of personal self-denial but an act of quasi-magical efficacy. Parliament ordered a fast to repel the plague of 1648, and Puritan congregations held fasts to cure sick members of the community and even to produce favourable weather. Some Puritan clergy claimed to perform exorcisms by fasting; this practice, however, proved uncomfortably close to papistical magic, and was forbidden.[20] However, other fasts continued to be performed; the Quakers Katharine Evans and Sarah Cheevers fasted for 11 days during their imprisonment on Malta, not to influence their captors, but to influence God. During Sarah Wight's fast, she was visited by numerous women suffering from despair; one explained that her church had held a fast for her.[21] All these stories suggest that fasting was a last loophole in the Reformation's attempts to outlaw practices which empowered the believer in relation to God. Such practices had in the medieval Church frequently been predicated upon the believer's body as the site of such power, and their irrepressibility might point to an uncanny return of what had been forgotten or repressed by orthodox Protestant culture.[22]

This way of practising fasting may have opened up a specific site of negotiation for women, since women's association with food and fasting is a surprising constant in western culture.[23] Caroline Walker Bynum points out that in Western culture women are particularly linked with food production and distribution *rather than* with food consumption. From breastfeeding to the kitchen of the godly household, food production is under female control.[24] However, such food production is characteristically represented as somehow selfless; woman's role is to feed and not to eat, to nurture rather than to be nourished. In this cultural context, women prophets' refusal of food can be read as a confirmation of that culture's understanding of women's relation to food. Both women prophets and their amanuenses represented prophetic utterances in terms of food and nourishment. 'Nothing but honey dropped from her mouth', writes Fisher, describing Martha Hatfield's tranced utterances ($A_4{}^{R-V}$). Refusing to nourish their own bodies in order to transmit nourishment to others, women prophets reproduced precisely the ideology of women's relations to food.

But these women's nurturative relationship with their congregations also subversively foregrounded women's power over food, their power to give or withhold nourishment from others. Equally importantly, women prophets constantly deployed tropes of hunger, food, feeding and satiation in order to describe their privileged relation to God. Sarah Wight characteristically uses these tropes when being urged to eat:

> Her brother spake aloud to her, to take some what to refresh her body. Shee then heard him, and answered: I cannot; I have what I did desire; I have a crucified Christ: I am so full of the Creator, that now I can take in none of the creature. I am fild with heavenly Manna. (p. 31)

Subsequently, Wight rebukes another questioner:

> Do you think, I doe not eat? How do you thinke I live? Being asked what she did eat? Shee said: No eye of men sees it, but the eye of God. None could taste the sweetness of the manna, by looking on it, none but they that eat of it. (p. 34)

She insists that 'Jesus Christ feeds me', and says, 'I have enough: he feeds me with delights'. Jesus also substitutes for drink: 'hee not only hath drops, but he flows in of himself' (p. 57) – and for food: 'God hath given me Christ to feed upon: and his flesh is meat indeed, and his blood drink indeed' (p. 58). In Wight's utterances, Christ is alternately figured as a food provider and as food itself. In either case, the figure is of plenitude, abundance and pleasure: 'a full Christ', overflowing with nurturative power. This representation renders Christ analogous to Wight herself. Like women, Christ is a provider of nourishment to others. But in producing these images as responses to offers of earthly food or drink, Wight not only facilitates the representation of Christ as a *copia* of nourishment, but also foregrounds her own privileged relationship to this quasi-maternal source of sustenance. For this privileged position is signified not only by Wight's reception of heavenly food from Christ, but also by the way her use of food allows her to represent herself – a woman – as an imitation of the suffering Christ, mortifying her own flesh in order to nourish others.[25]

Similar patterns of representation occur in the writings of Trapnel. Like Wight, she connects her inedia with her pleasurable reception of heavenly nourishment:

> I could not eat of anything
> Nothing will now go down,
> For I have tasted other meat
> In viewing of the crown. (*Legacy*, p. 49)

Again like Wight, Trapnel repeatedly uses food imagery, drawn especially from the *Song of Songs*, to tell the story of her unions with God. She also associates her speeches with nourishment.[26]

Women's fasts also worked to allow them to rewrite the socially constructed narrative of femininity, and particularly to disrupt the understanding of the passage from childhood to womanhood. The use of food imagery in Trapnel and Wight represents the woman both as an infant, nourished by the always plenitudinous maternality of God, and also as a mother, an *imitatio christi* who in turn provides nourishment for a hungry congregation. In such tropes, two life stages understood as distinct – infancy and motherhood – are combined and held in paradoxical suspension and unsettling play. This undoing of important hierarchical categories also depicts the possibility of moving from infancy to maternity without passing through marriage. In their own narratives, women prophets are able to obtain the role of mother without subjecting themselves to (earthly) patriarchal authority. Thus, although the infantilization of the woman prophet feeding on Christ appears to confirm her status as *femme couverte*, her self-representation also opens out a space for imagining female autonomy.

Trapnel's writings also display concern about food distribution in the community. This is a sign of Trapnel's political engagement. Other radical Protestants also described the uneven distribution of wealth in terms of a contrast between the feasts of the rich and the hunger of the poor. But in Trapnel's text this thinking becomes entangled with her self-representation as a maternal food provider. Addressing the army, she asserts that God will:

> welcome all of you
> And say, oh here is that,
> Which is more costly food for thee,

And far more delicate
Then all thou hast of that thou stolst
From the Commonweal poor,
For to feast thy carcass withall,
Which is to be no more. (*Cry*, pp. 25–6)

Here Trapnel's characteristic antithesis between earthly and heavenly food is motivated by a similar contrast between the plenteous provision of the latter and the uneven distribution of the former. Her gesture at the need to redistribute this wealth is occluded by her contemptuous understanding of it as the producer of a mutable body, but the move does point to the soldiers' failure to perform the *imitatio Christi* repeatedly enacted by Trapnel herself. Trapnel further associates herself with God as a provider of nourishment by distinguishing herself from the soldiers' immoderate consumption.

Again like Wight, Trapnel repeatedly responds to anxious attempts to force food upon her:

> I was judged by diverse friends . . . to be under a temptation for not eating; I took that Scripture, Neglect not the body, and went to the Lord and enquired whether I had been so, or had any self-end in it to be singular beyond what was meet; it was answered me, No, for thou shalt every way be supplied in body and spirit, and I found a continuall fullness in my stomach, and the taste of diverse sweetmeats and delicious foods therein, which satisfied me. (*Cry*, p. 5)

Again, food imagery functions to represent God as a source of fullness and plenitude. But here Trapnel touches on the anxieties generated among observers by her subversive behaviour. The source of that anxiety appears to be both the woman's exceptional relationship with God, and her display of this in her writings and on her body. Trapnel's attempt to soothe these anxieties by stressing God's agency and by describing her special feeding was perhaps more likely to exacerbate them.

Trapnel, Hatfield, Wight and their amanuenses all repeat that the women's inedia is produced not by the women themselves but by God. Wight frequently characterizes herself as incapable of eating: 'I cannot, I cannot', she repeats. Trapnel likewise insists that 'nothing will now go down'. When begged to take food, Hatfield replies: 'I would take food, if God would give me leave, but I cannot, I cannot' (p. 9). Just as Trapnel represents her body as resistant to the intake of food, so Fisher and Jessey report that Hatfield and Wight repeatedly vomit food they have swallowed (Fisher, pp. 2–3; Jessey, p. 21). Such moves appear to represent inedia as analogous to the prophetic voice itself; a sign of divine agency operating through the erasure of female agency. But as with the prophetic text, the possibility of female agency is constantly and anxiously made present by the insistent denials of it, and that possibility generates subversive meanings. The women's utterances on the subject of food also suggest a *contemptus mundi* at odds with post-Reformation teaching. When Trapnel and Wight refer to food as 'the creature' or as 'creature-refreshing' they raise the possibility of the return of ideas banished by the Reformed churches. Moreover, these ideas appear to be produced by God himself on their bodies, suggesting a divine cause for their break with Protestant orthodoxy.

Seventeenth-century men and women by no means took for granted a connection between female inedia and divine agency, or even religious discourse. Inedia could also be read as a sign of 'natural' illness, or of diabolic agency. Radical Puritans, who often stressed bodily signs such as trembling, weeping and fainting as part of religious experience, were perhaps more likely to understand such behaviour as proofs that God was at work. Despite this, Cotton Mather associates a case of women's fasting with witchcraft, while John Reynolds makes a clear and careful distinction between fasts caused by illness and fasts understood as religious experiences. Reynolds's criteria suggest that something other than a battle between competing authoritative discourses was at stake in making these distinctions:

> Certainly, the Infinitely Wise labours not for nought . . . [hence] abstinants, if miraculous, should confirm some doctrine rejected, or refuse some error received . . . . Our blessed Saviour and his *prodromi* procured not the least detriment to their health [by fasting].[27]

Reynolds links an authentically religious fast with both the production of authoritative doctrine or meanings and the maintenance of bodily health. From his criteria, it is evident that fasting and prophecy/religious discourse were culturally linked. In Reynolds's terms, prophecies could authenticate fasts. It is also striking to note his insistence on the maintenance of bodily health, since both Trapnel and Hatfield stress the fact that inedia does not debilitate them. Fisher writes of Hatfield:

> she grew very fat, and her flesh very firm and solid, and she did look very fair and fresh. Whereas you might rather apprehend, that shee was a lean, dried and withered anatomy. (p. 73)

On the other hand, as I have suggested, the texts link fasting with illness at other points. Trapnel repeatedly stresses her physical weakness, while Jessey and Fisher at first describe the fasts of Wight and Hatfield as the results of illness. In their texts, the associations of femininity with physical weakness and assertions of God's sole agency in causing the women's inedia jostle in a manner which appears contradictory, but which produces the same meaning: that the female body is a sign from which female agency is evacuated. This can be read as an attempt to contain the subversive meanings of fasting produced in the women's texts and practices.

Just as prophecy could authenticate fasting, so fasting could authenticate prophecy. A letter on Trapnel's Whitehall trance associates her inedia with proof that God is at work:

> I am ascertained (from those I can believe as if I saw it my selfe) that she Eate nothing all that tyme, no, nor drunke, save once in twenty-four houres a little (and but a very little) small beer . . . I have sometimes said, that I thinke God in this dispensation doth teach his people, that when our communion with him is enlarged, a very little of the creature will satisfie us.[28]

This writer uses many of the same figures as the women themselves: the term 'communion' suggests that Trapnel's trances are a form of eating, and this sets her renunciation of earthly food against her heavenly nourishment. This 'enlarged' communion is the producer of the 'very little' of 'the creature'. This opposition suggests the paradox represented by the woman prophet. To be open to God, to pour forth a continuous stream of utterance, meant to be closed to other sensations. Repeatedly, women prophets' amanuenses stress the closure of their senses to earthly stimuli. Sarah Wight can neither hear nor see during her trances and raptures; her eyes are propped open at one point to allow her to recognize her mother, but they immediately close again (Jessey, p. 27). Trapnel similarly is often insensible of those around her: in Cornwall, those who come to arrest her cannot make her hear them, and when they pinch her to bring her to herself she does not feel it (Report, p. 22). When the trance ends, she is unaware that anyone has been present. Martha Hatfield's closure to the world is literalized in the involuntary clenching of her jaw so that her family cannot force food through her shut teeth (The Wise Virgin, pp. 72–3). Fasting can be read as part of this bodily closure; it figures the separation of the woman's body from sense and the world.

Hence the fasts of women prophets seem to have offered them a way to control and manage the problem of the female body through a renegotiation of the split between body and spirit. For the meticulously detailed fasts of these women not only display the continued existence of a female self separable from the female body and able to control it. Their constant, contemptuous references to earthly food, their opposition between heavenly and earthly food, also allow them to locate themselves more and more firmly in spiritual rather than physical spheres. This was entirely understandable in a seventeenth-century context. The only potential area of gender egalitarianism made available to women was the Pauline notion of spiritual equality before the Lord.[29] Some women tried to develop this loophole in social law in their prophetic writings. Elizabeth Poole, arguing strenuously against the execution of Charles I, ingeniously inserts a vindication of her own prophetic status into her polemic:

> You never heard that a woman might put away her husband, as he is the head of her body, but for the Lord's sake she suffereth his terror to her flesh, though she be free in the spirit of the Lord.[30]

Poole's text shows the basis for women's desire to situate themselves outside or beyond the body. Her radical split between the free spirit and the subject flesh is theatrically staged by the display of the ill, weak or fasting body of the woman prophet as a conduit for the voice or voicing of authority.

III

Similar disavowals of the subject body are encoded in tropes of physical dissolution and disembodiment. 'I had a glorious vision of the New Jerusalem', writes Trapnel, 'which melted me into a river of tears.' Again she writes:

> They say these are convulsion-fits and sickness, and diseases that make thy handmaid to be in weakness, but oh they know not the pouring-forth of thy spirit, for that maketh the body to crumble, and weakens nature. (*Cry*, p. 29)

Increased elevation to a spiritual plane here necessarily brings about the bodily dissolution desired. Similar tropes occur in the writings of Jane Lead. In her description of the soul's progress to ultimate bliss, the passage of the seventh gate

> causes an unalterable Transmutation of all gross matter, and the vile Body's shape into a heavenly consistency: such a celestial body wisdom's Virgin shall have power to put on.[31]

During her visions, Lead represents herself passing from her body into a metaphysical state of being:

> I was insensible of any sensitivity as relating to a corporeal being, and found my self . . . being very sprightly and airy, in a silent place. (*Fountain*, III, 1700–1702, pp. 66–7)

Such metaphysical transcendences meant that women could foreground their insubordinate souls, and narratively discard their subject bodies. But writings of this kind also operated to reinforce both women's physical subjection and the social inferiority which purported to be based on women's physical weakness. Writing out of the body ultimately reproduced the ideology of women's bodily inferiority, even as it allowed women to construct a more stable sense of self.

Elsewhere, women prophets sought to rewrite the specificity of the female body in metaphysical terms. Jane Lead represents the transmission of mystical knowledge in terms of female reproduction. God is to bring forth 'virgin offspring in corporeal figures', though 'not in the ordinary way of generation'. Lead must await the 'travelling hour' as a sign that the 'ghostly birth' is forming in her. 'The glory of Israel' is

> to be sealed up, as in an unknown Pavilion, or hiding Place of Strength: which must be till it hath attained every measure and part, to the growing big, and filling up the Birth's place, with Breasts full of Milk, the Spring Word of the Spirit diffusing into them, the natural course of the Bloody Issue of Sin also stopping, all which will be evident Signs unto you, that are still apt to be questioning, whether this Ghostly Birth is in you forming. (*Fountain*, I, 1696, p. 440)

At first sight, we might read this as a validation of the reproductive female body. That body is associated with terms suggesting plenitude and completeness. The womb is 'a hiding place of strength', where 'strength' could refer both to the womb and to what hides there; the body is 'growing', the womb 'filling', the breasts 'full'. But this validation turns out to depend on the female body's metaphoricity. Only as a trope for a spiritual state can its reproductivity be described with such enthusiasm. This is gestured at in the ambivalent phrase 'the bloody issue of sin also stopping'. Whether menstruation is a metaphor for sin, or a sign of sin's workings within, its disavowal as sin works not only to valorize pregnancy, but also to position the reproductively able female body as a source of pollution. It is perhaps this earthly body which must be disavowed in order to construct the female body as an acceptable *sign*.

Elizabeth Hincks uses a slightly different trope of the reproductive female body. She rewrites the Puritan metaphor which likens God to the mother's breast, combining metaphors from female reproduction with the figure of God as nourishing mother also used by the fasting women:

> And his [St Paul's] seeking unto God, is as a sucking child.
> That seeketh for its mothers breast, that is tender and mild.
> And when the child had suckt its fill, the Breast likewise is eased
> The child then he is satisfied, and mother also pleased.[32]

Like Lead, Hincks transfers the maternal body from earth to heaven. As Elaine Hobby has noted, however, she foregrounds a specifically female knowledge – the knowledge of breastfeeding an infant – to construct herself as specially placed to understand God's relationship to believers.[33] Like the women fasters, she presents woman as a direct imitation of a nurturative maternal deity. And just as their metaphorization of themselves as mothers who replicate a maternal God opens up a space for women to achieve female adulthood without marriage, so Hincks's troping of God as mother bypasses the role of the father in producing children.

In these maternal metaphors, there is an underlying linkage between female reproduction and the production of the Word of God. In the writings of other women prophets, this linkage becomes explicit, and a further connection figures the transmission of the Word in prophecy as female reproduction. Elizabeth Poole describes the onset of a prophetic trance: 'the pangs of a travelling woman were upon mee' (A Vision, p. 1). Eleanor Douglas is more flagrantly transgressive. She metaphorizes her own prophetic works as the infant Christ:

> To the Reader: This Babe, object to their scorn, for speaking the *truth*, informing of things future, notwithstanding thus difficult to be *fathered* or *licensed*. That incision to the quick, hath under gone; without their benediction, in these plain swathe bands, though recommended unto thy hands.[34]

The pamphlet in which this extraordinary passage appears is dated 25 December 1651; Douglas is specifically comparing the appearance of her volume with the birth of Christ. The metaphor of swaddling bands, applicable both to book and baby, was especially associated with Christ's birth, while the difficulty of 'fathering' or 'licensing' it refers to Mary's lack of secure paternity for her child. The metaphoric link between literary works and children was of course common in the seventeenth century,[35] but Douglas's metaphorization of her book as Christ the child is truly startling. The polyvalence of the metaphor of Christ as Word allows her to represent herself both as a conduit for the Word of God and as the bearer of God, the producer of ultimate meaning.

IV

The disturbing power of such a self-representation can be gauged from the anxiety about women who announced themselves pregnant with Christ. These women were responding to the same radical millenarianism which helped to produce women prophets, but their concretization of those discourses was particularly unsettling. The story of one such woman, Mary Adams, reveals that her power to disturb was understood in gendered terms. The anonymous and hostile author of *The Ranters Monster* writes that 'she said that she was the Virgin Mary, and that she was conceived with child by the Holy Ghost'.[36] Like Douglas, Adams claims to be the producer of absolute meaning. But it is her display of feminine (re)productive power as the means by which this meaning is produced which causes the greatest alarm, as the narrative reveals. Adams gives birth to a monster:

> she was delivered of the most ugliest ill-shapen *monster* that ever eyes beheld; which being dead-born, they buried it with speed, for it was so loathsome to behold, that the womens hearts trembled to look upon it . . . . (*Ranters Monster*, p. 3)

The narrative follows the standard monstrous birth pattern: a transgression by one or both parents is made visible in and physically replicated by their offspring. But monstrous births were also signifiers of female imaginative and reproductive power acting without the constraint of paternity. The literature on monstrous births abounds with tales of women who produced abnormal infants because their imaginations were fixed on something inappropriate at the moment of conception. Ambroise Paré describes a woman who gave birth to children covered in fur because she looked at a picture of John the Baptist wearing skins while they were conceived. Another woman gave birth to a black infant, even though she and her husband were white, because she gazed at a picture of a Moor above her bed. In these cases what is absent is the mark of paternity; the child fails to replicate the father, as patrilinearity demands, and becomes a mirror not even of the mother, but of the mother's imagination.[37] The link between that imagination and the child's appearance turns on a pun on the word conception. Implicitly, female brain and female womb become interchangeable metaphors for each other.

The meanings of this linkage become apparent in the case of Anne Hutchinson, excommunicated from the Boston church in 1638, after speaking at meetings and teaching other women at her house. Another woman, Mary Dyer, chose to accompany her into exile.[38] John Winthrop, the hostile chronicler of their case, records that both were pregnant when they left Boston:

> The two fomenting women in the time of the height of their errors produced out of their wombs, as before they had out of their brains, such monstrous births as no chronicle (I think) hardly ever recorded the like. Mistress Hutchinson, being big with child . . . brought forth not one, but thirty monstrous births or thereabouts at once . . . none at all of them of human shape . . . . Looke as she vented misshapen opinions, so she must bring forth deformed monsters.[39]

What is significant about Winthrop's narrative is the explicit connection he makes between women's reproduction and their imaginations. Like most of the women prophets I have been discussing, Hutchinson was an antinomian; through the signifier of monstrous births, antinomianism is troped as the loss or absence of patrilineal control over ideas and actions.

This set of metaphoric relations between the female imagination and the female body helps to interpret the disturbing power of women prophets. The monstrous birth narratives discussed above represent a gender/political threat through the metaphor of the female body. But the link is not simply metaphorical; the woman's uncontrolled imagination or thoughts actually produce physical results, in the form of monstrous births, which themselves become signs for the loss or absence of patrilinearity and control. It is striking that writers like Puttenham describe the genre of prophecy in precisely the same terms. For Puttenham, the ambiguity or amphibologia of prophecies is an indirect threat to the social order because it threatens the order of rhetoric:

> all our old British and Saxon prophecies . . . turn them on which side you will, the matter of them may be verified, nevertheless carryeth such force in the heades of fonde people, that by the comfort of those blind prophecies many insurrections and rebellions have been stirred up in this Realme, as that of Iacke Straw, & Iacke Cade in Richard the seconds time.[40]

Hobbes put it more directly; for him prophecies were 'many times the principal cause of the event foretold'.[41] Just as the imaginings of women at the moment of conception produced the real event of a deformed child, so the disorder of prophecy produced genuine social chaos in the form of rebellion. Clearly, the discourse of loss of control spoken from a female body aroused greater fears of the chaos generated by women's brains and bodies.

Moreover, as with the birth of monsters, the central question is when reproduction subversively becomes production. Just as the wife was properly supposed to be a mere conduit for her husband's self-reproduction, so the woman prophet was supposed to be a mere container for the divine male voice. But the possibility that her own brain or imagination would become involved, disrupting this patrilineage, was never far away. The representation of this possibility both expresses and manages the fear of female reproduction as that which patrilinearity has had to repress. The fear is of what Catherine Gallagher terms 'semiotic riot': the uncontrolled woman produces meanings which threaten to undo bodily and discursive order:

> if the mother is not properly constrained then semiotic riot is the result. One's name may mean nothing; one's property may have no natural relation to one's name. One's self-representations may prove to be mere mental constructions . . . if one's mother was capable of the biological equivalent of system-making, of generating an illegitimate and unprecedented progeny.[42]

Gallagher lays bare the link between female reproduction and semiotic chaos. She differs from Neil Hertz in arguing that the fear of maternity unconstrained by paternity is central to fears of semiotic and consequent social disordering. But it is Hertz who makes the valuable point that by turning this threat into a symbol, writers control and manage its meanings.[43] The troping of semiotic and social chaos as a monstrous birth restores and replicates the notions of normality and patrilineage by pointing to their opposites. And in insistently linking the female body and the female brain, the trope insists that feminine production can only ever be bodily, restoring the female to the sphere of the physical and denying her access to a disembodied spiritual or mental identity.

V

Women prophets resisted such readings of their bodies and texts by seeking to represent them as signifiers of control and stability rather than chaos and disorder. If some women created anxiety by representing themselves as the Virgin Mary, others made use of the cultural status of the virgin female body. That body was the (valorized) binary opposite of the kind of grotesque, uncontrollable body described by Winthrop. Closed, with clearly understood boundaries, the virgin female body stood for order and containment. It could also stand for male property, as a defined, commodified and easily policed object.[44] Characteristically, women prophets set the virgin body against the problematically open body, just as they set heavenly food against creaturely nourishment. Trapnel, for instance, writes of the birth of Christ:

> When in womb and birth, O it
> Had there no bloody gore,
> A virgin pure, white and clean,
> Such as none was before.
> A virgin cleane, a glorious state,
> That was brought forth here,
> O it was of a glorious make,
> And without filth appeared. (Legacy, p. 64.)

The virgin birth of Christ is here explicitly contrasted with the polluting normalities of woman's reproduction. 'No bloody gore' is produced at Christ's birth; he appears 'without filth'. Elsewhere in her writings, Trapnel identifies herself with the Virgin Mary, calling herself 'hand-maid' after the Magnificat. She also identifies herself as the virgin Bride of Christ, who is to wed him at the Second Coming.[45]

Jane Lead also identifies with the virginal female body, although she was a widow who had borne at least one child. Drawing on the writings of Jacob Boehme, she valorizes the Virgin Wisdom, or Sophia, who for her is a feminine aspect of the Deity, 'a virgin hid in God from all eternity'. At certain points in the narrative, the figure of the Virgin Wisdom becomes a self-representation. This is facilitated by Boehme's doctrine that Adam originally contained an image of the Virgin Wisdom, lost before the Fall: for Lead the end of mystical progress is the recovery of this 'original virginity' and 'virgin crown'. God also tells Lead that she is to 'personate' the Virgin Wisdom, that Sophia will 'draw over her virgin veil of purity' to make this possible.[46] Philippa Berry suggests that, in men's writings, Sophia's combination of material and spiritual attributes meant that she could mirror a transcendent dimension and also link the writer to it, allowing him to fashion an identity which negotiated his troubling physicality.[47] But in the writings of women, identification with figures like Sophia and the Virgin Mary facilitates a different kind of negotiation with the body. By representing their bodies not as open and uncontrolled but as closed to everything except God, they presented those bodies as sealed containers for the meanings instilled into them from outside, producing not a multiplicity of monstrous texts but a single unitary text whose origin was not in doubt.

Most importantly, women prophets were able to revive the positive associations of virginity in order to construct a space for a conditional autonomy. Despite patriarchal endorsement for female virginity, an alternative and troubling reading of it can make it stand for female autonomy and power. By understanding all women as married or to be married, Protestants tried to close off this possibility. But women prophets appear to have revived it. Already we have seen that female prophecy was often in conflict with norms of female behaviour, especially with marital duties and obligations. Arise Evans describes Elinor Channel's struggle to get to London as a swerve away from marital and domestic obligation. Anna Trapnel defends her autonomy as an unmarried woman during her examination in Cornwall:

> AT: I am a single person, and why may I not be with my friends anywhere?
> Justice: I understand you are not married?
> AT: Then having no hindrance, why may I not go where I please, if the Lord so will? (*Report*, p. 26)

A similar kind of movement is made by Jane Lead. She writes of her marriage:

> Being dead wherein we were held fast, we should be discharged from the law of the first husband, to which we were married, after the law of a carnal command . . . that first Husband who so long hindered my marriage with the Lamb. (*Fountain*, I, pp. 69–71)

Trapnel and Lead use almost the same word to describe a husband: 'hindrance', the opposite of 'helpmeet', which was the standard word used to describe a wife in Puritan discourse. But both stop short of representing themselves as autonomous *femmes soles*. They are still *femmes couvertes*, covered by male authority, which is, however, divine rather than human. It is ironic that the woman prophet's identity as an autonomous public figure, able to move freely about the country, was underpinned by her troping of herself as the bride of Christ and as a virgin body. In seventeenth-century ideology, virginity and marriage were understood to make the female body private, to contain it within the home. Seventeenth-century radical Protestantism has long been understood as a force which helped to erode the order of property for men. Here, it can be seen to undermine the status of woman as property. Because Trapnel and Lead belong to God, they cannot belong to men.

Through fasting, food imagery, and the metaphors of bodily dissolution and female reproduction, women prophets explore the contradictory possibilities of a female body autonomy and an autonomy beyond or outside the gendered body. The genre of prophecy, in which the female body is a mere cover for the masculine voice, paradoxically shaped and enabled both moves. It allowed a glimpse of a space in which gendered subjection was confined to the disavowed flesh, while the escaped spirit had freedom. But it also formed the basis for a metaphorization of female prophecy as a female reproduction which erased or occluded the mark of an earthly father or husband, raising the disturbing possibility that woman might not be a mere conduit for male words, truths, or self-replications, but an agent in producing them. The management of this unsettling spectacle through the troping of women's brains and bodies as the makers of the monstrous, testifies to the power of such female self-representations to disrupt the homosocial order of rhetoric and property.

Gender and status in dramatic discourse

Margaret Cavendish, Duchess of Newcastle

Susan Wiseman

The *Crocodile* is a Hieroglyphicke of Honour or nobilitie. The *Hippopotame*, of Impiety, Ingratitude and Baseness. 1. These two have continuall warre.[1]

I

> I cannot chuse but mention an erroneous opinion got into this our Modern time and men, which is, that it should be thought a crime, or debasement for the nobler sort to Act Playes, especially on publick Theatres . . . . for certainly there is no place, wayes or meanes, so edifying to Youth as publick Theatres, not only to be spectators but Actors; for it learns them graceful behaviours . . . .[2]

So writes Margaret Cavendish, Duchess of Newcastle, in one of the many preambles to her first volume of plays written in the 1650s and published, after delays, in 1662. She negotiates the relationship between nobility and 'public' theatre, advocating theatre, including public theatre (now in these changed times passed out of fashion) as the cultural capital of the nobility. We see clearly her concern with status, or class, and her desire to claim the theatre for the nobility. But what about the relationship between gender and theatre? How did women writing during the Civil Wars and Interregnum enter and use dramatic discourses, and how were women positioned by these discourses?[3]

Writing, publication, performance and reception are shaped by the configurations of gender present in dominant discourses; the aim of this essay is to read the issues of status, or class, and gender in Cavendish's plays in terms of dramatic, theatrical and social contexts.[4] Women had written and published plays before the Civil War (Elizabeth Cary, Lady Falkland's *The Tragedy of Mariam*, 1613, is an example), but the 1650s and 1660s saw a marked increase in the number of plays published by women, and eventually their arrival on the stage: the dramatists of the Restoration included Katherine Philips, Elizabeth Polwhele and Aphra Behn. It is impossible to 'account for' the entry of women into dramatic discourses as writers rather than objects, but some of the changes in kinds of performance brought about by the Civil War and Restoration may have facilitated the passage of women into the profession. One such change is from the distinctly demarcated 'private' dramas (performed before invited audiences at court and great houses) and 'public' theatres of the 1630s and early 1640s to the blending of courtly and public performance after the Restoration, with the increased presence of the court at the public theatre.

Cavendish desired to be 'singular', and for someone reading her prodigious and various literary and scientific output, it is often difficult to avoid replicating her own version of herself as completely self-invented.[5] However, while she constituted herself as 'singular', her contemporaries regarded her as eccentric, even offensive, and regarded her behaviour as antisocial and repugnant. Pepys's well-known comments address themselves to something the Duchess of Newcastle was herself much concerned with in her plays: theatre and display. However, for Pepys, it is the Duchess herself who is displayed and observed.[6] Dorothy Osborne heaped scorn on Cavendish, and a closer acquaintance, Mary Evelyn, disapproved of her dress and conversation.[7] In 1667 Charles North wrote of her, 'The Dutchess Newcastle is all y^c pageant now discoursed on: Her breasts all laid out to view at a playhouse and her scarlet painted nipples'.[8] This neatly pinpoints the contrast between Cavendish's idea of the uses of theatre as a locus for the staging of an ideal self and the way she was perceived by at least one contemporary. Although women might enter theatrical discourse as the generators of texts, they continued to be constituted by dominant patriarchal paradigms and, in terms of theatre, to be placed as the object of the watching male eye.

Some critical approaches to Margaret Cavendish have treated her writing as 'women's autobiography', or read her as a woman writer.[9] As Sara Heller Mendelson and Catherine Gallagher note, such scholars have attempted to use Margaret Cavendish's writing 'to establish a pedigree for modern feminism'. Mendelson's aim is 'to reconstruct women's mental and material world in all its rich complexity'.[10] But this aim, though helpful in that Mendelson does distinguish between different purposes of reading, is also problematic because this world cannot be reconstituted, despite the evidence of various kinds that can be found, interpreted and reinterpreted. As Natalie Zemon Davis notes, gender needs to be studied as a part of the overall 'cultural network' (again, not

that this can ever be fully understood, reconstructed or articulated).
Davis argues that 'we should be interested in the history of both women
and men, that we should not be working only on the subjected sex any
more than an historian of class can focus exclusively on peasants'.[11]
If one is attempting, as I am here, to trace discursive changes in relation
to some sense of literary and cultural context, Davis's remark offers a
way of focusing an argument around contradictions within texts in
relation to contextual factors. The relationship between status and
gender, which concerns Davis, is an issue of central importance in
Cavendish's plays and is interwoven with the contestation of class values
fought out in the English Civil Wars and negotiated throughout the
Protectorate.

In terms of the relationship of drama to the society that produced it
during the 1650s, Cavendish is significant as a member of both an elite
group (as Duchess of Newcastle) and a non-elite group (as a woman).
However, her femininity and her elevated social status are further
qualified by details of her immediate context – most importantly by the
likelihood that she wrote a great deal of her dramatic and other output in
exile.

II Family and war: a context

Cavendish was writing during the 1650s; her plays and circumstances
serve to illuminate the fractures and disjunctures of power and gender
ideologies, of assertions of loyalty and contingent action in both these
areas. Douglas Grant comments, 'The disadvantage of writing plays
during the interregnum was the impossibility of their being produced.'[12]
But for a woman writing plays we could also see the Civil War bans on
drama as in some ways inaugurating a new and temporary equality in the
status of plays by men and women as long as neither sex was likely to
have plays staged. A comparison of her plays with other contemporary
plays, both within and without her immediate circle (particularly those
by the marginalized and exiled aristocrats of the 1650s such as Killigrew),
makes her writing practice appear much less eccentric.[13] For example,
ten-act plays were not unheard of in the explosion of dramatic genres in
the 1640s and 1650s; Killigrew wrote them, and pamphlet plays were also
published in two parts.[14]

Despite unpropitious circumstances for public performances, it seems
that the Duke of Newcastle's daughters may have staged their
entertainments at home in the 1650s (*Playes*, 1662, A12v). In private
performance, as in masque, a household celebrated itself; such perfor-

mances also dramatized the political and social concerns of those who wrote and performed them. An obvious example is the series of entertainments written by Mildmay Fane for private performance at Apthorpe during the 1640s; in 1641 'the youth and Servants' there acted 'Tymes Trick upon the Cards'.[15] The new emphasis thrown on private (or family) performance in which women participated during the Civil War and Protectorate may in itself have contributed to altering attitudes to women's later public performance. Things had changed so much during the 20 years between Stuarts that when Charles II returned he could not have masques at court because no one 'could make a tolerable entry'.[16] But although sophisticated masquing skills had been lost, drama continued to be written and even performed.

Newcastle's daughters apparently wrote their two plays or fairly short entertainments with their father in mind, addressing passages directly to him.[17] The Duke's first plays, co-written by Shirley, were published in 1649 and his daughters' plays seem to belong to the 1640s.[18] So we do have a *family* who wrote plays or in various ways participated in playmaking. This has not been considered as a signficant part of Margaret Cavendish's specific context as a writer. Although they did not live together, there are some similarities between the unpublished plays of the Duke of Newcastle's daughters and those of his wife, who, like his daughters, addresses him in dedicatory verses and features him in her plays and writings. Both share the topic of 'Tranquility'. In their private entertainments, the women of this family shift from mere actors to authors, from ciphers filled by the discourse to manipulators of the codes.

The Civil War context of 'The Concealed Fansyes' is suggested mainly in the language of siege and military discourse. It is more explicitly present in another entertainment composed by the two sisters called 'A Pastorall' which is in the same manuscript book containing poems to various relatives. One poem, 'On hir most sacred Majestie', suggests an intimate identification of these young women with the royal cause through the person of Henrietta Maria, who is portrayed as a hero who can tame 'Armyes of Rebells':

Your Eye if looke, it doth an Army pay
And soe, as Generall, you doe lead the way (fol. 9)

The pastoral explores the relationship between solitude and war and moves from the representation of the forces of darkness – witches – in the first antimasque to the country people bewailing their losses by plunder in the second antimasque. Not all the figures are those expected in pastoral. Two country wives and Goodman Rye and Goodman Hay discuss the strange beasts called satyrs which have come into the country, 'halfe Men, halfe Beasts' – presumably cavaliers. When Henn, one of the low, country figures, asks, 'what will they plunder', Hay replies, 'Noe they understand not that phrase; Plunder', and Rye explains, 'But I will tell you, they are very loving people'. The play dramatizes a war in which the poor county people suffer from plunder and 'ladies' are captured. These plays (which may have been performed) give no more than a glimpse of the ideologies of gender in relation to private theatre. With no cast list, they cannot be the basis for a full argument about women's acting even during the Interregnum. It seems helpful to see the 'Pastorall' as influenced by the pastoral drama of Henrietta Maria's court, like Walter Montagu's *Shepheards Paradise* in which the Queen danced for the King with a cast of women. This is to be set against the picture given in the cast list of the recently rediscovered *Cupid's Banishment* (1617), a masque put on by Ladies Hall, an academy for daughters of the elite, for the patron Lucy, Countess of Bedford, and homage to Anne of Denmark.[19] In it girls took crowd parts, but nearly all the major roles were played by men, including a Mr Richard Brown as Diana. Only one generation divides the Cavendish sisters from the Ladies Hall girls; the same Richard Brown who played Diana gave the manuscript of the play to his daughter: she who later married John Evelyn, and castigated Margaret Cavendish's improperly theatrical and pedagogic style.

The Cavendish family's plays can be considered as a nucleus of dramatic writing, most of it by aristocratic women, which is imbricated with the circumstances of the Civil War and which uses (and in the case of Margaret Cavendish, transforms) prewar dramatic genres. After the Restoration the writers must have had some inside knowledge of the London stages. The Duke wrote plays with assistance from professional dramatists both before and after the war; one of his re-entries into public life after the Interregnum was through the performance of *The Humorous Lovers*, which was mainly written by Shadwell. Newcastle was influential as a patron (even Dryden accepted the Newcastle patronage, despite his sneerings at Shadwell).

III   Acting, theatre and the reader

In Margaret Cavendish's writing, contradictions emerge around the issue of the court, power, gender, sexual desire and representation as they converge on the signifier 'theatre'. Her dramatic (and non-dramatic) writing plays with and redefines the marginalized position of women in relation to the 'theatre' of public affairs on the one hand, and the theatre of representation on the other. As Sophie Tomlinson has observed, there is a tension throughout Cavendish's writing between the real theatre and '"Fancy's" power to substitute the scene of the mind for the theatre of the world'.[20] The play *The Female Academy*, for instance, explores women's negotiation and colonization of both these forbidden 'theatres' (see below p. 167) by the female protagonists of the plays. The connotations of 'theatre' as a metaphor within the plays work to relocate and redefine the relationship between femininity and the public sphere. Interchangeable meanings of 'theatre' liberate transformations of gender and role within the texts. Within these dramas, the interchangeability of acting/ action makes transformations of role possible for the figured female nobility.

Although Cavendish herself describes her brain as the only stage on which her plays/fantasies are acted, her plays are not, as has been asserted, completely without a sense of the stage. The instruction she gives for the reading aloud of the plays is that they are not to be read as narrative, but as if staged, requiring a kind of mental acting from the reader: 'Playes must be read to the nature of those several humours or passions, as are expresst by Writing: for they must not read a Scene as they would a Chapter; for Scenes must be read as if they were spoke or Acted' (*Playes*, 1662, A6v). She writes of herself that 'For all the time my Playes a making were,/My brain the Stage, my thoughts were acting there' (A2r), and the reader is to re-enact them.[21] She suggests that the plays, for her, are the manifestations of her 'contemplations' and seems to be aware of the reader as engaging in her or his own fantasy. Her comments constitute, if not a full theory of performance, at least a commentary on the dramatic structure of the plays and on the importance of theatre as an idea.[22]

The signifier 'theatre' corresponds to several related signifieds in Cavendish's writing and functions in a number of symbolic ways: acting on stage and acting in the world. The political triumphs of women are woven into an analysis of and commentary on the contemporary situation through the use of the idea of theatre. Cavendish's theatre may then be (merely?) the theatre of the imagination and the triumphs of her heroines imaginary ones (imagined by both the play and its 'Noble Reader'). But meanwhile the notion of opposition between a 'real' world and an 'imaginary world' (in which noble women triumph) is problematized by the extension of the idea of 'theatre' to embrace both. Within the play, the acting out of a role (in an imaginary 'world') and the acting of that role become interpenetrative; the reader is invited to engage with the text at the point where the 'roles' are acted out.

An example of this interconnection, and of what Denise Riley calls Cavendish's 'scholastic flamboyance', is *The Female Academy*, published in the 1662 volume of plays.[23] It approaches the relationship between femininity, fantasy, linguistic and intellectual pursuits in what is for Cavendish a tautly structured five-act play exploring the ideas of education and rhetoric for girls and women, and combining the secluded all-female academic locus with (eroticized?) educational/dramatic display. The scholars at the female academy belong to the female nobility which Cavendish represents as unjustly constrained; they are 'of antient Descent, as also rich' (First Lady, Act I scene 1, p. 653). Their learning 'to speak wittily and rationally, and to behave themselves handsomely, and to live virtuously' (First Lady, Act I scene 1, p. 653) is achieved through 'discoursing'. Each lady is given a topic on which she speaks in public – although nobody is allowed to enter the academy, men and women are allowed to stand on the other side of a grate to hear the young ladies talking. A situation is set up similar to the one depicted in the frontispiece to Cavendish's *Poems and Fancies*, in which the figure of the author sits looking at the viewer, who is separated from the female figure by a railing in the foreground of the picture.[24] In the play, the listening men are allowed to watch the women orate upon the public stage, but they are marginal, silenced onlookers to the discourses, which turn increasingly to the twin topics of language and love. Here, as elsewhere in Cavendish's plays, the women represented as sexually exciting to men (as these young women overwhelmingly are to male viewers) are women displaying themselves both educationally and sexually within a masculine preserve. Other examples are the women dressed as pages, or as generals; all are women in control of positions usually held by men. Moreover, the play presents the male gaze as controlled by and subjected to the female object of the gaze, rather than vice versa.

It might be worth asking how readers might enjoy these representations. One answer might be found in Freud's study 'A child is being beaten', in which the ability to move fairly freely amongst the subject positions offered in any scene of the fantasy is a hallmark of the 'mature' fantasist. Freud's study suggests analogies with the role of a reader in manipulating and appropriating narrative, and the read play offers an ideal site for shifting identifications and wishful fantasy.[25] Moreover, the ways in which Cavendish's plays act out scenarios in which women are on display, desired but also triumphant, offers the reader, particularly the female reader, material for elaboration in fantasy.

The topics given to the speakers in the female academy include 'whether women are capable to have as much wit or wisdom as men' (Act

I scene 2, p. 654). The topic of discourse is proposed twice. The first speaker says, 'there are two sorts of discourses ... as there is discoursing within the mind, and a discourse with words' (Act I scene 4, p. 657); the second makes a similar distinction but adds a third kind – 'discoursing by signs, which is actions or acting' (scene 16, p. 666). From here it is a small move to the next topic, theatre:

> Lady Speaker: A Theatre is a publick place for publick Actions, Orations, Disputations, Presentations whereunto is a publick resort; but there are two Theatres, which are the chief, and the most frequented; the one of War, the other of Peace; the Theatre of Warre is the field, and the battels they fight the Plays they Act, and the Souldiers are the Tragedians, and the theatre of Peace is the stage, and the Plays there Acted are the Humours, Manners, Dispositions, Natures, Customes of men thereon descried and acted, whereby the Theatres are as schools to teach youth good Principles .... the designer of the rough Plays of War is a General or Council; the designer of the smooth Plays of Peace is a Poet, or a Chief Magistrate ...
> (*The Female Academy*, Act IV scene 21, p. 669).

Here the two kinds of 'theatre' and of 'play' are indistinguishable: the play of peace can be staged by *either* a poet or a chief magistrate, so that the theatre of the world and the theatre of the stage interchangeable. The theatre and war both offer training in public roles and duties; the speaker is later at pains to defend the direct relationship between drama and history, and the 'Natural' rather than the 'Romantical' acting style (*The Female Academy*, Act IV scene 22, pp. 669–71). This substitutable relation between representation and 'reality' is echoed in the poem 'A Dialogue Between Peace and War' in *Poems, or Several Fancies* (1668): 'War' gets the last word in the dialogue:

> A School am I, where all Men may grow Wise:
> A Theatre, where noble minds do stand:
> A Mint of Honour, Coyn'd for Valour's Hand.
> I am a Throne, which is for Valour fit;
> And a great Court, where Royal *Fame* may sit:
> A field, in which ambition much doth run:
> Courage still seeks me: Cowards do me shun.[26]

Cavendish is again connecting and slipping between theatre, education, the court and public action. Turning on the dual meaning of the 'theatre', her texts manage to expand the metaphor so that all human action becomes representation (and implicitly vice versa). The court is, of course, the stage of exemplary and corrupt human action in peacetime just as the battlefield is the theatre of war and the playhouse the school of manners. Here the manners of the world are represented and the young men are educated (as by the orations of the young ladies in the female academy) in the right ways of thinking about the world.

The idea of the theatre offers the reader scenes of domination to elaborate. The notion of acting is here synonymous with action: through representation, a woman 'acting' the part of a general may take public 'action'. The slippage between the theatre *and* the world, and the theatre *of* the world, serves very specific semiotic purposes in *The Female Academy*, *The Convent of Pleasure* and other Cavendish texts. The metaphor permits the fantasy of the acting woman slipping through the plurisemic signifier 'theatre' into a world of actual action.

Elsewhere the literal theatre seems to liberate women not from the *constraints* of gender, but by implication, from the very marks of gender. We might remember here Cavendish's fascination with the 'female actor' she booked rooms to see on the mountebank's stage in Antwerp:

> Upon this Profess'd Mountebank's Stage, there were two Handsom Women Actors, both Sisters, the one of them was the Mountebank's, th'other the Fool's Wife . . . his Wife was far the Handsomer, and better Actor, and danc'd better than the other; indeed she was the Best Female Actor that ever I saw; and her Acting a Man's Part, she did it so Naturally as if she had been of that Sex, and yet she was of a Neat, Slender Shape: but being in her Dublet and Breeches, and a Sword hanging by her side, one would believe she had never worn a Petticoat, and had been more used to Handle a sword than a Distaff; and when she Danced in a Masculine Habit, she would Caper Higher, and Oftener than any of the Men . . . .[27]

The commercial theatre is shown here as releasing the female protagonists from the characteristics of gender. The spectator is presented as being in the same position as the male viewers in *The Female Academy*. Cavendish reports on her own viewing, and the reader watches her watching; she went 'to see them act upon the Stage, as I caused a room to be hired in the next House to the stage, and went every day to See them, not to Hear what they said for I did not understand their language' (p. 407). The experience of watching the theatrical spectacle is such that when the pleasure is withdrawn (owing, we are told, to magistrates fearing the plague), she says, 'my Fancy set up a stage in my brain and the Incorporeal Thoughts were the several Actors, and my Wit play'd the Jack Fool', until 'the Magistrates of the Mind' chase her imaginary theatre away. Thus the theatre for Cavendish represents a locus of multiple possibilities – it liberates women from gender constrictions, and it liberates the 'incorporeal' imagination into making fictions. Here we see a movement from the 'acting' or third kind of discourse described by the young lady on the educational/erotic stage of the female academy towards something else fitting the description of the first kind, that is 'discoursing in the mind.'

The multiple idea of theatre operates most obviously in Cavendish's plays in relation to the heroines of her texts. Here sexual politics is closely entwined with the theatre of war. For example, in *Love's Adventures* (which follows patterns drawn from romance) the Lady Orphant has been promised by her now dead father to Lord Singular. He has vowed never to marry; she disguises herself as a man and joins the army as his page. Unlike Viola in *Twelfth Night*, the Lady Orphant establishes an impeccable army record: she makes an excellent man, defends herself against false accusations and persuades her Lord to allow her to fight alongside him, distinguishing herself first in the field and then in the council of war. Lord Singular's role is to be astonished and impressed by Orphant/Affectiona-ta's wisdom and courage (a scenario played out also in Cavendish's *Bell in Campo*). Eventually the scene returns to England, where her guardians are about to be tried for murder because of the disappearance of their charge. At the trial she reveals all – that is, her sexual identity:

> Affectionata: Most Reverend Judges, and grave Jury, sentence me not with censure, nor condemn me to scandals, for waiting as a Man, and serving as a Page; For though I dissembled in my outward habit and behaviour, yet I was alwaies chaste and modest in my nature.[28]

She and Singular declare a mutual passion and leave the stage with her reputation, chastity, honour, money and, above all, obedience to her father still intact – and nuptial pleasures soon to come.

A complex debate about the issue of sexuality and disguise has developed in recent critical writing.[29] How can we think of 'women' or female parts in plays written in the 1650s but published in the early 1660s? Certainly, it seems likely that during the 1650s the shifts that were taking place in the ethos and political implications of acting made these plurisemic disguises even more unstable. But while the meanings generated by women on stage were transformed by the arrival of the actress at Restoration and the gender reversals re-reversed, refigured in breeches parts, there was in the read texts of the Interregnum the *possibility* of complete gender congruity between part and actor; the 'women' in Cavendish's plays, as read, can be considered as bearing traces of femininity alone. These dramatic texts, published as women actors first began to appear on the public stage, draw on codes of *both* public and private, aristocratic and commercial theatre. In the prewar theatres these two codes of theatrical representation configured gender slightly differently, especially because of the masque tradition which troped feminine dramatis personae, played by women, as representations of the society's ideal values. If it can be accepted that the 1650s brought together these two codes in Sir William Davenant's public but masque-like productions such as *The Cruelty of the Spaniards in Peru*, then that fusing constitutes a shift in theatrical uses of gender. Cavendish's plays seem to place an imaginary woman's body on stage, but, interestingly, use disguise in a way very similar to prewar plays. One might contrast *The Female Academy*, where gender distinctions appear to be stable, and *Love's Adventures*. *Love's Adventures*, a text structured in part for reading, locates erotic, attractive power both in the relationship between femininity and public action, and in disguise and potential discovery. Is Affectionata eroticized through the female reader's identification with the page role, the marriage role, or a combination of both?

For several reasons – the reiterated idea of the two kinds of theatre, the analysis of the female actor liberated into a 'natural' masculinity, and the triumphant heroines of the plays acting out masculine roles in the theatre of war – the multivalent metaphor of the theatre generates repeated scenes of the transformation of power and gender. The plays by Cavendish discussed here rely on a particularly gender-related version of what Kathleen McLuskie calls the 'vital if ill-defined connection between the theatre and the world'.[30] The theatre functions as a place where problems of gender become superable for the heroine; a reader is permitted a fluid definition (or lack of definition) between the theatres of representation (whether imaginary or in actual performance) and the theatres of the world. The multiple signifieds of 'theatre' serve to link power, fantasy and gender in ways which figure the transcendence of the cultural meanings of femininity for the heroines (and for the reader?). It is perhaps the very absence of an actual playhouse, a circumstance particular to the 1650s, which permits such an intimate link between all the world and the stage of the imagination.

Some of Cavendish's female protagonists appear on stage in the same manner that a woman is on display at a court, performing what Ann Rosalind Jones calls the court lady's spectacular function, a 'generalized erotic function directly opposed to the silent fidelity demanded of the private woman'.[31] Here, where the courtly lady is constructed by the text, she perhaps becomes available to a reader in the position of the courtier. Her erotic function may be grounded in insistence on her chastity, like that of a *femme forte*, but the heroine's assumption of masculine roles and prerogatives constitutes a representation of a society radically transformed in terms of gender relations. The nobility of the heroine is central in such a transformation; Cavendish's writing speaks in several ways to royalism and patriarchal discourse.

IV Royalism and patriarchal discourse

Sherry Ortner has argued that 'the sex/gender system . . . can be best understood in relation to the workings of the "prestige system", the system within which personal status is ascribed, achieved, advanced and lost.'[32] Writing, and especially dramatic writing, offers Cavendish an opportunity to renegotiate the place of women in the prestige system, momentarily. As Ortner suggests in relation to Polynesia, prewar seventeenth-century English society regarded the aristocratic hierarchy as (ideally, if not actually) the custodians of the society's encompassing ideals. This is made literal in the language of patronage. On the other hand, it also relied implicitly on the continued use and exchange of women as bearers of values (including some of prewar England's 'ideal' values). Some, at least, of the developments of the 1650s suggested that some women were amongst those who would benefit from the fall of the old hierarchy and values which Cavendish in the main wished to preserve. The theatre provides a metaphor which can resolve, in writing, such intractable contradictions.

Attention to the fluidity of the 'theatre's' female protagonists alerts the reader to a whole set of further slippages taking place in Cavendish's texts around royalist ideologies and the status of women. The texts slide away from positions which some critics (like Jacqueline Pearson and Kathleen Jones) have chosen to read as 'feminist' in a relatively unproblematic way. Such readings take no account of the cross-currents of class and gender (or status and gender) in Cavendish's texts;[33] they dehistoricize and isolate the 'feminist' element in them by insulating them from their particular circumstances of production and consumption. On the one hand, as her endless prefaces and her heroines declare, Margaret Cavendish is a woman writing. But she is also the wife of a peer who enters the writing market at the level of buying authors to write plays for him. It is worth asking how questions of gender as raised in her plays relate to the framework of contemporary political thought: on the one hand to Hobbes's analysis of rational, radical self-interest (plus authority), and on the other to Filmer's *ad absurdum* elaboration of the divine right and his immensely literal paternalism which took the father of a family as God-the-father printed small. The position of female subjects under a system of gendered subjecthood derived from God was, at least in theory, Filmer's position of obedience to the *de jure* parenthood of husband and state; and, although Hobbes suggested that women were the primary 'owners' of children (in the state of nature 'every woman that bears children becomes both a mother and a Lord'), men owned women.[34] Moreover, as Scochet has demonstrated, generalized patriarchal thinking permeated even the most radical political documents of the Civil War.[35]

Patriarchal thinking was powerful in debates dealing with the politically ideal. As Margaret Ezell's book *The Patriarch's Wife* suggests, it is more difficult to map the relationship between political discourse and its implication for individuals and the material decisions of daily life. That is not to say, as at some points Ezell seems to suggest, that patriarchal discourse was nothing more than a disposable meta-language.[36] During the Civil War, as Brian Manning notes, 'stripped of the trappings of government, the monarchy was seen to rest, not upon the love of the people, but upon the interests of a class'.[37] Clarendon said of Newcastle that he 'loved monarchy, as it was the foundation and support of his own greatness'.[38] The same could, perhaps, be said of his wife. These negotiations of gender and class issues can, I think, best be read in relation to the stabilizing, patriarchal discourses which supported monarchy, but which also syncretically supported the structure of the family; the same metaphorical thinking held the king in place as head of the state and the father as head of the family.

Cavendish argues, on the one hand, that women are unjustifiably marginalized, and on the other, for the primacy of the monarch. Her arguments circle some central issues – conversation, public display and action, marriage and remarriage (see *Bell in Campo*) – issues which concerned all women, but which she usually presents through the predicament of a particular noble figure. Even as they rail against it, her heroines (such as the Lady Sanspareile) endorse the division of the world into binary opposites based on the masculine right to authority; Cavendish attempts to claim status as a writer not by repudiation of gender hierarchies but by what Ann Rosalind Jones calls 'subtle appropriations and reshufflings of the prevailing notions of feminine virtue'.[39]

On the topic of gender relations and the rights of women, Cavendish is highly contradictory. She suggests that marriage is not desirable for all women and approaches positions which assert female autonomy, only to back away; she combines a conception of the wife's role in marriage which might have been taken from the educationalist Juan Luis Vives, with a telling critique of the power relations between the sexes. She follows the gendered ascription of qualities and its implications for woman's engagement with the world and particularly the public sphere: 'The minde and the body', she writes, 'must be married together; but so as the minde must be the husband; to govern, and command, and the wife to obey, and reason which is the judge of the minde must keepe the senses in awe.'[40] She is not the only woman entering patriarchal discourse in support of monarchy and the family. In 1649 Elizabeth Poole wrote of Charles I that, although he had broken his side of the patriarchal contract, the country (as wife) was still subject to his authority. 'And although this bond be broken on his part; You never heard that a Wife might put away her husband, as he is head of her body.'[41] But at the same time as Cavendish and Poole are objects in patriarchal discourse, patriarchy and patriarchal discourse are precisely the object of *their* discourse. We might want to see this double movement, this use of words by that which ought under patriarchy to lack language itself, as disrupting the patriarchal paradigm even as it asserts its centrality.

The play *Youths Glory and Deaths Banquet* will allow us to map these contradictory relationships more clearly. Here the Lady Sanspareile comments on political questions: the area which Cavendish believed closed to women's action or comment. Delivering a commentary on 'justice', she declares that 'humane Justice [belongs] to Monarchical Princes . . . For which Justice Gods and Princes are both feared and loved'. Through this analogy monarchy becomes inseperable from justice (*Youths Glory and Deaths Banquet*, Part 2 scene 1, p. 155). Earlier she has commented in a Hobbesian way that the 'Marshall Law' is 'the Supream Authority, placing and displacing, and is the Monarchical Power, that doth not only protect all other Laws, but commands them with threats' (*Youths Glory*, Part 2 scene 1, p. 150). To such supreme and threateningly enforced authority there seems little chance of relationship unless she is a ruler. Lady Sanspareile addresses a female monarch as follows:

> most glorious Princess, you and your Subjects are like the Sun, and the rest of the Planets, moving perpetually, keeping their proper Sphere . . . .
> (*Youths Glory*, Part 2 scene 1, p. 156)

As Gallagher notes, Cavendish's insistence on order can only coincide with the recognition of the rights of women to power at the very top of the hierarchy – only a queen both confirms the perpetual order *and* takes an active part in it.[42] Even for a queen some elements in the monarchical discourse – being feared, displacing, threatening – are apparently unavailable or inappropriate. Cavendish's prose writing contains a range of contradictory opinions about politics, ranging and often sliding from the orthodox to the eccentric.[43] An example of such slippage and reorganization can be seen in *The Worlds Olio* where she comments, 'Womens tongues are like Stings of Bees; and what man could endure our effeminate monarchy to swarm about his ears?' She implicitly links the bid for authority by a female with a danger (a 'swarm'); she goes on to link that bid for authority with speech, through which the 'effeminate monarchy' attempts to seize power. She continues:

> True it is, our sex make great complaints, that men from their first Creation usurped a Supremacy to themselves, although we were made equal by nature, which Tyrannical Government they have kept ever since, so that we never could come to be free, but rather more and more enslav'd, using us either like Children, Fools, or Subjects, that is to flatter or threaten us, to allure or force us to obey, and will not let us divide the world equally with them, as to Govern and Command, to direct and Dispose as they do; which slavery hath dejected our Spirits, as we are become so stupid that Beasts are but a Degree below us . . . . (*The Worlds Olio*, A4r)

A slippage takes place here: the views initially attributed to her complaining sex in general seem to become absorbed into the text as its own complaint. From condemning 'effeminate monarchy' the text moves rapidly to apparently sponsoring a feminist position. Cavendish seems on one hand to subscribe to a state ideology of contempt for female rule, on the other to evade or escape her text's marginal or actively transgressive status as literary production under this patriarchal state. The initial attribution of the 'complaints' to loci external to the text opens an aporia alongside the official, unified 'I's' agreement with the absolutist position, and allows an ambiguous, unowned intervention of other views. In short, assertions of a feminist kind rest uneasily in Cavendish's texts with a conceptualization of authority wholly derived from the male, ruling, speaking figure.

Yet Cavendish returns again and again to the theme of female wisdom and women's ability to make laws and to organize military campaigns and to orate. Again and again her heroines, like Lady Contemplation, Lady Sanspareile and Lady Orphant, take on male roles and respect, so that in effect they answer the case against female rule and government. The Lady Sanspareile is quickly sketched in as a paragon of wit and learning; granted a proper education by an esteemed father, she goes on to astonish the world with a series of orations on all subjects from politics through marriage to the theatre. She is so impressive that one surprised 'gentleman' comments that he could wish for 'that I never wisht before' – to be a woman, 'but such a woman as the Lady Sanspareile' (*Youths Glory, Playes*, 1662, scene 13).

One of the most prolonged explorations of these contradictions between power and femininity comes in one of the earlier plays, *Bell in Campo*.[44] Here too the only resolution is coincidence of these qualities through a woman raised to the top of the hierarchy: in this case a female general. This play also reflects Cavendish's engagement with the Civil War: the triumphal entry may well be a reading of Henrietta Maria's triumphal entry into Oxford in 1643.[45] *Bell in Campo* tells the story of the war between 'this Kingdom of Reformation', and 'the Kingedome of Faction' (Act I scene i), contrasting the sad fortunes of women left behind by war-going husbands with the career of the Lady Victoria, who is elected to head an army made up of 'women of all sorts' (Act I scene ix). Part of the play is given over to the wise law-giving of the Lady Victoria, but most of Acts III, IV, and Part Two, Acts II, III and IV interweave the reported successes of the Female Army with the sad fates of war widows. The successes bring the Masculine and Female armies closer together, and the second part ends with the plan for Lady Victoria's triumph:

1. Gent   ... the Lady Victoria shall be brought through the City in triumph, which is a great honour, for never any makes triumphs in a monarchy but the King himself; then that there shall be a blank for the Female Army to write their designs and demands; also there is an Armour of gold and a Sword a making, the hilt being set with Diamonds, and chariot all gilt and imbroidered to be presented to the Lady Victoria, and the City is making great preparation against her arrival.

2. Gent   Certainly she is a Lady that deserves as much as can be given from Kings, States, or Poets.
(*Bell in Campo*, Part Two, Act IV scene 18)

This passage and the closely juxtaposed list of female demands focus the contradictions between monarchist ideology and rhetoric on the one hand, and the claims Cavendish also articulates for noble, aristocratic women on the other. Again a heroine, 'liberated' from the restraints of gender, outdoes the men in fields traditionally barred to her sex. The list of demands returns from celebration of heroism to analysis of women in their domestic relations, as they articulate demands for domestic autonomy which seem petty in comparison to the great triumphs of the Lady Victoria. The demands of the women include that they:

... shall sit at the upper end of the
Table above their Husbands.
Thirdly, that they shall keep the Purse ...
Tenthly, They shall go to Playes, Masks, Balls, Churchings,
Christenings, Preachings, whensoever they will, and as fine and bravely attired as they will. (Part Two, Act V scene 20)

When the play shifts from a single aristocratic woman to women in general, it shifts its discursive field from the fantasized triumphs of war to the issues of the battle of the sexes fought out in comic drama, conduct books and in the antifeminist tracts of the earlier seventeenth century. The right to power, for women in Cavendish's writing, is a privilege attendant upon birth and status; her plays dramatize the differences between noble women warfarers and other women, especially citizen women.

V Gender, class and mobility: the Civil War context

These positions about gender remain contradictory even taking into account that some are spoken by Cavendish in an authorial persona, and others by the central figures in plays so often taken by commentators to be, unproblematically, 'Margaret'. These contradictions have perplexed a range of writers on Cavendish. Treating her life and writing as one text, a recent biographer says of her 'disapproval' of the roles some women found during the civil wars and after: 'Why such an insistent advocate of greater freedom for women should condemn those who exercise such freedom is difficult to assess'.[46]

While Cavendish does not seem to be exactly 'an insistent advocate of freedom for women', slippage between critique and valorization of patriarchal institutions does occur. Her fleeting, momentary critique of sexual politics is discongruent and dissonant with her usual insistence on nobility and royalty.

The two positions can be linked using something to which critics of Cavendish's plays have paid little attention – the representation of gender in relation to social mobility. In William Cavendish's plays, women of the lower orders are represented as sexually interested and available. In the plays by his daughters Brackley and Cavendish, such women are limited to ladies' servants or farm women (who, though called by animal names such as 'Henn', are represented sympathetically as suffering from the depredations of an alien war). Margaret Cavendish's representation of citizen women, maids and servants insists on their desires for social mobility. For example, the citizen women who appear momentarily in *The Female Academy* are angry at being excluded from the academy orations or discourses which are held exclusively for a noble audience. Their recourse is to the men's academy: the men, they say, will not turn them away but make them welcome (*Female Academy*, Act II scene 11, p. 662).

One of the most detailed treatments of social aspiration and femininity occurs in a plot developed autonomously through Part One of the play

The Matrimoniall Trouble. In this plot, Bridget Greasy, a 'Cook-maid',
is accused of stealing by Thirsty the steward, who berates her initially for
her unskilful making of 'pudding in guts':

> Thirsty: you are a Slut, and did not take all the dung out of them, nor wash,
> nor scrape nor cleanse them as they should have been, but you
> order the guts as you do the dishes, the one is dungy, the other
> greasie; besides, my Master complains, that his Fowl tastes rank,
> and his Brawn tastes strong, and his Beer tastes musty, and that's
> because you are so lazy, as not to shift your Brawn into fresh
> sousing drink, nor make the brine strong enough in the powdering
> tub, nor thrust your fingers far enough into the Fowls rumps to
> draw them clean . . . . Besides, your sluttery is such, as you will
> poyson all the House: for in one place I find a piece of butter, and a
> greasie comb, full of nitty hairs lying by it; and in another place
> flour and old worn stockings, the feet being rotted off with
> sweat.[47]

At this point the master, Sir John Dotard, comes in; the rest of this plot
traces Bridget Greasy's rise through the ranks to become his wife. Much
of her progress is reported disapprovingly by other servants who
comment on her hypocrisy and thieving. Her entry to a more powerful
sphere, unlike that of noble ladies to the theatre of the world, does not
imply gender solidarity on the writer's part. Sara Mendelson comments,
'class interests are certainly more obvious than gender solidarity among
seventeenth-century women.'[48] Even this formulation is inadequate,
though, to the specific case of the interrelationship of class and gender in
Cavendish's plays and in her writing generally. Cavendish's multiple
'theatres' are open only to the noble female. Her emphasis on the sexual
attraction and power of the noble female is underpinned by commitment
to a hierarchical structure in which the femininity of the lower orders
must be kept under control. The sexual desirability and desires of women
of the lower orders endanger the security of the noble woman and are
constructed as disgusting and transgressive. The same is true of their
actions in the world; Cavendish speaks approvingly of the breaking up of
a conventicle of 'preaching sisters' which she had nevertheless gone to
see. The theatre preserves the noble ladies' sexual attraction while
elevating them to masculine roles; it allots to lower-class women (and the
sexually desirous courtiers in *The Presence*) all the negative and
grotesque attributes of femininity.[49] Socially mobile women – particularly in the plays in the 1662 volume – connote danger and chaos.
Citizens' wives remain the focus of animosity throughout Cavendish's
plays. Often they act as grotesque foils to deserving or vulnerable
women, like the citizen's wife in the play within a play in *The Convent of*

Pleasure, who goes looking for her husband in the tavern and stays there to drink with the men.

What is at stake throughout Cavendish's writing is the intransigent interrelationship between patriarchal or monarchist ideals and the desire to disrupt gender ideology. I began this piece with Cavendish's analysis and valorization of the potential of the theatre as an educator of the nobility. Peter Stallybrass writes of the class aspirant that, 'like the members of the elite, the class aspirant has an interest in preserving social closure, since without it there would be nothing to aspire *to*. But, at the same time, that closure must be sufficiently flexible to incorporate *him*.'[50] Here I have attempted to integrate the ingredient of gender with the vexed issue of class and pinpoint the slippages in Cavendish's operations of patriarchal and monarchist rhetoric. As a royalist woman, Cavendish the writer faces an intractable dilemma. She wishes to support the idealized class order, but to disrupt gender ideologies. S. D. Amussen, following Christopher Hill, argues persuasively that in the early seventeenth century, 'the existence of the gender hierarchy was secure. But the class hierarchy was challenged; the criteria for determining status, the conception of the moral superiority of the wealthy and the inferiority of the poor were also called into question.'[51] To suggest reform in gender hierarchy was to point, inevitably, towards the current instability of class hierarchy. Cavendish, writing at a time when this instability was barely beginning to lessen, mounted only limited challenges to gender hierarchy.[52] Her own position as a wife whose husband endorsed her work indicates immediately the interrelationship of class and gender hierarchies: to suggest that one (gender) might benefit from reform is to point, inevitably, towards the instability of the other (class).

The very circumstances of social change and mobility which contributed to Cavendish's becoming a playwright simultaneously threatened her position as an aristocrat. These circumstances, read back into her plays, account for the slippages and the insistence on designating the socially mobile as the dirty, low, waste parts of society. At every juncture the assertion of class stability and of fixed lowerness stands surety for the noble ladies' liberation from gender constraints and entry into the theatre of the world.

The Jacobite vision of Mary Caesar

Valerie Rumbold

The unpublished manuscript book of the Jacobite Mary Caesar (1677–1741), an autobiographical text of some 30,000 words, is familiar to historians for its commentary on political events and personalities in the first half of the eighteenth century, and to students of literature as a source of contemporary response to Pope and Prior.[1] As a friend of Pope, Prior and Swift, an intimate of the Harley circle and the wife of an MP and leading Jacobite conspirator, Mary Caesar was in an excellent position to record political and literary anecdotes. Her book is, however, far more than the sum of its anecdotal parts: in particular, it represents a poignant attempt to integrate an increasingly negative experience of life with a faith in the ultimate triumph of Jacobite virtue.

Superficially at least, it may seem strange to subject a book like Mary Caesar's to specifically literary analysis. Although she writes a beautifully clear hand, she is highly eccentric in spelling and punctuation; and to the reader who goes to her for historical narrative, her handling of her material is likely to appear simply as being of the same level of eccentricity, not to say incompetence. The fault, however, is not so much with her as with readers' expectations of chronologically ordered narrative and explicit evaluative commentary, requirements which are indeed met by the best-known seventeenth- and eighteenth-century autobiographical writings, whether by women or by men. In contrast, Mary Caesar follows no one chronological scheme, ordering different sections of her book in different ways, often referring to the events of the present principally in order to reflect on events of the past, sometimes transcribing substantial passages of prose and verse by others, and making no consistent attempt to explain the significance of events and personalities in terms accessible to the uninitiated reader. In effect, despite her occasional use of dated entries, the title of 'Diary' or 'Journal' raises expectations that it is not her aim to fulfil.[2] Her book, sometimes almost reminiscent of the commonplace-book tradition, is rather a work of meditative reflection, in which chronological and causal ordering take second place to the integration of experience with her Jacobite ideology. Moreover, though not actually written in cipher or under the figure of feigned names and situations, which were the typical strategies of conspirators like Charles Caesar when communicating by post, Mary Caesar's book presents the Jacobite faithful – the only reader actually mentioned is her husband – with allusions and double meanings whose recognition offers the pleasures of complicity and solidarity. For the casual reader, however, this esoteric mode can simply be a further obstacle.

One way of assessing the distinctive character of Mary Caesar's book is to consider what she leaves out, for simple omission is in fact one of her most characteristic strategies. It is, for example, from her correspondence, not from her book, that we learn that the Mr Freeman whose election defeat she coolly records is actually her brother, and that she had helped her son to plan a successful elopement with his son's intended bride.[3] This coup was so relished in the neighbourhood that it became the subject of a ballad, *Upon the Royston Bargain: or, The Alehouse Wedding*; but it was not the stuff of which her book was to consist.[4] Similarly, she makes no mention of the sudden death of this son in 1740, nor of the illnesses that necessitated her own trips to Bath, nor of the distressing circumstances of her husband's imprisonment for debt in 1735.[5] When she mentions his dangerous illness, it is only in passing, as she records with thanksgiving his recovery and return to parliamentary business.[6] Just as there is no purely private sorrow in her book, so there is no discussion of courtship, children or feuds and affinities within the wider family, all topics which, as the family correspondence amply and often movingly shows, were by no means lacking in dramatic incident and emotional repercussions for all concerned.

Instead, leaving aside what would perhaps have been the most obvious interpretation of her prescribed role as private woman, she writes exclusively about the areas in which the feminine sphere can properly overlap with the public and political, in effect transforming the public into the private: she dwells on her role as messenger to Tory prisoners and promoter of subscriptions for Tory poets; she recounts her reaction to parliamentary debates which she has attended; she reads and discusses the memoirs of statesmen; and she reflects on her private contacts with the men who actually take part in affairs of state. At the heart of her

Jacobite commitment, moreover, lies not the pragmatism of a professional politician, but a personal and affective devotion to the Stuart
family, and to the memory of Queen Anne and her servant the first Earl of
Oxford as founders of her husband's fortune. These were focuses of
political feeling which, far from emphasizing the potential threat of a
woman's interest in affairs of state, effectively assimilated her passionate
devotion to acceptable models of wifely and Christian piety. What is
remarkable, however, is her decision to omit from her writing all
reference to the domestic interests which first spring to mind in
connection with such models.

The opening of her book, which immediately establishes her
assimilation of the political to the conjugal, is more than usually
revealing of the writer's strategies and preoccupations, not least with the
problem, to which she never explicitly alludes, of how she as a woman
can be justified in taking on the role of author. On 30 May 1724, alone at
their estate at Benington in Hertfordshire, she heard from her husband in
London of the death of their friend and benefactor Robert Harley, first
Earl of Oxford. Had her husband been at home, their mutual
commiseration would perhaps have blunted her commemorative urge;
but as it was, she took up her pen and began her book: 'The Loss Lord
Oxford is to Mr Caesar, maks me reflect on the many changes of His
Fortune, since I had the Honor and Happines of being His Wife'.[7] She
may be the writer, but her husband is the authoritative presence, as she
adopts the vicarious narrative stance that is to characterize her book.
Unlike Lucy Hutchinson, who prefaces her account of her husband with
the implausible claim to be no more than 'his pale shade', or the
Duchesses of Marlborough and Buckingham and Lady Mary Wortley
Montagu, who express a clear sense of their sex as impediment to
participation in political life, Mary Caesar never articulates the issue of
authority as one of gender. This was probably because her husband,
already the legitimizing subject of her writing, explicitly encouraged her
to see herself as a commendable exception to her sex: on one occasion,
for example, he wrote that he was glad to hear, 'that you begin to get up
your Spirits, (news that perhaps would not please all Husbands) but
you who know so well how to govern them can't have too much'.[8] By
far the most important instance of the help he gave her is enshrined
in the exchange which, while it constitutes the most authoritative
imprimatur for her book, also reveals the depth of her 'feminine'
deference:

My Begining to wright was for amusement. when maloncarly on the Death of
Our Great Friend Treasurr Oxford, and the Absence of Mr Caesar, to whom I

had not the least thought of showing it to, Not Thinking it could haue stood the Test of His Good Understanding.'

Yet the combination of pride in her labours and confidence in her husband did in the end induce her to show him her book; and the first of her five sections closes with his giving it the seal of his approval:

> Mr Caesar was att London when I wrot this. but so Parssial when att Home. to say it should be Lay'd Upon the Table in my Picture.[10]

When we read on and discover how important portraits were in their cult of Tory virtue, we recognize that he could not have paid her a compliment better calculated to encourage her.

Mary Caesar never explains her unease about writing in terms of gender, but it is invariably the prospect of having her work read by men that prompts her expressions of inadequacy. Her anxiety focuses ostensibly on spelling, apparently for her representative of a whole range of expertise in which she felt deficient. The men in her circle spelled in ways far closer to modern standard forms, and most were accomplished writers both in prose and in verse. In contrast, it seems unlikely that Mary Caesar had received any training in writing beyond the mechanical accomplishment of writing a good hand; and although she shows herself vigorous in language, deft in the management of rhythm and well able to shape her material to her purposes, she always comes back to her sense of technical incompetence, especially when faced with the task of writing letters to her male friends. Lord Orrery teased her, 'Another objection I have about your Spelling, (and it is ye greatest) is that you fill half your Letters merely upon that subject'; and when Pope told Oxford that she 'never wrote a letter but to a good purpose', his gallantry was at least in part a defence of her reluctance to write at all.[11] In her book, she records such comments in a sequence of brief notes (which show her writing in her least ambitious style, almost in the manner of a commonplace book). The sequence demonstrates how, supported by these treasured compliments, she advanced from initial panic to eventual pride in her correspondence:

> Righting was Never my tallent, so allways avoid'd it. if possible, which made the then Lord Harley say, at Wimple to Lady Harriat and Mr Prior. we must go to meet her at Royston Races, for she is in earnest haveing rote.
>
> But how terrifid'd when my Lady told me, they had shewn it to Mr Prior, tho she at the same time said he lik'd it. laughing told me He would not say how well, but bid me right on and never mind spelling.
>
> Pope says sometimes too many letters in my words. Never too many words in my letters.
>
> Dean Swift, There is one part of Pope's Compliment which I can Not Make you for I could not with the striacest search find one letter to many in any of your words, though I found a thousand words too few in your letter.

Part of the Deans I rote Lord Oxford who says Your transcribing Swifts letter apears to me like a very curious Jeweller, that taks care to set a fine Gem in the best light.

Dublin Lord Orrery 1732 A letter from Mᵣ Caesar ought to be answer'd by a head much less perplecect with intricate afairs and a hart les fill'd with sorraw Then mine are at Presant. In the midst of my Affliction it gives me some pleasure to find my Self remembered, by you Mᵐ, and indeed I have an Hereditary right to your fauour. let me therefore claim a Constant Correspondance with you.

At Lord Lansdowns telling Lord Orckney in that how little Lord Orrery knew me, He said twas Charity. O but my Speling is bad. Lord Lansdown Answer'd I did not observed it, but I'me shure your Stile is good.[12]

From this it is clear that she repeated each friend's compliment to the next, almost extorting from them the commendations that she so craved. She offers an amusing precedent, however, for copying them into her book: 'Now take Sanction with Pope, who Introduces his Works with the Complements made him, therefore it Aught by me to be done, to Palliate my perceverence'.[13] She is shrewdly aware of Pope's manœuvres for establishing his literary supremacy; she also feels that her 'perceverence' requires an imprimatur.

Writing had evidently come to be of immense importance in Mary Caesar's life, and one of the reasons is clear from the timing of her book. It dates entirely from the years after 1724, that is, from the period when Charles Caesar's most daring political intrigues were over, and hence from a time when there was less scope for the practical service to the cause that had previously occupied her.[14] During the Gyllenborg plot of 1716–17, for example, in which her husband was one of the prime movers of a plan for a Jacobite rising backed by foreign troops, the Caesars had been surprised in their sleep by government agents; and she, knowing that there was nothing incriminating in the house, had acted the part of an innocent with such verve that one of them, impressed but not convinced, paid her the treasured compliment that 'there are Women that have as much Resolution as men'.[15] While her husband and other Tory leaders were imprisoned in the Tower, she was zealous in visiting and in comforting their families, despite the fact that she had children of her own to be consoled in their father's absence.[16] Although these were years of great danger, they were evidently for her the high point of her career, when the absence of the men – whose prerogatives she was far from resenting – thrust her into the front line of the secret campaign. Soon after the commencement of her book, however, such heady experiences had become a thing of the past. Although on Oxford's death in 1724 Charles Caesar had replaced him as one of the leading figures in English Jacobite affairs, his eminence proved shortlived, probably because his cautious realism became increasingly unpalatable to his associates. Whatever the Caesars understood of the manœuvrings that had relegated them to the margin of affairs, these were, for Mary at least, years of waiting and hoping in which writing emerged as one way of channelling the loyal zeal which no longer found its outlet so readily in action.

It is also clear from the book itself and from comments in letters to Mary Caesar that writing became an integral part of a lifestyle which amounted almost to a domestic cult for the edification of family and friends in the Jacobite faith. Documentary archives, pictures and poetry took on particular importance, and were ritually displayed to guests as well as serving as objects of Mary Caesar's private contemplation. To understand the function of these elements in the exemplary lifestyle over which she presided is also to grasp the basic strategies of her writing, since for Mary Caesar writing, housekeeping and hospitality all partake of the same consecrated energy.

The correspondence which makes up her archive, though carefully purged of treasonable expressions, is couched for the most part in a Tory or at least anti-government vein that she, confident that true Toryism was necessarily Jacobite, was happy to accept as evidence of solidarity. A prime example of a case in which such reading was fully justified is her correspondence with the Gyllenborgs, now safely returned to Sweden, who write of their desire to imitate on their own country estate 'your good order neatness and pretty contrivances'.[17] Their stress on the virtues of good housekeeping in rural retirement is standard country party rhetoric; but they had shown by their participation in one of the boldest of Jacobite invasion plans that such language carried for them the extra charge of opposition to the specific corruptions of court and city under a Hanoverian king. Whig correspondents, on the other hand, needed to be constantly on the alert to avert Mary Caesar's partisan readings: Lord Dupplin, for example, a Whig grandson of the first Earl of Oxford, teases Charles Caesar about the inhibitions he feels in writing to him, having seen 'those terrible repositorys which adorn your Lady's closet'.[18] Clearly, for a non-Jacobite to express friendship for the Caesars was to risk being written into Mary Caesar's propaganda. The third Earl of Essex, an ambassador who had previously been married to one of the Tory Hydes, reacted to the confection of royalist precedents and Jacobite double meanings that she sent to congratulate him on the birth of a son by politely but strenuously dissociating himself from her treasonable implications: to a man in his position, engaged in the diplomatic service, her insinuations could only have been an embarrassment.[19]

In the portrait gallery which provided the icons of Mary Caesar's Jacobite faith, pride of place was given to a group of royal portraits presented by their subjects: Elizabeth (given to Sir Julius Caesar, founder of the family), Anne (given to Charles Caesar) and the Old Pretender (given to Mrs Caesar).[20] The royalist message was further reinforced by a set of hangings representing the Restoration of 1660, a silent admonition to anyone sceptical of the feasibility of James's return. James's agent Anne Oglethorpe, who delivered his picture to Mary Caesar in 1717, reported, 'She shows it to everybody and cannot be a moment without looking at it'; but in later years the owner elaborated her sharing of such images, as she shows in describing how she used her gallery as a kind of ritual induction when she welcomed her former opponent Lord Cowper into the ranks of the Jacobite faithful:

> Who when Att Benington I Shewing him the Restoration Hangings. Turning quick to me He Said. They that Once thought they Serv'd thier Country by Endeavouring to Keep Him Out. Found they Had No way to Save it, but by Bringing Him Home. Seaing in my Closet a Picture he lookt through a glass Earnestly Appon it for Soom time. then Said it had Not Only a Sweet but A Sensible Countenance. and a Likeness to Both Parents More then Usual. He was Not Happier in His Expresstion then in the Most Pleaseing Delivery and Sʳ John Denams Unimaictable Discription of the Thames May Aptley to His Conversation be Apply'd
> Tho Deep, yet Clear. tho Gentle yett Not Dull.
> Strong without Rage, without O're Flowing Full.[21]

This is a beautiful example not only of Mrs Caesar's use of pictures, but also of her typical literary procedures and preoccupations. Cowper is recorded as making his profession of faith in just her own manner, not by openly stating his hopes, but by citing a historical precedent in terms that, on the literal level at least, even the most loyal Hanoverian could hardly argue with. His comments on the portrait of the Pretender not only encapsulate the principal articles of the Jacobite faith (the personal suitability and legitimate descent, often contested, of James Stuart), but also highlight what is a frequent theme with Mary Caesar, the continuity and synthesis of desirable qualities in legitimate monarchs, and, by association and adoption, in their chosen servants. Her choice of lines by Denham, one of the favourite poets of her Tory pantheon, to praise Cowper as an associate dignified by a similar confluence of virtues, is a particularly apt way of marking his adoption into the circle of the Jacobite faithful. The whole passage demonstrates the coherence and selectivity of her vision, as she shapes her recollections into writing which is in effect the sister-art of the portraiture that prompts Cowper's profession.

Mary Caesar's favourite portrait painter was apparently Sir Godfrey Kneller, who had painted the portrait of Queen Anne presented by her to Charles Caesar; and in Mrs Caesar's account of her own sitting with Kneller she again shows the polarizing force of her selectivity:

> he allso play'd on the Lute, which he told me had taken too much of his Time, but it had giveing him the Advantage of judging of the Sound of Voices, which he Said he did. when drawing Queen Anns Picture, Asking if the Crown Should be On Her head, the Queen Answerd No, I'le have it Lye by me on the Table, I knew what She Ment. But then rejoic'd to think of a German King Soon after being in his room as he was painting which he did with Such Ease as if playing with the pencil, and talking of the politeness of the Upper Germany I Came from thence but the King Came from the Lower Germany.[22]

No doubt Kneller was fully aware of his sitter's taste for discreet subversion, as he praised the royal voice that she had so admired, hinted slyly at Queen Anne's recognition of her brother's superior right, and insinuated that the present King left something to be desired in the matter of polish. Again, however, what may seem on first sight to be simply a discursive recollection of a favourite painter is clearly moulded by Mrs Caesar's political programme; and the eulogy of his art which follows (not quoted), which even leads her into the unusual concession of quoting a (non-partisan) poem by a Whig poet in his praise, reflects the lustre cast over him in her eyes by his creation of the image of Queen Anne which was the focus of her domestic devotion.

Poetry too plays a major role in Mary Caesar's cult of Jacobite virtue; and although Shakespeare provides several phrases that she adapts to the praise of her heroes, it is hardly surprising to find that her great love is for the poetry of Tory loyalists, especially those personally known to her. Poetry for her is the handmaid of politics; and this is clear in her appreciation of Pope, who despite his Tory sympathies remained wary of implication in her Jacobite schemes. The function of Pope's work for her is beautifully illustrated in her recollection of her emotions at the conclusion of the Peace of Utrecht:

> O the Delight I Felt in hearing Her Magisty from the Thrown Deliver That Speech Which Gave Her So Much joy.
> At Length Great Anna said – Let Discord Ceace
> She Said, the World Obey'd, and all Was Peace.[23]

She also recalled with pleasure how, 'in the Happy Day's of Queen Ann', Pope had written, also in *Windsor Forest*, that 'Rich Industry Sits Smiling on the Pleine/And Peace and Plenty Tell a Stuart Reigns'; and she threw herself into the task of securing subscriptions for Pope's *Odyssey* with extraordinary enthusiasm, no doubt seeing Pope's translation of this pre-eminent classic as asserting the centrality of her political grouping to the national culture.[24] She was most explicit about her desire to recruit him as laureate to 'James III' when he sent her a copy of one of his works with a covering note in which he attempted to atone for the indiscretion of having praised her arch-enemy Bolingbroke as 'All-accomplished St. JOHN'.[25] Pope's poetic note gracefully transferred the resented epithet and made a joke at his own expense:

> O all-Accomplish'd Caesar! on thy Shelf
> Is room for all Popes Works – and Pope him self.[26]

She responded with verses which punningly insist on the metaphorical greatness that requires not a shelf but a whole new building; but her praise is strictly on her own terms, as she classes his works with the writings of the statesmen most revered in her memorial archive, and demands from him the avowal of Jacobitism which would in her eyes represent a triumphant continuity with the early promise of *Windsor Forest*:

> 'Tis true Great Bard Thow on my Shelf Shall Lye
> With Oxford, Cowper, Noble Strafford by.
> But for Thy Windsor a New Fabrick Raise
> And There Triumphant Sing Thy Soverain's Praise.[27]

Far dearer to her than Pope, however, was the poet and diplomat Matthew Prior, who, to quote one John Lockman, 'in Anna's golden Days,/Was proud to hail Thee in his deathless Lays'.[28] Characteristically, it was not his gallantry but his loyalty that she treasured most:

> The World Knew Mr Prior to be a Fine Poet but Mr Caesar who had the Pleasure of his Friendship Esteem'd that As the least Qualification he was Master of, being Superiour to all Temptation, True to His Trust. and to His Friend. His Conversation was Not more Plesant then Instructing but with Such an Air of Politness and Good Breeding, that a Stranger Entering the Roome would Not a thought Him a Poet, As Naver being Full of Him Self nor Satirocl on others. See Him a Young Man Riseing in King Williams Ciurt. and yet even then with what Decency did He Treat His Unhappy Sovereign in His Carmon Seculare for the year 1700
>> Janus, Mighty Deity
>> Be Kind; and as Thy Searching Eye
>> Does Our Modern Story Trace
>> Finding Some of Stuart's Race
>> Unhappy, Pass ther Annals By:
>> No Harsh Reflection Let Rememberance Raise
>> Forebear to Mention what thou Canst Not Praise.[29]

Again it is her husband, Prior's fellow conspirator, who holds the centre of the stage. As the passage unfolds, however, her own feelings, unaffectedly in harmony with the husband who authorizes her commentary, emerge both through her pleasure in remembering Prior and through her meditation on his works. She has already mentioned in passing that she helped to collect subscriptions for the publication of his poetry, and, as we might expect, there was a strong political motive for her efforts, insofar as the impoverished and imprisoned poet was at the time under pressure to incriminate his former master Oxford: 'But Alas they knew Little of that Great Man who After being the Queens Minister and Plenipotentiary in France ... Rather Chose to Support Him Self by Publishing His Works by Subscription'.[30] On the other hand, she also esteemed him for his freedom from the vein of professional self-advertisement that she detected in Pope: Prior was for her a man 'Naver ... Full of Him Self nor Satirocl on others', less a career poet than a loyal servant of the cause – who could also turn his hand to poetry.

Whether the objects of interpretation are letters, paintings or poems, Mary Caesar sees in them and their creators only what serves her Jacobite faith. How, privately, she dealt with the fact that Essex's reply to her congratulations was in effect a rebuff, or that Kneller was happily devoting his skills to immortalizing the Hanoverian court, we cannot know. In her book, however, one thing is clear: on the rare occasions when she alludes to collaboration with the usurping power by those she admires, its significance is consistently minimized. Kneller's teasing about his anticipation of a German king is capped by his insinuation that the king comes from the less cultivated part of Germany; Prior's 'Riseing in King William's Ciurt' is palliated by a delicacy towards the former dynasty which she interprets as loyal respect to 'His Unhappy Sovereign'. Acquaintances like Dupplin, or to a lesser extent Pope, were evidently aware that their association with Mary Caesar laid them open to repeated attempts, not so much to convert them as to impose a Jacobite reading on every expression of political or ethical idealism. Hers is an imagination which assimilates everything admirable to its own political creed.

This aspect of her writing is particularly noticeable in her treatment of family history. The Caesars emerge free of any embarrassing deviation from royalist virtue, every hint of hiatus smoothed over by selective emphasis and association. Typically, her family history is prompted by one of her favourite Tory poets; equally typically, the subject is a portrait, this time of Queen Anne:

> Mistaken Zeal was the First Marys Share
> Elizabeth was Form'd for Regal Care
> In Ann Alone These Happy Nations Find
> Prudence and Piety Togethar joyn'd.[31]

The lines are by the Duke of Buckingham, whose widow Catherine, illegitimate daughter of James II, remained the revered patroness of the Caesars. Although by no means as committed a Jacobite as his wife, he was a key writer for Mary Caesar, especially since his works had been distinguished by government suppression on their first appearance.[32] There is, however, something characteristic in her attraction to these particular lines, for they celebrate that synthesis and continuity which she herself finds in royal and royalist history. These are themes that she proceeds to elaborate, presenting the Caesars as a noble family confirmed in their honours by a long tradition of royal favour:

> M[r] Caesars Ancesters and Him Self Has Been Highly Honner'd by These Great Queens. Queen Mary Christined S[r] Julius and Added the Name of Caesar to that of Adelmare. He Being Grandson by the Female Line to the Duke de Caearine But by the Masculine Line, from Baron Adelmare Made Count of Genoa in the Raign of Charles the Great, to Whom He was Related.[33]

This descent from an actual Julius Caesar was a source of much august playfulness, as the Caesars' acquaintances vied with each other in variations on the imperial pun; but as important as the name itself was the fact of its having been bestowed by a royal godmother. The association with imperial Rome is reactivated by the quasi-maternal patronage of the childless queen, and the family's nobility is further asserted by the claim to kinship with the founder of western Christendom. What cannot be brought into the synthesis is rigorously excluded, whether it is purely personal material about Charles Caesar's ancestors or negative commentary on their royal patrons. In the reign of Elizabeth, for example, the Caesars had an early taste of persecution:

> S[r] Julius Father Assisting the Countes of Lennox. (Who Was Mother to Lord Daryly, After Col'd King of Scotland as Husbond to the Queen, and Father to King James the First) And Lending Her His Plate So Enseins'd Queen Elizabeth that She Sent Him to the Tower Whare He Dy'd.[34]

Yet Mrs Caesar, eager to trace the Caesars' distinction to as many sources of royal favour as possible, is not content simply to rest her case on this service to the ancestress of the Stuart line (whose future royalty she deftly indicates), but stresses equally the greatness and bounty of the vengeful Queen to the next generation:

> But That Great Queen Made Amends to His Son Who Served Her in Many Places, and had Ordre'd Him to Continnue the Name of Caesar. Honnering Him With Her Prescence in His House there to be Entertand with Her Court Two Day's and One Night. His Lady Being With Child the Queen Gave Him

One of Her Own Smokes [smocks]. Therein To Rop [wrap] His Childeren to Make Them Fortunate.

Again a childless Queen is presented as symbolic parent, re-endorsing the honorific Caesar name and clothing the child with her own personal linen. The absence of negative commentary is striking, as Mrs Caesar directs the reader to a positive judgment by equating Sir Julius's service with honour, and such honour with 'Amends' for a father's death in prison. Similarly, when she comes to Charles I, she is less than explicit about and very ready to excuse the wrong done to one of the Caesars in the name of Charles I, 'Which that Good King No Sooner Heard then Orderd a Redress. tho Not Done. As Some Times Dus Hapin'.[35] In the case of a rightful king it was easy for Mary Caesar to take the will for the deed, especially as his son, once restored, atoned (like Elizabeth) by favours to another member of the family:

> But to return if King Charls the First, Had Sufferd a Hardship to be Done to the yonger Son of Sr Julyas. He after Made Sr Charls His Eldest. Master of the Rolls. in the Begining of the year 1639 He Dy'd the 6 of December 1642 But before so Blestd to have it In his Power to Lend that Good King Great Sums of Money, for Which the Talles Still Remain, Sr Charls's Soon. Not Haveing An Earl of Tullibardin to make Lord Clarendon Remember Caesar.[36]

Yet despite her wry sense of the leverage required to extract justice from kings (she even tells the tale of a technically successful but actually unpaid petitioner of Charles II who responded to his expressions of regret by saying 'I'me Very Sorry to See your Magisty has No Better Intrest'), there is no irony whatsoever in her sense of the privilege of being hereditary creditor to the House of Stuart.[37]

Mary Caesar's almost hagiographical fusion of family history with Tory piety is most strikingly demonstrated in her management of the potentially embarrassing gap between the generation of Caesars whose royal subsidies were swallowed up in the Civil War and the generation whose pride it was to serve Queen Anne.[38] Charles II, a king under whom Sir Henry and Sir Charles actually refused to hold office, is brought into a paragraph which makes so much of the royal grant of knighthood, Sir Henry's serving in the Restoration parliament, the continuity provided by the figure of Lord Clarendon, and Sir Charles's having been father to the servant of Queen Anne to whom the writer is married, that the reader is swept up uncritically in the symbolic arch which is to land the Caesars safely in the age of Anne:

> He [Sir Henry] was Chose for the County of Heartford to serve in the Bless'd and Healing Parliament. and Mea'd Sr Henry by the King in Lord Clarendons Lodgings in White-hall. and the same King Made His son Sr Charls at

Cambridg Who serv'd for the same County. and Was Father to Mr Caesar Treasure of the Navy to Queen Ann of Bless'd Memory.[39]

In a work of published propaganda, such strategic omission might be suspected of deliberate distortion for partisan ends; but in this purely private work it suggests rather the self-deception of a sincere zealot.

There is, moreover, a particular and poignant motive which strengthens Mary Caesar's commitment to the idealization of her husband's family: it is – although her book rigorously refuses to discuss it – the apostasy of her own. Until 1714 it had been her ancestors, the Freemans of Aspenden, who had most consistently represented the Tory interest in that part of Hertfordshire, regularly competing against the Caesars at elections.[40] Her silence arises from the fact that in the crisis of 1714 her brother Ralph had turned to the Hanoverians, while Charles Caesar committed himself to the Pretender. Mrs Caesar makes not the slightest reference to these matters – although she once refers in passing to 'my Good Father Who was Perfect in Every Virtue' – and when she records Mr Freeman's election defeat in her book she gives no hint that he was her brother, although in daily life their enmity was a major preoccupation.[41] Their quarrel may indeed have gone back to her marriage, which united her with her brother's principal rival in local politics; but it is clear that once Mary and Charles had embraced Jacobitism, and embraced it moreover as a simple continuation of their existing Toryism, there was no possibility for Mary of priding herself on her connection with a family now represented by a Hanoverian Tory. Her husband's family were the beneficiaries of her disillusionment.

The distorting idealization practised by Mary Caesar involves not so much telling lies about the past as weaving a web of associations between favoured topics which excludes enquiry into what lies behind and between. In this context, it is interesting to read the verse tributes to the Caesars by their friends and admirers which Mary Caesar preserved among her papers, for in these too there is a comparable dwelling on comforting associations as earnest of a continuing destiny. In an undated poem on Charles and Mary's wedding anniversary, for instance, they are praised for having 'guarded both their King & Liberty'; and Caesar's promotion to Treasurer of the Navy is recalled in glowing terms:

When Anna's Danger taught Her to beware
Designing Ministers, & to prefer
Her loyal Patriots, strait she thought on You.[42]

On another anniversary, one Philogamus stressed Mrs Caesar's role, likening her, in one of the imperial allusions so beloved of their friends, to Venus, legendary ancestress of the Roman Caesars:

With heavenly Charms thus Cytherea glow'd,
Alike from her a Julian Issue flow'd.

Mrs Caesar's children, according to Philogamus, have been born to confront the national crisis as heroic defenders of church and king:

Leaders in War and Counsellours of State,
Form'd to Support a Sinking Nations Fate:
Resolv'd to hand, with Zeal undaunted, down
The Public Rights with hazard of their Own,
And guard unhurt the Mitre and the Crown.

Even more striking, for its explicit universalizing of the Caesars' values, is a poem by their neighbour Edward Cobden celebrating the opening of the Caesars' domestic chapel on their wedding anniversary in 1720. In the poem, Cobden addresses Mrs Caesar as 'so beautifull an Epitome of y^c Creation' and exhorts her 'to multiply such glorious Abridgements of y^c Universe' in her children. The bold stroke of dignifying such exemplary persons as 'Epitome' or 'Abridgement' of the world is highly significant, asserting that there is no general principle in nature not expressed in such distinguished adherents of the cause. To claim that the order of nature is fully expressed in Mary Caesar's beauty and fertility, her Anglican piety and her Jacobite commitment, is to close one's eyes both to a nature working itself out in a history which pushes the Caesars to its margins, and to the potential for relativism implicit in the fact that nature has produced Whigs as well as Tories. Yet for a writer rooted exclusively in one political tradition, the other can be excluded as mere perversion, with no claim to have nature behind it. For Mary Caesar and her friends, drawing on a Renaissance mode of courtly compliment which underlines their commitment to old ways, nature is imbued with values which reach their apex in a group of royal servants with the monarch at their centre. It is a view which banishes from sight not only the shortcomings of the great and the intransigence of destiny, but also the experience of behind-the-scenes uncertainty, negotiation and pragmatism, so familiar to many of Mary Caesar's most admired friends in life, but so thoroughly excluded in her presentation of them. The notion of an epitome or abridgement of nature seems to promise a straightforward concentration, the vital energies of nature focused in microcosm; but the art of abridgement practised in these poems and carried to its extreme in Mary Caesar's book amounts to the suppression of everything resistant to Jacobite idealism.

The fervour of this idealism is most impressively evoked when Mary Caesar recollects her only face-to-face meeting with a monarch of the Stuart line. Here her rhetoric meets its ultimate object, as the reader is presented with a verbal icon which radiates absolute and ineffable qualities:

> And tis as Impossible for me Even to Attempt the Beauties of that Excellent Queens Mind, as for Kneller to have Exprest the Gracefullnes of Her Motion, Which was Agreable in Every Action. Even to the Moveing Of Her Hand. And the Queens Walking. Stroke Not More Awe. then Her Speaking to me Gave joy and Pleasure, Which Revives with Thinking of It. Fancying I hear the Musick of Her Voice, for Such it Was when She Spoke. And Piety and Good Breading was So Intirely the Queens, that They Seem'd Allmost to Dye with Her.[43]

From the pen of a court poet such praise might fall with a somewhat hollow ring, especially when written of a woman whose first impression on the eye is one of bloated and unwieldy corpulence. But Mary Caesar does not pretend that the Queen was pretty or quick on her feet: like Prior, she follows the precept 'Forbear to Mention what thou Canst Not Praise'. In effect, her memory of the Queen fulfils the devotional function of renewing in the writer the pious transport of hearing the royal voice speaking personally to her. There is delightful spontaneity here, as her effort at recall breaks into a recollected joy, 'Which Revives with Thinking of It. Fancying I hear the Musick of Her Voice'. For the modern reader this is perhaps the most sympathetic instance of her capacity to see in monarchs, and by association in their servants, an incarnation of ultimate values.

But Queen Anne is dead, and as Mary Caesar says, 'Piety and Good Breading . . . Seem'd Allmost to Dye with Her'. In her book, which begins with a death and is, unknown to her, to end with the death of Charles Caesar himself, bereavement is never far away, and elegy is a dominant mode. It is the loss of a good man and his irreplaceable virtues that characteristically prompts her highest flights, flights which rekindle in her the ardour of devotion and shift the balance of emotion from lament to assurance. Her response to the death of Oxford at the beginning of her book had been to recount the high points of her married life to date, kindling with enthusiasm as she wrote. Similarly she responds to the last of her husband's political bereavements, the death of Lord Strafford in 1739. Strafford was one of the last survivors of her husband's colleagues from the reign of Anne.[44] Others found him stupid, proud and tedious; but to the Caesars he was forever dear as negotiator of the Peace of Utrecht and a loyal promoter of the Stuart cause:

> Mine alass Seems Nothing when Recollecting what I saw Mr Caesar felt when he told me he had Lost a True Friend, I soon guest the rest, that Death had now Seiz'd the Last Minister of Queen Ann his Great and Dear Friend the Earl of Strafford who had Abided with him On the Rock, no Storms nor Beatings of

the waters Could Tearify them, They Stood Firm and Unshaken Seaing Some Come from, Others go to the Crown. But the most Wonderfull was a set of Men, Not haveing Strength of Mind Longer there to Abide Looking Out. Saw a Bunch of White Feathars sproting On the surface of the Glittering Water that Gentlely Play'd att the foot of the Rock, thather they Flew, They Pursu'd (What) Rebellion in Every Light. Lord Strafford when takeing His Last leave of us, speaking of them with contempt smiling say'd to Mr Caesar, Our case is Very hard being forc'd to help support them against Sr Robert Walpole, who has not ill Nature annufe to Use Us so ill, as they would do if in Power. The Dutchis of Buckingham still when we meet Morn the Lose of the Agreabill Polite and Noble Earl of Strafford Ever Ready to Serve, with Head, Hand, and Heart.[45]

This bereavement, to which Mary Caesar responds characteristically by contemplating her husband's emotion, demands an unusual grandeur of commemoration, which she provides in the biblically resonant allegory of the rock. The white feathers allude to the insignia of the Prince of Wales, then the alternative focus to the Pretender for opposition to the government; and those who pursue them are rebels 'in Every Light' because they oppose not only 'James III' but also the king they have set up in his place. The image of the rock certainly communicates the heroism that Mrs Caesar sees in the loyalty of her husband and his colleague; but it also hints at something of the bleakness of their situation, as elderly men, once powerful but now at odds with those they feel ought to be their allies. In a paradoxical way, loss and exclusion are positively charged by the restatement of ideals which they evoke – from Mrs Caesar herself and from those whose words she incorporates into her lament. In effect, this remarkably, even wilfully, positive book draws its strength to a surprising extent from such elegiac affirmation, supported where possible by inspirational historical parallels and by the very few encouraging events that it falls to her share to record.

There are in fact two irreconcilable contours to the experiences recorded in Mary Caesar's book, which covers the period from 1724, when she was in her late forties, to shortly before her death in 1741. To the casual reader, susceptible to the affirmations contained in her elegies and unchallenging of the silences behind her weaving of encouraging associations, the book seems to proceed on a plateau of steadfast faith, varied only by the excitement of promising developments and the deferral of hope as, one by one, they peter out. The end of the book, an abrupt cry of anguish at Charles Caesar's death, comes as a shock for the reader. This impression of a plateau of faith is, in effect, strong testimony to Mary Caesar's ability to shape refractory experience into exemplary form; for, far from resting in serene expectation, the Caesars' fortunes took a downward curve from soon after the commencement of the book to their deaths, and although there were at times signs that recovery might be on the way, they were never permanently fulfilled. The extent to which Mary Caesar is able to resist recording this downward slide in her book is remarkable. Clearly, one of the functions of her writing is as a devotional activity for the sustenance of faith, and its success may be judged by her persistence in a positive engagement with the political process, and with her husband's part in it, which is only broken by his death. The utter desolation which then ensues marks the limitations of a faith sustained not so much by confrontation with loss and disillusion as by evasion of their threats.

Mary Caesar's strategies for maintaining the conviction of high destiny despite increasing difficulties can be appreciated by comparing the Caesars' fortunes as represented in her book with other sources. At first Oxford's death had meant promotion for Charles Caesar, who shared with Strafford and Orrery the management of the Pretender's affairs in England; but in 1729 Strafford and Orrery hinted to James that owing to crippling losses in South Sea stock it seemed possible that Caesar had taken bribes from Walpole; and after 1731 he is mentioned no more in the Stuart correspondence.[46] No mention of his debts, his exclusion from active Jacobite service or any suspicion of his associates' loyalty to him is made in Mary Caesar's book; and while she may not have fully understood the extent of his fall from favour, their poverty, along with his increasing ill health, was an ever-present anxiety. Still, however, she makes impressive use of her characteristic devotional strategies to light herself through periods of anguish hardly hinted at in her book. From outside sources we learn, for example, that in 1734 Charles Caesar came bottom of the poll, and having lost parliamentary privilege was imprisoned for debt. Typically, she not only found strength in the emblematic words of a Tory poet, but also enacted the kind of ritual sharing that figures so prominently in her writing. In this case, she found the mirror of her faith in the words of Lord Lansdowne:

> A Passage thear so reliv'd my mind, I rote it in my Pocket Book. Dineing that day at Mr Gors I show'd it Him and Mr Comptton, saying as the carecter Tallid so I hop'd Would the Event
> Vertue Like yours; Such Patience in Adversity
> And in Prosperity Such Goodnes
> Is Still the Care of Providence.[47]

Her prophetic appropriation of the lines seemed vindicated when in 1736 her husband's supporters secured his re-election to parliament – and hence his release from prison – at their own expense, news which even she admitted 'Could Carsly gane belefe'.[48] To her London home came visitors to report rejoicings 'beyond Imaganation' in the Hertfordshire constituency, where the absent Charles Caesar had been chaired by proxy; the streets had been illuminated even where his opponent's interest was strongest, and 'there Ceas'd not the Cry of Caesar For Ever Even from Children that Lispted it'. Mrs Caesar's delight in the triumph of the cause that she presents as so demonstrably dear to the people makes this one of the emotional high points of her book; and the coincidence of her husband's restoration to public life with increasing difficulties for Walpole filled her with hope; but when Walpole failed to fall she confessed:

> I Abridg'd the Afair of the Excise with all the Exactness I was Capable of. Thinking it Might have been the Cause of Some Great Revers. But Like Unto a Flash of Lightning the Spirits of the People Came and went . . .[49]

Typically, however, having paused briefly to blame the intrigues of 'Faulse Bretheren', she continues to follow the campaign against Walpole with enthusiasm apparently undiminished, making no allusion to her son's death, and referring to her husband's extremely poor health only to note his recovery and return to the House.[50] On the last New Year's Day of her life, 1 January 1741, faithful as ever to her sustaining hope, she exchanged epigrams with the young Lord Quarendon:

> The Dutchess of Buckingham Sending to Mr Caesar and I to Pass the First day of this Year 1741 at Buckingham House it gave me Pleasure and Pain for what is so Pleasing as to be distinguisht by Those One Highly Honners. and it floung my Mind Back On the Dismall 1641 which I thus Exprest
> Sad Forty One, Britton Still feels Her Crime,
> May This, Showr Blessings On Our Suffring Isle.
> Lord Quarendon thus Wrot Under.
> In Beter Times may matchless Caesar Sing
> Still live, to Love her Country – and her King.[51]

Later that year, however, Charles Caesar died, leaving a distraught widow and an estate ruined by debt.[52]

Beyond the pain of bereavement, Mrs Caesar had lost her vital link with the world of political action that had been crucial to her self-image throughout her married life. Again she turned to the Tory poets. On the last page of her book, without any transition from the parliamentary business which she had written up a few weeks previously, under the newspaper cutting reporting her husband's death, she has written with a shaking hand:

> Alas, there's no Expression
> To tell my Dismal Woe.[53]

At the bottom of the page she has added, 'DB page 189'; and if, following her hint, we turn to this page in the first volume of the Duke of Buckingham's *Works*, we find the conclusion of his lament 'On the Loss of an only Son, Robert Marquis of Normanby'.[54] The Duke has written, 'Alas, there's no Expression/Can tell a Parent's Woe!'; and Mrs Caesar, by echoing his lament over a child of Stuart blood, proclaims the inexpressibility of her emotion by a symbolic association with this cutting off of dynastic hope. It is a poignant reversal of the prophetic sharing of inspirational texts so often enacted in her book. Her principal sharer is dead, and the implicit faith that has previously irradiated her elegies no longer sustains her. Having arranged this painfully appropriate closure, she stops writing, abandons her files of correspondence, and abandons herself to grief.[55] Within three months she was dead.

Mary Caesar had once confided to the poet Mary Barber that she would have liked to write the history of her own times, no doubt envisaging a vindication of Tory truth from the calumnies of the Whig Gilbert Burnet.[56] The very notion of such a project suggests comparisons which help to define exactly what Mary Caesar was doing in the book that she did write. Whether we compare her writing with Burnet's *History* or – to take an example far more congenial to her – with Clarendon's *History of the Rebellion*, it is clear that these commentators are concerned to set before the reader a framework within which the details they record can be understood. This is something which in her private book Mary Caesar has no need to consider; yet the extreme allusiveness of her writing, which requires a high degree of familiarity with her subjects before it can be understood at all, suggests that the bent of her interest did not lie in the direction of large explanatory structures. The suspicion that the larger claims of generic history would have proved burdensome to her can also be related to the difference between the style she has evolved for herself and the more measured dignity of the professed historian. Even Burnet, who attempts nothing like the elaborate periods of Clarendon, was conscious of writing in a tradition which spurred him to emulation, paying particular attention to De Thou as his 'great Originall'; and even his relatively unpretending style breathes the assurance of one for whom the world of letters holds no terrors.[57] In comparison, Mary Caesar is acutely conscious of failure in even the most basic conventions of educated written usage. With her shorter-breathed style, closer to the spoken word, her strengths are less those of authoritative formulation and evaluation than of imaginative celebration. Although she writes in prose, she is more the court poet than the court historiographer, as she cherishes the symbolic act or the telling remark, drawing her material together not in a structure of analysis but in a series of passages, loosely connected at best, which kindle with the enthusiasm of her discovery of the archetypal patterns on which her royalist understanding of the world depends. This understanding of nature is itself a problem for a would-be historian, since it allows so much of the political process simply to be labelled as perversion and ignored as such. Her exceptional reluctance (even in comparison with Burnet or Clarendon) to acknowledge either the pragmatism of some of those who support her cause or the fears and grievances of those who oppose it suggests that as a historian she would offer little beyond interesting anecdote set in the frame of an intense but blinkered personal vision. Interestingly in this connection, she had herself little respect for generic history, preferring memoirs, as did many in an age that loved to stress how (in her words) 'things of little consequence in them Selves, are Sometimes the Cause of Great Events'.[58] In her characteristically elitist phrase, memoirs have the advantage of being 'Most Commonly wrote by such as have been intrusted', whereas mere 'Compilers of Histories' are 'forc'd to gather from such as know as little as does themselves, and Load it with words, to swell the Volume'.[59] It is noteworthy that both Clarendon and Burnet take pains at the outset to dispel any such suspicion, both, like Mary Caesar, using the notion of trust. Clarendon declares that he is not 'altogether an incompetent person', as he was both 'a member of Parliament in those councils before and till the breaking out of the Rebellion' and 'had the honour to be near two great kings in some trust'.[60] Burnet, for his part, claims, 'I have lived in such intimacy with all who have had the chief conduct of affairs, and have been so much trusted, and on so many important occasions employed by them, that I have been able to penetrate far into the true secrets of counsels and designs'.[61] Behind Mary Caesar's words to Mary Barber must have lain some similar sense of privilege which would set her above mere 'Compilers of Histories' and enable her to show the mysteries of political events in a true light.

Yet readers must surely wonder how far Mary Caesar really had penetrated 'the true secrets of counsels and designs', not only because as the wife of a politician rather than a politician herself she stood at one remove from the events and discussions that preoccupied her, but also because her single-minded idealism placed the whole realm of self-interested calculation and pragmatic ambiguity beyond her interpretative scope – except, of course, when dealing summarily with those, like Bolingbroke, who had definitively fallen from grace. Moreover, a position of trust in the Tory circles on which she looked back through the narrow focus of Jacobite commitment could only be exploited, under the Hanoverians, in a secret and dangerously treasonable kind of history. Mary Caesar would have needed a second restoration to make the history to which she had privileged access either publishable or convincingly central to national experience. Although both Clarendon and Burnet saw the tide turn against them in later life, neither lived to see his worst fears for the nation realized, and both had had the crucial experience of seeing their favourite candidate ascend the throne after years of threatening uncertainty. At least once they had been able to focus their idealism on actual moments when the nation had seemed to embrace their vision in the person of the monarch. For Mary Caesar, however, after the joy of her husband's appointment under Queen Anne, there is no focus for her vision which can be elaborated without taint of treason. She has no scene to rival Clarendon's celebration of the Restoration, only Lord Cowper's pious response to its typological representation in the hangings at her house at Benington. Instead of the coming together of disaffected aristocrats which had brought Burnet's beloved William to the throne, she could point only to plots which had brought her husband and friends into prison and into danger of their lives, without ever, in effect, bringing the Stuart heir she so idolized nearer to his goal.

Thus Mary Caesar lacked not only the literary assurance of the educated man, and the open-mindedness which would have enabled her to appreciate subtleties of motivation in friend or foe, but also the historical circumstances which would have allowed her to present her special knowledge as part of a public claim for the centrality of her political and ethical values. Yet to give prominence to these negatives is perhaps to accept too readily the primacy of the mode of formal history which, as far as we know, she never attempted. The woman who had confided to her book, 'Righting was Never my tallent, so allways avoid'd it. if possible', was probably all too aware of the obstacles. In effect, the private and devotional book that she did write has its own kind of achievement: in it she draws strength from her husband's legitimizing presence at its centre to express her idealism with confidence, strenuously shaping experience to fit the distinctive mould of her faith. In the note of celebration that rings out from her laments over deaths and defeats, and not least in the abrupt yet poignantly allusive abandonment to final despair which marks the limitations of such quasi-religious faith, she gives us a fascinating and moving insight into the fulfilments – and evasions – of the particular brand of Jacobite idealism she had forged for herself.

Notes

Introduction

1 Denise Riley, *'Am I That Name?'*
Feminism and the Category of
'Women' in History, Macmillan,
1988, p. 1.

Hobby

Thanks to Isobel Grundy and Sue
Wiseman for suggestions and
corrections; to Simon Shepherd for
countless relevant conversations;
and to Christine White for both
these kinds of help and so much
more.

1 William Brathwait, *The English*
Gentlewoman, 1632, p. 41.

2 Good general histories of these
developments include H. N.
Brailsford, *The Levellers and the*
English Revolution, Christopher
Hill, ed., The Cresset Press, 1961; C.
Hill, *The World Turned Upside*
Down: Radical Ideas During the
English Revolution, Penguin, 1974;
B. Coward, *The Stuart Age*,
Longman, 1980; J. F. McGregor and
Barry Reay, eds., *Radical Religion in*
the English Revolution, Oxford
University Press, 1984. For women's
position in the period, see Mary

Prior, ed., *Women in English Society*
1500–1800, Methuen, 1985; and
Antonia Fraser, *The Weaker Vessel:*
Women's Lot in Seventeenth-Century
England, Methuen, 1984 (this work,
whilst including much useful
material, is marred by the author's
inclination to believe that women
were as passive as law-makers and
conduct-book writers would
have them be). For details of
women petitioners, see note 11
and 12.

3 My figures differ from those of
Patricia Crawford, who sees the
1640s as a more significant
watershed. Although on the whole I
agree with her identifications of
women's texts in the period, I
believe the significance of her figures
is distorted by her listing only
numbers of texts published, not
numbers of authors. Of the texts she
identifies as published by women in
the 1640s, 51 were written by Lady
Eleanor Douglas, ten published as
the works of Queen Henrietta
Maria, and six were translations of
Marguerite de Valois.

4 Germaine Greer, Jeslyn Medoff,
Melinda Sansone and Susan

Hastings, eds., *Kissing the Rod: Seventeenth-century Women's Verse*, Virago, 1988, focuses on poetry; Moira Ferguson, ed., *First Feminists*, Indiana University Press, 1984, on 'feminists'. The introductions to both volumes go some way, however, towards alerting their readers to the wide range of other materials produced in the period.

5 For a more extended analysis of these features, see Elaine Hobby, *Virtue of Necessity: English Women's Writing, 1649–1688*, Virago, 1988.

6 Bradstreet's claim to be regarded as America's first poet is, for instance, taken for granted by Louise Bernikow in *The World Split Open: Women Poets 1552–1950*, The Women's Press, 1974. In *Virtue of Necessity*, I argue that the existence of Philips's 1650s published poems suggests that she was not as averse to publication as is usually claimed. Other published poems of the decade include books by An Collins, Elizabeth Major and the anonymous *Eliza's Babes* poet (see below); Anna Weamys's *A Continuation of . . . Arcadia*, 1651; and a song by Mary Oxlie in William Drummond's *Poems*, 1656, and one by Mary Knight in Henry Lawes's *The Second Book of Ayres*, 1655.

7 The question of whether women's subordination was natural or desirable was a popular topic of learned or ironic debate amongst men in the period. The many published discussions include William Austin, *Haec Homo*, 1637; Charles Gerbier, *Elogium Heroinum*, 1651; Thomas Heywood, *The Generall History of Women*, 1657; William Hill, *A New-Years-Gift for Women*, 1660.

8 Amongst her detractors were Henry More, William Waller and Dorothy Osborne. See my *Virtue of Necessity*, p. 131.

9 The Marquess of Newcastle himself seems to have gone to considerable lengths to defend his wife's writing, and dedicatory epistles by him in praise of her preface many of her works. It would therefore be wrong to assume that she perceived him as an obstacle to her writing and intellectual endeavours, though it would also be naive to assume (as many have) that, just because they both published assertions of his support, that was the end of the matter. A husband's support, or the approval of some other male authority, was extremely useful in persuading the reader to accept a woman's publishing. On the specific inflection given to the word 'fame' by Margaret Cavendish, see also Jean Gagen, 'Honor and Fame in the Works of the Duchess of Newcastle', *Studies in Philology*, 56, 1959, pp. 519–38.

10 Cavendish's critics, including her biographers Douglas Grant, Kathleen Jones and Sara Mendelson, have been too ready to read her statements as naively self-revealing, allowing little scope for her attempts to manipulate her reader so as to make her writing for publication less unacceptable. (Grant, *Margaret the First: A Biography of Margaret Cavendish Duchess of Newcastle*, Rupert Hart-Davis, 1957; Jones, *A Glorious Fame: The Life of Margaret Cavendish, Duchess of Newcastle, 1623–1673*, Bloomsbury, 1988; Mendelson, *The Mental World of Stuart Women: Three Studies*, Harvester, 1987.) This 'transparent' reading of Cavendish commonly extends to reading the

statements of her fictional
characters, especially those of her
philosophical virgins in her *Playes
and Orations* and of her letter-
writers in *CCXI Sociable Letters*, as
if they give direct access to the
author's opinions and experiences.
For a more extended discussion of
this problem, see Elaine Hobby,
'The Fame of the Honest Margaret
Cavendish' (unpublished MA
dissertation, University of Essex,
1979); and S. Findley and E. Hobby,
'Seventeenth-Century Women's
Autobiography', in Francis Barker,
ed., *1642: Literature and Power in
the Seventeenth Century*, University
of Essex, 1981.
11 See Ellen MacArthur, 'Women
Petitioners and the Long
Parliament', *English Historical
Review*, 24, 1909; Patricia Higgins,
'The Reactions of Women, with
Special Reference to Women
Petitioners', in Brian Manning, ed.,
*Politics, Religion and the English
Civil War*, Edward Arnold, 1973.
Mass political petitions presented by
women to Parliament during the
decade include *To the Parliament
. . . the humble petition of . . .
women*, 1653; *To the Supreme
Authority . . . severall Wives and
Children*, 1650; *These several
Papers*, 1659; *Unto every individual
Member . . . Women-Petitioners*,
1653; *The Womens Petition*, 1651.
12 Those who published petitions
for restitution of property or the
resolution of other personal
grievances were Mary Alexander,
Susannah Bastwick, Margaret Beck,
Mary Blaithwaite, Frances Clarke,
Anne Henshaw, Rebecca, Lady
Jermyn, Anne Levington, Mary
Love, Katherine Pettus, Anne Smyth,
Margaret Somerset, Katherine Stone
and Mary Walker. Between them
they spanned the political spectrum.

Many of these petitions were not
entirely women's writing, since they
were drafted by lawyers on the basis
of information provided by the
women. For further details, see my
unpublished Ph.D. thesis, 'English
Women's Writing, 1649–1688',
University of Birmingham, 1984. Far
more petitions in defence of
individual women and their families
were presented to Parliament than
were ever published: see the relevant
volumes of the *Commons' Journals*
for details.
13 'Assaulted and pursued chastity',
in *Natures Pictures*. The reversal is
not quite as abrupt as this summary
would suggest, since the heroine and
her women soldiers first conquer the
man's army.
14 *The Worlds Olio*, sig. A5; see
also Anna Maria van Schurman,
The Learned Maid, 1659, which also
assumes that women worthy of
being educated must be financially
secure.
15 T. O'Malley, ' "Defying the
Powers and Tempering the Spirit":
A Review of Quaker Control over
their Publications 1672–1689', *The
Journal of Ecclesiastical History*, 33,
1982.
16 She was a noted prophet during
the 1630s, apparently moving freely
in court circles. Having successfully
predicted the death of the Duke of
Buckingham and of both her
husbands, she ran into trouble,
however, when she began to
prophesy the overthrow of Charles
I. Much of the rest of her life was
spent in prison, her release being
obtained on at least two occasions
after petitions were presented by her
daughter, Lucy, Countess of
Huntingdon. See Christopher
Hindle, *A Bibliography of the
Printed Pamphlets and Broadsides of
Lady Eleanor Douglas*, Edinburgh

Bibliographical Society, 2nd edition, 1936.

17 For this practice, see M. Plant, *The English Book Trade*, Allen and Unwin, 3rd edition, 1974, p. 144; and F. Siebert, *Freedom of the Press in England, 1476–1776*, Illinois University Press, 1952. The suggestion that *The Appearance* has been deliberately destroyed is a speculation, based on the facts that only one copy of it survives, and that that copy is a partial one, breaking off where I indicate. It seems to be the only one of her texts so mutilated, and is alone in its apparent assertion of the author's own divinity. I have not, however, traced any record of a prosecution over this specific pamphlet.

18 See also Anna Trapnel, *A Voice for the King of Saints*, where the author presents herself as Christ's spouse.

19 McGregor and Reay, p. 19.

20 This summary is an over-generalization about the women who wrote religio-political pamphlets. Amongst the first women to enter this arena was Mary Pope, who was firmly opposed to the radicals, and throughout the Interregnum some women wrote to oppose millenarian positions.

21 Her experiences are described in *Anna Trapnel's Report and Plea*, part of which is published in *Her Own Life: Autobiographical Writings by Seventeenth-Century Englishwomen*, ed. Elspeth Graham, Hilary Hinds, Elaine Hobby and Helen Wilcox, Routledge, 1989.

22 Dorothy Waugh's experiences are described by her in 'A Relation', in *The Lambs Defence*, 1656.

23 See, for instance, Sarah Blackborow, *A Visit to the Spirit in Prison*, 1658, and *Herein is held forth the Gift*, 1659; Margret

Lynam, *For the Parliament*, 1659; Rebeckah Travers, *For Those that meet to Worship*, 1659.

24 Hill, op. cit., p. 99.

25 Elizabeth Hooton *et al.*, *False Prophets and False Teachers*, 1652, p. 1.

26 *These several Papers*, 1659.

27 For a similar use of imagery, see also Hester Biddle, *Wo to thee City of Oxford* and *Wo to thee Towne of Cambridge*; Anna Trapnel, *Anna Trapnel's Report and Plea*.

28 Similar arguments are made in many Quaker pamphlets, including Richard Farnworth, *A Woman forbidded to speak in the Church*, 1654, and in the collectively written *The Saints Testimony*. This twist at the priest's expense, though, is Cotton and Cole's, perhaps drawing on the tendency in the Book of Isaiah to speak of weak or ineffectual men as women (Isaiah 3.12; 19.16).

29 The most extended example is Anna Trapnel, *A Legacy for Saints*, 1654.

30 In accounting for these developments simply in terms of the activities of sectaries, I am oversimplifying: the decade also saw Catholic works by Saint Bridget and Gertrude More. Also, sectaries' works were not confined to conversion narratives. In 1650, for example, Frances Cooke published an account of her near-death in a storm at sea, justifying her incursion into print by explaining that she had promised God to 'studie to glorifie his Name all the dayes of my life' if he saved her (p. 2): 'I know it is a great mercy to blesse God for mercies, and they which have a heart to bless God for his mercies, ought to have a tongue to prayse him for the same, and a pen to record them' (p. 3).

31 The term 'natural and legall
estate' was commonly used to
describe those people whom
sectaries perceived as still ruled by
the Ten Commandments (the Law,
hence 'legal estate'), and in a state of
natural sin, who have not yet
accepted Christ as their saviour (or
not been accepted by God). There is
an extract from Parr's work in
Graham *et al.* eds., *Her Own Life.*
See also John Rogers, *Ohel or Beth-
shemesh*, 1653, p. 349: 'The Church
must bee satisfied that they are
Beleevers, and in the true faith of
our Lord Jesus, whereof every
member whom they admit, doe give
in some evidences, or make some
account, or other'.
32 See O. Watkins, *The Puritan
Experience: Studies in Spiritual
Autobiography*, Schoken,
1972.
33 Her criticisms of Quakers were
answered by Edward Burrough in
*Something in answer to . . . Jane
Turner*, 1654.
34 She had entered the public eye
before, in 1647, when Henry Jessey's
account of her trances was
published as his *The Exceeding
Riches of Grace.*
35 Published in Edmund Calamy,
The Godly Man's Ark, 1656. For a
more detailed discussion of the male
prefaces to these works, see *Virtue
of Necessity*, chapter 2.
36 In general, the materials
discussed in section two of the essay
were written by Quakers, the
materials in section three by
Baptists, but this is an
oversimplification.
37 Hilda Smith's otherwise
interesting *Reason's Disciples:
Seventeenth-Century English
Feminists*, University of Illinois
Press, 1982, is marred by precisely
this mistake.

Medoff

Versions of this essay were delivered
at the annual meetings of the
Northeast Modern Language
Association, March 1988, and the
Modern Language Association,
December 1988.
1 [Edmund Curll, ed.],
*Miscellanea. In Two Volumes . . .
Viz I Familar Letters Written to
Henry Cromwell, Esq; by Mr. Pope
. . . III Letters from Mr. Dryden, to
a Lady, in the Year 1699*, E. Curll,
1727, vol. I, p. 151; repr. in Charles
Ward, ed., *The Letters of John
Dryden*, Duke University Press,
1942, p. 127.
2 Jeremy Collier, *A Short View Of
The Immorality, and Profaneness of
the English Stage*, S. Keble, R. Sare
and J. Hindmarsh, 1698, p. 145.
3 Matthew Prior, 'A Satyr on the
Modern Translators, 1684', *Poems
on Affairs of State*, 1697, vol. I, p.
207.
4 For Burnet's admonition, see his
letter to Wharton, 14 December
1682, in Pierre Bayle *et al.*, *A
General Dictionary, Historical and
Critical*, 10 vols., J.J. and P.
Knapton, *et al.*, 1734–41, vol. X, p.
126. Less than seven years after this
condemnation, the political tide had
turned, Burnet and the Whigs were
in power and Behn (a Tory) was
indigent and ill. The soon-to-be
Bishop of Salisbury advised Behn to
compose verses welcoming William
and Mary. In spite of initial protests
expressed in 'A Pindaric Poem to the
Reverend Doctor Burnet', Behn did
follow his suggestion to the extent
of writing a congratulatory poem to
Queen Mary. See Germaine Greer,
ed., *The Uncollected Verse of Aphra
Behn*, Stump Cross Books, 1989, pp.
159–62.
5 Robert Gould, 'The Poetess. A

Satyr', *Works*, (1709); quoted in Maureen Duffy, *The Passionate Shepherdess: Aphra Behn 1640–1689*, Avon Books, 1979, p. 280. *Punk* meant *prostitute*.

6 Feminist critics have noted that Harold Bloom's concept of 'the anxiety of influence' is predicated on a patriarchal understanding of the canon, a view which requires major rethinking or 're-visionary rereading' when considered in relation to women's writing. See Sandra M. Gilbert and Susan Gubar, *The Madwoman in the Attic: The Woman Writer and the Nineteenth-Century Literary Imagination*, Yale University Press, 1979, pp. 46–53; and Annette Kolodny, 'A map for Rereading: Gender and the Interpretation of Literary Texts', in Elaine Showalter, ed., *The New Feminist Criticism: Essays on Women, Literature, and Theory*, Pantheon Books, 1985, pp. 46–62. Ann Rosalind Jones's work on Renaissance women writers and fame has been influential on the present study, particularly 'Surprising Fame: Renaissance Gender Ideologies and Women's Lyric', in Nancy K. Miller, ed., *The Poetics of Gender*, Columbia University Press, 1986, pp. 74–95. Dorothy Mermin's important essay, 'Women Becoming Poets: Katherine Philips, Aphra Behn, Anne Finch', *ELH*, 57.2, Summer 1990, pp. 335–55, appeared after this essay was submitted to the publisher.

7 The use of battle imagery in poems praising women writers has been examined in Jane Spencer, *The Rise of the Woman Novelist: From Aphra Behn to Jane Austen*, Blackwell, 1986, pp. 26–7.

8 Abraham Cowley, *The Second and Third Parts of the Works of Mr. Abraham Cowley . . . The Third containing His Six Books of Plants, Never Before Published in English*, Charles Harper, 1689, p. 143. Behn translated part of this, inserting a section in which 'The Translatress in her own Person speaks'.

9 The elegy is reprinted in Germaine Greer, Susan Hastings, Jeslyn Medoff and Melinda Sansone, eds., *Kissing the Rod: An Anthology of Seventeenth-Century Women's Verse*, Virago, 1988, pp. 267–70. See Mary Ann O'Donnell, *Aphra Behn: An Annotated Bibliography of Primary and Secondary Sources*, Garland, 1986, p. 340, and Rosemary Foxton, 'Delariviere Manley and "Astraea's Vacant Throne"', *Notes and Queries*, 33.1, March 1986, pp. 41–2.

10 'To the Excellent *Orinda*', *Poems by the most deservedly Admired Mrs Katherine Philips The matchless Orinda*, H. Herringman, 1667, sig. a4–a4.

11 [Elizabeth Thomas], *Miscellany Poems on Several Subjects*, Thomas Combes, 1722, pp. 273–80. Subsequent references will be made within the text.

12 For a discussion of women writers of this period and their publication histories, see the introduction to Greer *et al.*, pp. 1–30. See also Elaine Hobby, 'Discourse so unsavoury' in this collection; and her *Virtue of Necessity: English Women's Writing 1649–1688*, Virago, 1988.

13 'To Mrs Jane Barker, On Her Ingenious Poems', in Jane Barker *et al.*, *Poetical Recreations: Consisting of Original Poems, Songs, Odes, &c. With Several New Translations In Two Parts*, Benjamin Crayle, 1688, sig. a^v.

14 Abraham Cowley, 'Upon Mrs

Philips Her Poems', in *Poems by the most deservedly Admired Mrs Katherine Philips The matchless Orinda*, H. Herringman, 1667, [sig. a3].

15 Jane Barker, 'Poems on several occasions, in three parts. The first refering to the times. The second, are poems writ since the author was in France, or at least most of them. The third, are taken out of a miscellany heretofore printed, and writ by the same author', Magdalen College Library MS 343, Oxford University. The quotations are taken from an unfoliated title-page to the third section of the manuscript.

16 Jane Barker, *Love Intrigues: Or, The History Of The Armours Of Bosvil and Galesia*, E. Curll, 1713; *Exilius, Or, The Banish'd Roman*, E. Curll, 1715; *A Patch-Work Screen for The Ladies*, E. Curll, 1723; *The Lining of the Patch-Work Screen*, A. Bettesworth, 1726. Barker's dissociation from Behn has been noted in Janet Todd, *The Sign of Angellica: Women, Writing and Fiction, 1660–1800*, Virago, 1989, pp. 50–1.

17 [Edmund Curll, ed.], *Miscellanea*, vol. I, sig. A4.

18 Thomas's reputation is discussed in Joanna Lipking, 'Fair Originals: Women Poets in Male Commendatory Poems', *Eighteenth Century Life*, new series 12.2, May 1988, pp. 58–72; and T. R. Steiner, 'Young Pope in the Correspondence of Henry Cromwell and Elizabeth Thomas ("Curll's Corinna")' and 'The Misrepresentation of Elizabeth Thomas, "Curll's Corinna"', *Notes and Queries*, new series 30, December 1983, pp. 495–7; 506–8.

19 Anon., *The Session of the Poets, Holden at the Foot of Parnassus-Hill, July the 9th. 1696*, E[lizabeth] Whitlock, 1696, pp. 39, 40–1, 43.

20 Both Etherege's and Behn's comedies were presented at Drury Lane a few weeks before the publication of the essay: Donald F. Bond, ed., *The Spectator*, Clarendon Press, 1965, vol. I, pp. 216–19.

21 Henry Grove and Theophilus Rowe, eds., *The Miscellaneous Works in Prose and Verse of Mrs Elizabeth Rowe. The Greater Part now first published, by her Order, from her Original Manuscripts*, R. Hett, 1739. Subsequent references will be cited within the text as 'Rowe'. Thomas Birch, ed., *The Works of Mrs Catherine Cockburn, Theological, Moral, Dramatic, and Poetical*, 2 vols., J. and P. Knapton, 1751. Subsequent references will be cited within the text as 'Birch'. Rowe's poems have recently been republished in Madeleine Forell Marshall, *The Poetry of Elizabeth Singer Rowe*, Studies in Women and Religion 25, Edwin Mellen Press, 1987.

22 [Catharine Trotter], *Olinda's Adventures: Or the Amours of a Young Lady*, in *Letters of Love and Gallantry and Several Other Subjects. All written by Ladies*, Samuel Briscoe, 1693. The 1718 edition has been printed in facsimile with an introduction by Robert Adams Day, Augustan Reprint Society no. 138 (William Andrews Clark Memorial Library, University of California, Los Angeles, 1969). Thomas Southerne acknowledged his debt to Behn's *The History of the Nun: Or, The Fair Vow-Breaker* in his dedication of *The Fatal Marriage: or, The Innocent Adultery*, Jacob Tonson, 1694; and to both *The History of the Nun* and Behn's *Oroonoko* in his dedication of *Oroonoko: A Tragedy*, H. Playford, B. Tooke, and S. Buckley, 1696.

23 *Agnes de Castro, A Tragedy*, H.

Rhodes, R. Parker, S. Briscoe, 1696, [A2]. Trotter's plays are published in facsimile in Edna L. Steeves, ed., *The Plays of Mary Pix and Catharine Trotter*, 2 vols., Garland, 1982.
24 BL Add. MS 4264, fol. 265. Subsequent references to Add. MSS 4264 and 4265, part of Thomas Birch's collection, will be cited within the text. Vol. 4264 contains four letters to Trotter signed 'E.B.', ff. 261–8.
25 Letter from Elizabeth Burnet to John Locke, 20 June 1702, E. S. De Beer, ed., *The Correspondence of John Locke*, 8 vols. incomplete, Clarendon Press, 1976– , vol. VII, p. 638. Subsequent references to the correspondence will be cited within the text as *Correspondence*.
26 [Catharine Trotter], 'To Mrs Manley. By the Author of *Agnes de Castro*', in Delarivier Manley, *The Royal Mischief. A Tragedy*, R. Bentley, F. Saunders, J. Knapton, 1696, [sig. A3ᵛ].
27 Evidence of Trotter's collaboration with Manley on assembling *The Nine Muses* exists in Lady Sarah Piers's undated letter to Trotter, BL Add. MS 4264, fol. 324.
28 C. E. Doble, ed., *Remarks and Collections of Thomas Hearne*, Oxford, 1885–1921, vol. II, p. 292; quoted in Gwendolyn Needham, 'Mrs Manley: An Eighteenth Century Wife of Bath', *Huntington Library Quarterly*, 14, 1951, p. 259.
29 John Oldmixon, *The Court of Atalantis, Intermixt with Fables and Epistles in Verse and Prose, By Several Hands*, 1714; reissued as *Court Tales*, 1717; quoted in Patricia Köster, ed., *The Novels of Mary Delariviere Manley*, 2 vols., Scholars' Facsimiles and Reprints, 1971, vol. I, pp. xxv–xxvi.
30 Lady Mary Wortley Montagu wote in 1709 that Manley would prove a scarecrow to other writers. See Robert Halsband, ed., *The Complete Letters of Lady Mary Wortley Montagu*, 3 vols., Clarendon Press, 1965–7, vol. I, pp. 15–16. Pope in 1733 got his friend Lord Peterborough to disavow his insult to Lady Mary which linked the pox and libelling, as applicable only to such as 'Mrs Centlivre, Mrs Heywood, Mrs Manley and Mrs Been' (*Complete Letters*, vol. II, p. 97). For an examination of the way Manley shaped her public and literary personae, see Carol Barash, 'Gender, Authority and the "Life" of an Eighteenth-Century Woman Writer: Delariviere Manley's *Adventures of Rivella*', *Women's Studies International Forum*, 10.2, 1987, pp. 165–9.
31 [Delarivier Manley], *Memoirs of Europe, Towards the Close of the Eighth Century*, 2 vols., John Morphew, 1710, vol. I, p. 289.
32 [W. M.], *The Female Wits; or, The Triumvirate of Poets at Rehearsal*, W. Turner, 1704; repr. Fidelis Morgan, ed., *The Female Wits: Women Playwrights of the Restoration*, Virago, 1981, p. 392. The play has also been reprinted by the Augustan Reprint Society with an introduction by Lucyle Hook (no. 124, William Andrews Clark Memorial Library, University of California at Los Angeles, 1967).
33 [George Powell?], *Animadversions on Mr. Congreve's Late Answer to Mr. Collier*, John Nutt, 1698, A4v–A5. In the seventeenth century, to 'flant' meant both 'to flaunt' and 'to wave a plume proudly'.
34 Catharine Trotter, *Fatal Friendship. A Tragedy*, Francis Saunders, 1698, A2v.

35 Anon., *A Letter to Mr. Congreve on his Pretended Amendments, etc. of Mr. Collier's Short View*, Samuel Keble, 1698, p. 36. I am grateful to Professor Kendall of Smith College for this information.

36 Catharine Trotter, *The Unhappy Penitent. A Tragedy*, William Turner and John Nutt, 1701, A4ᵛ.

37 William Forbes, ed., *An Account of the Life and Writings of James Beattie*, 2 vols., Archibald Constable, 1806, vol. II, pp. 243–4.

38 For a discussion of Cockburn's adoption of the role of 'good author', see Margaret J. M. Ezell's study of seventeenth-century women's writings, *The Patriarch's Wife: Literary Evidence and the History of the Family*, University of North Carolina Press, 1987, pp. 94–5.

39 Birch's notes and miscellaneous memoranda for Cockburn's works include the following entry, dated 9 July 1751 (three months after publication of the *Works*): 'Intended to have been publish'd in the *Edit.* of Mʳˢ Cockburns Works, projected in 1728. Letters between her & Mʳ Langham Edwards, Gentleman Usher to the late King, & Brother of Tho. Edwards Esq.' (BL Add. MS 4244, fol. 51). A copy of an undated letter from the Reverend Patrick Cockburn to an unknown addressee discusses his wife's plan to publish her collected works (BL Add. MS 4265, ff. 108–9).

40 Cockburn called the revised version 'The Honourable Deceivers'. Though Birch mentions the revision in his biography and records a manuscript copy in his notes, it has not yet been located. See Birch, vol. I, p. ix; BL Add. MS 4264, fol. 2; BL Add. MS 4265, ff. 108–109.

41 Among Birch's notes appears a list of queries, including questions about works he intended to omit or not mention. Here we find, in his hand, 'Life of Olinda'. See BL Add. MS 4265, fol. 43.

42 BL Add. MS 4264, ff. 271–2. See also ff. 269–70, 273–4, 333. The letters of Sarah, Lady Piers to Trotter, dating from Trotter's early appearance on the London scene in the mid-1690s and continuing until 1709, attest to a deep and passionate friendship and provide valuable information on the ways women poets supported each other's work (BL Add. MS 4264, ff. 284–338). The correspondence is discussed in Jeslyn Medoff, 'After Aphra: Women Writers and Their Public Personae 1660–1740' (in progress).

43 Robert Adams Day, *Told in Letters: Epistolary Fiction Before Richardson*, University of Michigan Press, 1966, p. 187; Fidelis Morgan, ed., *The Female Wits*, Virago, 1981, p. 31; Kendall, *Love and Thunder: Plays By Women in the Age of Queen Anne*, Methuen, 1988, p. 138.

44 John Duncombe, *The Feminiad: Or, Female Genius. A Poem*, M. Cooper, 1754, pp. 14–15.

45 Forbes, vol. II, pp. 243–4.

46 Sarah Hale, *Woman's Record*, Harper & Brothers, 1872, p. 265.

47 John Doran, *Annals of the English Stage*, ed. and rev. Robert W. Lowe, 3 vols., John C. Nimmo, 1888, vol. I, p. 242.

48 [Elizabeth Singer], *Poems on Several Occasions by Philomela*, John Dunton, 1696.

49 Rowe's editors noted, 'The last of her writings, which, by her consent, appeared in the public under her own name, were some copies of verses printed in the Miscellanies, in the year 1704' (Rowe, vol. I, pp. lxix–lxx). They refer to *Poetical Miscellanies: The Fifth Part*, Jacob Tonson, 1704, pp.

195–7; 337–4; 371–88; 484–94. The editors were apparently unaware that two of Singer's poems were identified as the work of 'Mrs Singer' in *A Collection of Divine Hymns And Poems On Several Occasions*, J. Baker, 1709, pp. 35–42; 110–15. For a list of each of Singer's known poems and their appearance in various miscellanies and editions of Rowe's works, see Henry F. Stecher, *Elizabeth Singer Rowe, the Poetess of Frome: A Study in Eighteenth Century Pietism*, Lang, 1973, pp. 230–4. Stecher has observed that Isaac Watts, who edited Rowe's posthumously published *Devout Exercises of the Heart* (1737) at her request, was also sensitive to the task of reinforcing her reputation (pp. 92–3).

50 John Dunton, *The Life and Errors of John Dunton, Late Citizen of London; Written by Himself in Solitude. With an idea of a New Life*, S. Malthus, 1705, p. 245.

51 John Dunton, *Athenianism: Or, The New Projects of Mr John Dunton*, John Morphew, 1710, p. 23.

52 The threatening letter to Dunton by one 'J.W.', possibly Isaac Watts, dated 5 November 1718, is reproduced in John Nichols, ed., *The Life and Errors of John Dunton, Citizen of London*, J. Nichols, Son, and Bentley, 1818, vol. I, pp. xxix–xxx.

53 'A Poetical Question Concerning the Jacobites', *Athenian Mercury*, 29 May 1694, vol. 14, no. 3. See also *Poems on Several Occasions*, part I, p. 27.

54 'To Celinda', *Athenian Mercury*, 28 September 1695, vol. 18, no. 22. See also *Poems on Several Occasions*, part II, p. 27.

55 *Athenian Mercury*, 18 June 1695, vol. 17, no. 23. See also *Poems on*

Several Occasions, part II, pp. 6–8.

56 [Elizabeth Rowe], *Philomela: Or, Poems By Mrs Elizabeth Singer [now Rowe] of Frome in Somersetshire . . . The Second Edition*, E. Curll, 1737, p. [xx]. Some of Singer's early poems were available in the early part of the century through the *Athenian Oracle*, a republication of most of the material in the *Athenian Mercury* (four volumes in various editions, 1703–1728).

57 'Verses, occasion'd by the Busts in the Queen's Hermitage, and Mr Duck being appointed Keeper of the Library in Merlin's Cave', *The Gentleman's Magazine*, May 1737, vol. VII, p. 308. See also Birch, vol. II, pp. 572–4, for a revised version.

58 Myra Reynolds, ed., *The Poems of Anne Finch, Countess of Winchilsea*, University of Chicago Press, 1903, p. 6.

Barash

1 Abel Boyer, *The History of the Reign of Queen Anne, Digested into Annals. Year the First*, A. Roper and F. Coggan, 1703, p. 78.

2 For two accounts of the myth of the Amazons, see Page Dubois, *Centaurs and Amazons: Women and the Prehistory of the Great Chain of Being*, University of Michigan, Ann Arbor, 1982; and William Blake Tyrrell, *Amazons: A Study in Athenian Mythmaking*, Johns Hopkins University, Baltimore, 1984. For a discussion of how this mythology is reworked in seventeenth-century literature, see Simon Shepherd, *Amazons and Warrior Women*, St Martins, 1981. Antonia Fraser claims erroneously, in *The Warrior Queens*, Knopf, New York, 1989, pp. 24–5, that Queen Anne was not figured as a

warrior woman.

3 Susanna Centlivre, dedication to *The Platonick Lady*, J. Knapton, 1707, sig. A2v.

4 Sarah Fyge Egerton, 'The Essay, Addressed to the Illustrious prince and Duke of Marlboro [i.e. Marlborough] after the long Campaign, 1708', Henry E. Huntington Library, MS EL 8796. Quoted with the kind permission of the Huntington Library.

5 Elizabeth Elstob, trans. and ed., Madeleine de Scudéry, *An Essay Upon Glory*, J. Morphew, 1708.

6 On Anne as Augustan monarch, see Howard Erskine-Hill, *The Augustan Idea in English Literature*, Edward Arnold, 1983, pp. 238–41; and Howard D. Weinbrot, *Augustus Caesar in 'Augustan' England*, Princeton University Press, 1978, especially p. 51, where he claims that the Augustan ideal gained strength under Anne.

7 Catharine (Trotter) Cockburn, 'On His Grace the Duke of Marlborough after his Victory at Blenheim, 1704', in Thomas Birch, ed., *Works by Mrs. Catherine Cockburn, Theological, Moral, Dramatic and Poetical*, J. and P. Knapton, 1751, vol. II, pp. 561–4.

8 Catharine Trotter [Cockburn], *The Revolution of Sweden*, James Knapton and George Strahan, 1706, sig. A4v.

9 Edward Gregg, *Queen Anne*, Ark, 1980, pp. 297–300. For a discussion of the ways in which Anne is attacked as a woman after 1709, and of Delarivier Manley's defence of Anne's political authority as part of her challenge to other women's pattern of constructing mythical female communities around the queen, see Carol Barash, *Augustan Women's Mythmaking: Women Writers and the Body of*

Monarchy, 1660–1720 (Princeton Ph.D. Dissertation, University Microfilms International, 1989), chapter 7.

10 Catherine Gallagher, 'Embracing the Absolute: The Politics of the Female Subject in Seventeenth-Century England', *Genders*, vol. 1, 1988, p. 25.

11 Egerton's *Poems* (1703) were dedicated to Charles Montagu, Earl of Halifax, a Whig minister; for more information on Halifax see note 32, below.

12 This is also true of the career of Catharine Trotter Cockburn; for a discussion of Cockburn's shifting political alliances, see Barash, *Augustan Women's Mythmaking*, pp. 341–7.

13 For a discussion of this contradiction in Astell's writings, see Ruth Perry, *The Celebrated Mary Astell*, University of Chicago, 1986, chapter 6; and for a theory of interpretation based on the inherent conflicts within 'ideology', see John B. Thompson, *Studies in the Theory of Ideology*, Polity, Cambridge, 1984.

14 For instance, Moira Ferguson's *First Feminists: British Women Writers 1578–1799*, Indiana University and Feminist Press, Bloomington, IN and Old Westbury, NY, 1985, by taking the 'feminist' bits of women's writing out of their original contexts, tends to reduce all women's writing to one political position, minimizing conflicts within individual texts and particularly among eighteenth-century women themselves.

15 Rachel Weil, 'And Women Rule Over Them: Sexual Ideology and Political Propaganda in England, 1680–1720' (Ph.D. dissertation, Princeton University, 1990). Although her death seems to have

goaded many women into print, Mary seems not to have been a significant influence on women writers during her lifetime; see Barash, pp. 302–308.

16 Cases can also be made for an increase in women's published writings in other politically pivotal years, like the 1640s, 1650s (above, p. 16) and 1680s; I am interested here in specific patterns initiated between 1695 and 1708.

17 On the 'female signature', see Nancy K. Miller, *Subject to Change: Reading Feminist Writing*, Columbia University Press, New York, 1988, especially pp. 14–17, 69–76 and 230–61; in the late seventeenth and early eighteenth centuries, however, men also write 'as women', suggesting that the female voice is in this period a privileged position from which to address certain issues.

18 See, for example, Delarivier Manley, *The Secret History of Queen Zarah and the Zarazians*, not paginated, 1705, p. 24; and Sarah Churchill, *An Account of the Conduct of the Duchess Dowager of Marlborough*, J. Bettenham for G. Hawkins, 1742, pp. 116–17.

19 For depictions of Mary as obedient wife, see Edward Howard, 'Pastoral Elegy on the Death of the Late Queen', published with his *Essay Upon Pastoral*, R. Simpson, 1695; translation of Latin epigraph to Mary II, Bodleian MS. Eng. Poet. F.13, fol. 74v; Gilbert Burnet, *History of His Own Time*, vol. II, Joseph Downing and Henry Woodfall, 1724, pp. 48–9; 55; 133–4; 137–8 and *passim*; and for Anne as bodily and/or maternal, David Hamilton, *The Diary of Sir David Hamilton*, Clarendon, Oxford, 1975; Delarivier Manley, *Secret Memoirs and Manners . . . from the New*

Atalantis, J. Morphew, 1709; and Jonathan Swift, *A Modest Enquiry into the Reasons of Joy Express'd by a Certain Sett of People, Upon the Spreading of a Report of Her Majesty's Death*, J. Morphew, 1714, all of which suggest that although her propagandists depict her as mother of church and state, the queen is physically dependent upon her closest advisors and therefore vulnerable to their manipulations. For a longer discussion of these matters, see Barash, chapter 7.

20 Several of the manuscript speeches in the British Library are in the queen's hand and many others have her corrections and changes; also see B. Curtis Brown, *Letters of Queen Anne*, Cassell, 1935, p. xii.

21 Delarivier Manley, *The Old and True Way of Manning the Fleet . . .*, J. Morphew, 1704.

22 See speeches of 27 February and 25 May 1702, in *A Collection of all Her Majesty's Speeches, Messages, Etc. from her Happy Accession to the Throne to the 21st June 1712*, 1712.

23 Chudleigh's *The Ladies Defence: or, the 'Bride-Womans Counseller'*, answer'd, John Deeve, 1701, was a reply to a 1699 sermon by John Sprint which advocated wives' complete subjection to their husbands; Egerton responds to [Robert Gould], *Love Given O're: or, a Satyr Against the Pride, Lust and Inconstancy, Etc. of Women*. 1683. See also Jeslyn Medoff, 'New Light on Sarah Fyge (Field) Egerton', in *Tulsa Studies in Women's Literature*, vol. 1, no. 2, 1982, pp. 155–75; and Felicity Nussbaum, *The Brink of All We Hate: English Satires on Women, 1660–1750*, University of Kentucky Press, Lexington, 1984, for the larger context of anti-feminist satire

in this period.

24 For the history of the theory of the monarch's two bodies, see Ernst Kantorowicz, *The King's Two Bodies: A Study in Medieval Political Theology*, Princeton University Press, 1957; Kantorowicz, however, does not discuss differences in gender. Marie Axton's *The Queen's Two Bodies: Drama and the Elizabethan Succession*, Royal Historical Society, 1977, argues that it was most often Elizabeth I's opponents who used the theory of the monarch's two bodies to discuss – and to attempt to limit – the queen's political authority. Axton has relatively little to say about the (female) monarch's literal body, which, I have elsewhere argued, was rendered more problematic from the execution of Charles I; see Barash, op. cit., pp. 25–60.

25 Mary Chudleigh, dedication to *Poems On Several Occasions, Together with the Song of the Three Children, paraphras'd*, Bernard Lintot, 1703. Subsequent references are to this edition and will be included in the text as *Poems*.

26 In Queen Anne's first speech to Parliament, she emphasized her vigorous support for the Church of England; she frequently used the word 'zeal' to describe this support. See *Collection of Her Majesty's Speeches*, especially speeches for 25 May 1702, 27 February 1703 and 27 October 1705.

27 See Katherine Philips, 'To the truly competent Judge of Honour, *Lucasia*, upon a scandalous Libel made by *J. Jones*', 'Upon the Double Murther of *K. Charles I*', and 'To My Excellent *Lucasia*, On our Friendship', in *Poems by the Incomparable Mrs. K. P.*, J. G. for R. Marriott, 1664; Jane Barker, 'An

Invitation to My Friends at Cambridge' and 'The Virgin Life', in *Poetical Recreations: Consisting of Original Songs, Poems, Odes, etc. With Several New Translations*, B. Crayle, 1688.

28 Both 'The Elevation' (pp. 33–4) and 'The Resolution' (pp. 45–68) sketch out paths of emotional authority parallel to justifications of the queen's rule in the political poems discussed below.

29 On the importance of pronouns to the inscription of female linguistic authority, see Monique Wittig, 'The Mark of Gender', in Nancy K. Miller, ed., *The Poetics of Gender*, Columbia University Press, New York, 1986, pp. 63–73.

30 Reason is coded male, for instance in 'A Pindarick Ode', when 'the more manly, and the brave,/ Themselves by Resolution save' (p. 68). Chudleigh attempts to make reason genderless, but her repeated discovery that reason is already possessed by men and marked as male, seems to go against the strain of feminist discussions of eighteenth-century women that finds women empowered by a genderless reason; for example, Ruth Perry, 'Radical Doubt and the Liberation of Women', *Eighteenth-Century Studies*, vol. 18, no. 4, 1985, pp. 472–94; and Hilda Smith, *Reason's Disciples: Seventeenth-Century English Feminists*, University of Illinois Press, 1982, especially pp. 117–39 on Astell.

31 It seems likely that this poem, which includes a scene of Anne's coronation, was actually written before the poem to Anne which appears earlier in Chudleigh's *Poems*.

32 Charles Montagu, Earl of Halifax (1661–1715) wrote verses on the death of Charles II that brought

him to the attention of prominent
Whigs. In 1688 he signed the letter
of invitation to William of Orange,
and by 1703, the year of Egerton's
Poems, Tories were attacking him
publicly and attempting to take
away his position as auditor of the
exchequer.
33 S.F. [Sarah Fyge Egerton], *Poems
on Several Occasions, Together with
a Pastoral*, J. Nutt, 1703, sig. A4.
Subsequent references are to this
edition and will be included in the
text as *Poems*.
34 See Medoff, 'New Light on
Egerton'.
35 Even Delarivier Manley, who
criticizes such a hierarchy,
nevertheless makes it a central
problem in her satires of Anne's
court; see Barash, chapter 7.
36 S.C., 'To Mrs. *S.F.* on her
incomparable Poems', in poems
prefatory to *Poems on Several
Occasions*. Although only the 'M.P.'
of the introductory poems can be
identified with confidence (as Mary
Pix), most of the authors inscribe
themselves as women, speaking of
Egerton in terms of 'our Sex'.
37 By the end of the volume, I mean
the last of the poems, not including
the pastoral.
38 See Chudleigh, 'To the Ladies',
Poems, p. 40.
39 See Egerton, 'To Mr N. Tate
Esq., on the Queen's Picture',
Poems, p. 114. Egerton also includes
an unfinished poem on William's
death, as if to mourn the death of
the male monarch is both a
necessary and an impossible gesture
after her proud defence of and
identification with Anne.
40 Mary Astell, *A Serious Proposal
to the Ladies, for the Advancement
of their True and Greatest Interest*,
T.W. for R. Wilkin, 1696, sig. A2.
Subsequent references are to this

edition and will be included in the
text.
41 Astell, *A Serious Proposal*, part
II, Richard Wilkin, 1697, p. 9.
42 Astell, *Some Reflections Upon
Marriage; occasion'd by the Duke
and Dutchess of Mazarine's Case,
which is also consider'd*, John Nutt,
1700, p. 29.
43 Astell, preface to *Reflections
Upon Marriage*, 3rd edition, R.
Wilkin, 1706. Subsequent references
are to this edition and will be
included in the text. Throughout
Reflections, the speaker refers to
women as 'you'; see especially pp.
24–5, where the second person
plural 'we' refers to men, and p. 96,
where the narrator addresses male
then female readers without
identifying him/herself.

Lilley

1 Women's elegy might also be
thought of as crossing the division
between poetry and prose, and
potentially contracting relations
with other genres such as
autobiography, letters, dedications
and prefaces, prophecy and
warning, testimonials, meditations
and advice. See, for example, Lady
Eleanor Douglas's *Sions
Lamentation, lord Henry Hastings
his funerals blessing*, London, 1649;
Briget Paget's dedication to the
posthumous edition of her husband
John's *Meditations of Death*, Dort,
1639; the many elegiac narratives
and interpolated poems of *The
Autobiography of Mrs. Alice
Thornton*, ed. Charles Jackson,
Surtees Society, vol. 62; Durham,
1875; Grace Lady Gethin's 'Of
Death', in *Misery's Virtues
Whetstone*, London, 1699; and the
moving collection of Quaker
testimonies by Joan Whitrow,

Rebecca Travers and others, *A
Short Account of the Dealings of the
Lord with Susanna Whitrow . . .*,
Dublin, 1677. I shall be dealing only
with poetry.
2 Ann Rosalind Jones, 'Surprising
Fame: Renaissance Gender
Ideologies and Women's Lyric', in
Nancy K. Miller, ed., *The Poetics of
Gender*, Columbia University Press,
New York, 1986, pp. 74–95 (p. 79).
3 Abraham Cowley, *Poetry and
Prose*, ed. L. C. Martin, Oxford
University Press, 1949. Subsequent
references are to this edition and
will be included in the text.
4 'An Epitaph on Elizabeth
Cromwell. Mother to His Highness
the Lo. Protector of Great Britain
and Ireland, &c. By J.L.', London,
1655, reprinted in John W. Draper,
ed., *A Century of Broadside Elegies*,
Ingpen and Grant, 1928, where it is
ascribed to J. Longe.
5 See John Norton's 'A Funeral
Elogy, Upon that Pattern and Patron
of Virtue . . .', in Bradstreet's
Several Poems, Boston, 1678;
William Cavendish, *A Collection of
Letters and Poems . . . to the Late
Duke and Duchess of Newcastle*,
London, 1678; *An Elegie upon the
death of the most incomparable
Mrs. Katharine Philips*, J.C.,
London, 1664; as well as memorials
by James Tyrrell and Thomas
Flatman prefacing Philips's *Poems*
(1678); and *Two Centuries of
Testimony in Favour of Mrs. A.
Behn*, John Pearson, 1872. William
Temple's 'Upon the Death of Mrs.
Catherine Philips' is printed in W.
Roberts, 'Sir William Temple on
Orinda: Neglected Publications',
PBSA, vol. 57, 1963, pp. 328–36.
Dryden's 'Ode on the Death of
Anne Killigrew' is the best-known
elegy for a woman writer in the
period (though Killigrew's writing

remains obscure). In *Redeeming
Eve. Women Writers of the English
Renaissance*, Princeton University
Press, 1987, pp. 179–80, Elaine V.
Beilin briefly discusses an early
exception to the absence of elegies
by women for other women writers,
a Latin elegy for Marguerite de
Navarre written jointly by three
sisters: Anne, Margaret, and Jane
Seymour, *Le tombeau de Marguerite
de Valois Royne de Navarre*, Paris,
1551. According to Beilin, however,
the poem 'glorified feminine virtue';
Marguerite de Navarre's and their
own literary production is offered as
a transparent vehicle for the exercise
and praise of a commendable
feminine piety.
6 The only known copy is now in
the Houghton Library, Harvard
University. It is reprinted in *Kissing
The Rod: An Anthology of
Seventeenth-Century Women's
Verse*, eds. Germaine Greer, Jeslyn
Medoff, Melinda Sansone and Susan
Hastings, Virago, 1988, pp. 267–70,
which unfortunately omits lines 73–
89 and 124–66. The editors suggest
that the 'Young Lady' may be
Delarivier Manley (p. 269). This
attribution was previously argued
for by Ra Foxton, 'Delariviere
Manley and "Astrea's Vacant
Throne"', *Notes and Queries*, n.s.
33, no. 1, 1986, pp. 41–2.
7 See Ruth Salvaggio, 'Verses on
the Death of Mr. Dryden', *Journal
of Popular Culture*, vol. 21, Summer
1987, pp. 75–91. This is a useful
survey but has little to say about the
Nine Muses and mistakenly claims
that it was written by eight women,
p. 84. For a fascinating discussion of
gender and 'the problematic of "the
muse"' in Bradstreet's public
elegies, see Timothy Sweet, 'Gender,
Genre, and Subjectivity in Anne
Bradstreet's Early Elegies', *Early*

American Literature, vol. 23, 1988, pp. 152–74.

8 All the Rochester elegies, and the poems occasioned by them, are conveniently collected in David Farley-Hills, ed., *Rochester. The Critical Heritage*, Barnes & Noble, New York, 1972, pp. 94–131. However, Farley-Hills prints the abridged text of Wharton's elegy as it appeared in Nahum Tate's *Poems by Several Hands*, 1685, which omits 47 lines and effectively all the polemical material. I therefore quote from the complete text in *Examen Miscellaneum*, London, 1702, pp. 15–19. The abridged text is also printed in *Kissing the Rod*, but the additional lines are given in the notes, pp. 288–9. The publishing history of the four poems by Behn and Wharton is confusing: each wrote an elegy for Rochester; Wharton responded to Behn's; Behn replied to Wharton's response. The latter was the first of the four to be printed, in Behn's *Poems upon Several Occasions* (1684), so all four must have been written prior to that date and circulated privately. Wharton died in October 1685, the year in which versions of the two elegies were first printed (in different collections). By the time Wharton's poem to Behn was printed in 1693, Behn was also dead (d. 1689) and the full-length version of Wharton's elegy for Rochester did not appear until *Examen Miscellaneum* (1702), by which time it had elicited further poetic responses, from Waller and several others.

9 Cavendish's pair of elegies seems to be glossed by a revealing passage from 'A true relation of my birth, breeding, and life': 'My eldest sister died some time before my Mother, her death being, as I believe, hastned [sic] through grief of her onely daughter, on which she doted . . . she dying of Consumption, my sister, her mother dyed some half a year after of the same disease, and though time is apt to waste remembrance as a consumptive body, or to wear it out like a garment into raggs, or to moulder it into dust, yet I finde the naturall affections, I have for my friends, are beyond the length, strength and power of time: for I shall lament the loss so long as I live . . .', *Nature's Pictures*, London, 1656, pp. 377–8.

10 Jane Barker, *Poetical Recreations*, London, 1688, pp. 59–60. Subsequent quotations are from this edition.

11 *A Poem on the Death of the Queen*, by 'A Gentlewoman of Quality', London, 1694–5, Wing P2692; *An Ode Occasion'd by the Death of Her Sacred Majesty*, by 'A Young Lady', London, 1695, Wing O132.

12 Ivy Schweitzer, 'Anne Bradstreet Wrestles with the Renaissance', *Early American Literature*, vol. 23, 1988, pp. 306–307 (pp. 291–312).

13 Seventeenth-century women's contribution to elegy, public or otherwise, has also been steadily overlooked in generic histories. For instance, Avon Jack Murphy's 'Selective, Annotated Checklist of Critical Elegies Written in England Between 1600 and 1670', published as an appendix to 'The Critical Elegy of Earlier Seventeenth-Century England', *Genre*, vol. 5, 1972, pp. 75–105, includes no elegies by women, and only one for a woman (Cowley on Katherine Philips). It should be remembered that the division between public and private elegies is often not straightforward, for example the royalist Katherine Philips's 'Epitaph on my truly honoured Publius Scipio' (1660), for

the parliamentary Major General, Philip Skippon, is accounted for by the fact that he was her mother's third husband.

14 See also Margaret Fell Fox, 'A Few Lines Concerning Josiah Cole', in *A Collection of the Books of Josiah Cole, 1671*. This may be Margaret Fox's only poem. I am grateful to Ra Foxton for alerting me to these Quaker testimonies, and providing me with texts. See M. R. Foxton, *Her Name in Print . . .*, unpublished Ph.D. thesis, University of Queensland, 1984, 2 vols. Volume 2, *Women's Writing in England 1660–1714*, is an invaluable generically annotated bibliography. For a useful chronology and biographical key to Philips's poetry, see Ellen Moody, 'Orinda, Rosania, Lucasia *et aliae*: Towards a New Edition of the Works of Katherine Philips', *Philological Quarterly*, vol. 66, 1987, pp. 325–54.

15 On the dangers of publication, see Philips's poem to her husband concerning 'The Double Murther', 'To Antenor, on a Paper of Mine Which J.J. [the republican, Jenkin Jones] Threatens to Publish to Prejudice Him'. A recent article by Elizabeth H. Hageman, 'The Matchless Orinda. Katherine Philips', in Katharina M. Wilson, ed., *Women Writers of the Renaissance and Reformation*, University of Georgia Press, 1987, contains an interesting discussion of Philips and publication, especially pp. 577–9. Conversely, the editors of *Kissing the Rod* suggest that Behn's royal elegies were 'futile bids for royal patronage', p. 263.

16 Anne Killigrew, *Poems [1686]*, ed. Richard Morton, Scholars' Facsimiles & Reprints, Gainesville, Florida, 1967, pp. 76–7. Subsequent quotations are from this edition.

17 Compare Margaret Cavendish's 'An *Elegy* on my *Brother*, kill'd in these unhappy Warres' and 'Of the *death* and *buriall* of *Truth*', as well as Katherine Philips's 'On the death of the Queen of Bohemia' and 'On the 3rd of September 1651'.

18 Mary Mollineux's 'Elegy' was published in a posthumous volume by her husband, Henry Mollineux, whom she met in 1684 when they were both imprisoned, and married in 1685: *Fruits of Retirement: or, Miscellany Poems, Moral and Divine: Being Contemplations, Letters, &c. written on a variety of subjects and Occasions*, London, 1702. I quote the last two stanzas (19–20) from the sixth edition of 1772, printed by Mary Hinde. It includes a five-page elegy by her husband in which he apostrophizes her as 'My Friend, my Friend, my dearest Friend, my Wife'.

19 A high proportion of these suffered at least some delay in publication. Anne Bradstreet's half a dozen elegies on her parents, grandchildren and daughter-in-law appeared in the posthumous *Several Poems* (Boston, 1678) under the heading 'Several other Poems made by the Author . . . which she never meant should come to publick view'. In *Kissing the Rod*, a number of familial elegies are printed for the first time from manuscript sources: 'On my Boy Henry' (d. 1656) by Elizabeth Cavendish Egerton, Countess of Bridgewater, and 'On the death of my Deare Sister the Countess of Bridgewater . . . 1663', by Lady Jane Cavendish Cheyne (these sisters were step-daughters of Margaret Cavendish); as well as three elegies by Mary Carey on the deaths of her children in the 1650s. Gertrude Aston Thimelby's elegies on her father, Baron Walter Aston

(1584–1639), wealthy patron of Drayton, and young son (after 1651), and on her sister's children, were published in a nineteenth-century family miscellany, *Tixall Poems*, ed. Arthur Clifford, Edinburgh, 1813. Doubtless there are many more that are undiscovered.

20 I do not want to suggest that Katherine Philips can provide an inclusive model, though she is a characteristically conflictual figure. Unless otherwise stated, texts are taken from *Minor Poets of the Caroline Period*, ed. George Saintsbury, Oxford University Press, 1905, vol. I, pp. 485–612, which follows the posthumous 1667 edition.

21 Philips's father, a successful London merchant, died when she was seven, but she was survived by her mother, husband and daughter when she died of smallpox at 32; she lived to see the fulfilment of her political desires in the Restoration, and to participate to some degree in the literary culture of the court of Charles II. Within her flexible and reasonably financially secure marriage she was free to pursue a retired but ardent writing life with relative independence. Philips's poems also bear elegiac witness to her intense relations with other women. In 'Wiston Vault' (1652–4), she subverts her wifely destiny in the burial ground of her husband's family, by imagining herself entombed in Lucasia's heart: 'Though ne'er stone to me, 'twill stone for me prove'.

22 Text from *Kissing the Rod*, p. 195, which prints National Library of Wales MS 776.

23 For the identification of 'F.P.', see Moody, p. 333.

24 *Female Poems on Several Occasions*, London, 1679.

25 Kate Lilley, *To Dy in Writinge: Figure and Narrative in Masculine Elegy*, unpublished Ph.D. thesis, University College London, 1987.

26 Letter to Poliarchus, i.e., Charles Cotterell, 29 January 1663/4, reprinted in *The Female Spectator*, eds. Mary R. Mahl and Helene Koon, The Feminist Press, 1977, pp. 159–61.

27 'Mrs. Thimelby on the Death of her Only Child', in *Tixall Poems*, pp. 85–6. Already orphaned and widowed, Thimelby subsequently became a nun in a convent at Louvain. See note 19.

28 The text, from Huntington Library MS H.A. 8799, is reprinted in full in both *The Female Spectator*, pp. 124–5, and in *Kissing the Rod*, pp. 226–7. As the notes in *Kissing the Rod* explain (p. 227), Elizabeth Langham was the sister of Henry Hastings, whose death in 1649 occasioned a memorial collection, *Lachrymae Musarum* (1649). That volume excluded an elegy which may be by his mother, Lucy Hastings (see *Kissing the Rod*, pp. 9–10), a prose lament by his grandmother, Lady Eleanor Douglas (see note 1), and a Latin elegy by Makin. The lack of a parallel volume to mourn Elizabeth's death is censured by Makin in her elegy: 'It asks a volume rather than a verse,/Which is confined only to her hearse.' (lines 32–3).

29 Anne Wharton, 'My Fate', final couplet, in *The Temple of Death*, London, 1695, pp. 251–2. Jane Barker's 'A Farewell to Poetry, with a Long Digression on Anatomy' and 'Resolved never to Versifie more' explore her inability to sustain vocal and textual productivity, the position of a woman writing.

Ballaster

1 Elaine Showalter, *A Literature of Their Own: British Women Novelists from Brontë to Lessing*, new revised edition, Virago, 1982, pp. 18–19.

2 See in particular: Janet Todd, ed., *A Dictionary of British and American Women Writers 1660–1800*, Methuen, 1984; Mary Anne Schofield and Cecilia Macheski, eds., *Fetter'd or Free? British Women Novelists 1670–1815*, Ohio University Press, 1985; Jane Spencer, *The Rise of the Woman Novelist: From Aphra Behn to Jane Austen*, Blackwell, 1986; and Dale Spender, *Mothers of the Novel: 100 Good Women Writers Before Jane Austen*, Pandora, 1986.

3 Apart from Madeleine de Scudéry, the best-known writer of the lengthy French romance in the 1650s, a number of women in France turned to the shorter *nouvelle* in the 1660s and 1670s, among them Marie Desjardins (Madame de Villedieu), Marie d'Aulnoy and Marie de Lafayette. See F. C. Green, *French Novelists, Manners and Ideas*, Dent, 1921; and English Showalter, *The Evolution of the French Novel 1641–1782*, Princeton University Press, 1972.

4 'Preface to Queen Zarah', reprinted in Ioan Williams, ed., *Novel and Romance 1700–1800: A Documentary Record*, Routledge & Kegan Paul, 1970.

5 Aphra Behn, 'Dedication', *Love-Letters Between a Nobleman and his Sister*, Part 1, London, 1684, not paginated.

6 A successful dramatist could expect anything from £50 to £100 from the proceeds of the 'third day' (traditionally ceded to the author) of a production, whereas the novelist commonly received a single payment of one to three guineas for a manuscript.

7 Aphra Behn, 'Preface' to *The Lucky Chance*, quoted in Fidelis Morgan, ed., *The Female Wits: Women Playwrights of the Restoration*, Virago, 1981, p. 19; Delarivier Manley, *Secret Memoirs and Manners of Several Persons of Quality of Both Sexes, From the New Atalantis*, vol. 2, in Patricia Köster ed., *The Novels of Mary Delariviere Manley 1705–1714*, vol. 1, Gainesville Scholars Facsimiles and Reprints, 1971, p. 524. Subsequent references to this edition will be included in the text as *Novels*.

8 See Patricia Parker, *Literary Fat Ladies: Rhetoric, Gender, Property*, Methuen, 1987, pp. 8–35.

9 Jacques Derrida, 'The Law of Genre', in *Critical Inquiry*, vol. 7, no. 1, 1980, p. 74.

10 On generic disturbance in the formation of the novel, see Lennard Davis, *Factual Fictions: The Origins of the English Novel*, Columbia University Press, 1983; and Michael McKeon, *The Origins of the English Novel 1600–1740*, Johns Hopkins University Press, 1987.

11 Anon., *Five Love-Letters from a Nun to a Cavalier*, repr. in Natascha Würzbach, ed., *The Novel in Letters: Epistolary Fiction in the Early English Novel 1678–1740*, Routledge & Kegan Paul, 1969, p. 11.

12 Aphra Behn, *Love-Letters Between a Nobleman and his Sister*, ed. Maureen Duffy, Virago, 1987, p. 184. Subsequent references will be included in the text as *Love-Letters*.

13 Anon., *Seven Portuguese Letters: Being a Second Part to the Five*

Love-Letters from a Nun to a Cavalier, London, 1681, p. 33.

14 Peggy Kamuf, *Fictions of Feminine Desire: Disclosures of Heloise*, University of Nebraska Press, 1982, p. 56.

15 Aphra Behn, *The Histories and Novels of the Late Ingenious Mrs. Behn*, London, 1696, pp. 401–16.

16 Charles Gildon, 'An Account of the Life of the Incomparable Mrs. Behn', prefixed to Aphra Behn, *The Younger Brother*, London, 1696, not paginated.

17 Aphra Behn, *Oroonoko and Other Stories*, ed. Maureen Duffy, Methuen, 1986, p. 69.

18 John Hoyle, a lawyer, was accused of buggering a poulterer, William Bistow, of Gracechurch Street, before the grand jury on 26 February 1687. Not surprisingly, since the penalty for sodomy was death, the jury returned a verdict of ignoramus and discharged him. See Angeline Goreau, *Reconstructing Aphra: A Social Biography of Aphra Behn*, Oxford University Press, 1980, p. 192.

19 Delarivier Manley, 'To the Author of Agnes de Castro', prefixed to Catharine Trotter, *Agnes de Castro*, London, 1696, not paginated. Orinda and Astrea are the romance names adopted by Katherine Philips and Aphra Behn respectively in their poetic writings.

20 *The Lady's Pacquet* was later reprinted separately with some additions as *Court Intrigues*, London, 1711.

21 Marie d'Aulnoy, *Memoirs of the Court of England*, London, 1707, p. 2.

22 Marie d'Aulnoy, *The Ingenious and Diverting Letters of the Lady — Travels into Spain*, London, 1692, sig. A3r.

23 This history is provided by Edmund Curll in his address 'To the Reader' prefixed to the fourth edition of *Rivella*, retitled *Mrs. Manley's History of her own Life and Times*, London, 1725, p. vi. See also Fidelis Morgan, *A Woman of No Character: An Autobiography of Mrs. Manley*, Faber, 1986, pp. 152–7.

Sharrock

1 Mary Astell, *A Serious Proposal to the Ladies, for the Advancement of their True and Greatest Interest*, 2 parts, London, 1697, part I, p. 15 (part I was first published in 1694 and part II in 1697). All subsequent references to this work will appear in the text with the abbreviation *SP*, part and page numbers.

2 Anne Finch, 'The Introduction', in Myra Reynolds, ed., *The Poems of Anne Countess of Winchilsea*, Unversity of Chicago, 1903, pp. 4–5.

3 Mary Poovey also analyses the differences between writing as an act of ideological defiance and the inhibitions expressed within eighteenth-century texts by women. Her primary concern, however, is to explore the 'strategies of indirection' adopted by these women in order to negotiate the ideological restrictions within which they were operating. See Mary Poovey, *The Proper Lady and the Woman Writer. Ideology as Style in the Works of Mary Wollstonecraft, Mary Shelley, and Jane Austen*, University of Chicago, 1984, pp. 41–2. As Mary Poovey indicates, a similar ideological ambivalence within two nineteenth-century women poets is discussed in Cora Kaplan, 'The Indefinite Disclosed: Christina Rossetti and Emily Dickinson', in Mary Jacobus, ed., *Women Writing and Writing about Women*, Croom Helm, 1979, p. 64.

4 Aphra Behn, *The Lucky Chance, or an Alderman's Bargain*, London, 1687, Preface, not paginated.

5 Bathsua Makin, *An Essay to Revive the Antient Education of Gentlewomen, in Religion, Manners, Arts & Tongues*, London, 1673, p. 5. It should be noted that the gendered identity of the writer is a subject of uncertainty. Given the loss of the manuscript, it has not been possible to ascertain whether it was written by Makin's hand or whether she commisioned a man to ghost-write it for her. Any attempts to attribute it directly to Makin have had to rely on the rather precarious evidence of the woman-orientated nature of her arguments. See Elaine Hobby, *Virtue of Necessity. English Women's Writing 1649–88*, Virago, 1988, pp. 200–201.

6 Mary Astell, dedicatory letter, in *A Collection of Poems humbly presented and Dedicated to the most Reverend Father in God William By Divine Providence Lord Archbishop of Canterbury*, 1689, printed from manuscript in Ruth Perry, *The Celebrated Mary Astell. An Early English Feminist*, University of Chicago, 1986, pp. 400, 401.

7 Mary Astell, *Letters Concerning the Love of God, Between the Author of the Proposal to the Ladies and Mr. John Norris*, London, 1695, pp. 1–2. All subsequent references to this work will appear in the text with the abbreviation *L* and page numbers. (As I will mention later, Astell was to decline referring to herself as an 'Author'. The use of the term here may well be a consequence of the text having been published by Norris only with Astell's rather reluctant consent. See Perry, p. 82).

8 Mary Astell, *Reflections Upon Marriage*, 3rd edition, London, 1706, 'Preface', not paginated. All subsequent references to this work will appear in the text with the abbreviation *R* and page numbers. (The text was first published in 1700 with the title *Some Reflections Upon Marriage*. I use the 3rd edition, as it is here that the 'Preface' is added in which she specifically identifies herself as a woman. The gender of the writer is not disclosed in the body of the text.)

9 Her disavowal of 'Authority' here indicates her sympathy with the new natural philosophy, as expounded by, amongst others, Descartes and Bacon. Although she does not concur with Descartes's mechanistic view of the universe, she sides with the empiricist approach in her dismissal of 'Antient and Modern Authors' and her de-gendering of the soul and intellect (*R*, 'Preface', not paginated). For a detailed discussion of Astell's philosophical position, see Perry, pp. 71–82.

10 Louis Althusser, 'Ideology and Ideological State Apparatuses (Notes towards an Investigation)', in *Essays on Ideology*, Verso, 1984, p. 36.

11 Margaret E. Rose, *Parody/Meta-Fiction. An Analysis of Parody as a Critical Mirror to the Writing and Reception of Fiction*, Croom Helm, 1979, p. 61.

12 Roland Barthes, *Criticism and Truth*, trans. Katrine Pilcher Keuneman, University of Minnesota, 1987, p. 89.

13 Astell's goal for the '*Religious Retirement*', as she calls it, is that it might serve as 'a Seminary to stock the Kingdom with pious and prudent Ladies . . .' (*SP*, 1, pp. 36, 43). Although the women are also to act as educators, the recurring emphasis on their virtue and discretion plays into the

stereotypical view of femininity as the expression of polite, religious restraint. For example, the anonymous author of the popular work *The Ladies Calling* (1668) expounds upon the reasons why women, unlike men, are innately equipped to act as exemplars of piety. See Anon., *The Ladies Calling*, Oxford, 1668, part I, pp. 79–82.

14 Mary Astell, *The Christian Religion, As Profess'd by a Daughter of The Church of England*, London, 1705, p. 36.

15 See Roland Barthes, 'The Death of the Author', in *Image Music Text*, trans. Stephen Heath, Fontana, 1984, pp. 142–8 (pp. 147–8).

16 Mary, Lady Chudleigh similarly adapted imperialist terminology in order to argue for the self-governing of a woman's intellectual self: 'The Tyrant Man may still possess the Throne;/'Tis in our Minds that we wou'd Rule alone;/Those unseen Empires give us leave to sway,/And to our Reason private Homage pay'. See Mary, Lady Chudleigh, *The Ladies Defence: or, The Bride-Woman's Counsellor Answer'd: A Poem*, London, 1701, p. 18. Alice Browne insists that, although a modest demand, this should not be dismissed as a 'sermon ideal'. See Alice Browne, *The Eighteenth Century Feminist Mind*, Harvester, 1987, p. 91. However, the reliance upon men to sanction Chudleigh's request severely impinges upon the inner freedom and the respect that a woman might receive, and this partial submission to the masculine world is already encoded within the imperialist vocabulary that she employs. In this way, her text offers a useful parallel to the problematic dependence upon male 'author-ity'

within Astell's writings, to which I shall be drawing attention.

17 Mary Astell, 'Ambition', 1684, repr. from manuscript in Perry, p. 405.

18 See Catherine Gallagher, 'Embracing the Absolute: The Politics of the Female Subject in Seventeenth-Century England', *Genders*, no. 1, Spring 1988, pp. 33–8.

19 See Regina Janes, 'Mary, Mary, Quite Contrary, or Mary Astell and Mary Wollstonecraft Compared', in Ronald C. Rosbottom, *Studies in Eighteenth-Century Culture*, vol. 5, 1976, p. 126.

20 In *Vindication of the Rights of Women* (1792), Mary Wollstonecraft also overlooks both the interests of working-class women and her own exclusion of them. By rendering the middle classes 'natural', she devises a supposedly egalitarian system in which the 'needy' and the servant classes are still considered indispensable and, one can assume, 'natural' appendages. See Miriam Brody Krammick, 'Introduction' to *Vindication of the Rights of Women*, ed. Miriam Brody Krammick, Penguin, 1978, pp. 41–4; and Timothy J. Reiss, 'Revolution in Bounds: Wollstonecraft, Women, and Reason', in Linda Kauffman, ed., *Gender and Theory. Dialogues on Feminist Criticism*, Basil Blackwell, 1989, p. 15.

21 Regina Janes attributes Astell's abandonment of her temporal aspirations for women to 'the other-worldly bent of her thought'. By sublimating both women and her demands for them, Astell then does not have to negotiate for change in this world. See Janes, p. 130. Joan Kinnaird, on the other hand, seeks to resolve the paradoxical

conjunction of Astell's proto-
feminism and conservatism by
arguing that she 'preached not
women's rights but women's duties
. . .'. See Joan K. Kinnaird, 'Mary
Astell: Inspired by Ideas', in Dale
Spender, ed., *Feminist Theorists.
Three Centuries of Women's
Intellectual Traditions*, Women's
Press, 1983, p. 37.
22 See Catherine Belsey, *The
Subject of Tragedy. Identity and
difference in Renaissance drama*,
Methuen, 1985, p. 218.

Grundy

1 Jane Austen, *Northanger Abbey*,
1818, vol. I, chapter xiv. See Natalie
Zemon Davis's sketch, 'Gender and
Genre: Women as Historical
Writers, 1400–1820', in Patricia H.
Labalme, ed., *Beyond Their Sex:
Learned Women of the European
Past*, New York University Press,
1980. Richard Steele wrote: 'History
. . . written by a woman, you will
easily imagine to consist of love in
all its forms' (*Tatler*, no. 36, 2 July
1709).
2 [Elizabeth Cary, Viscountess
Falkland], *The History of . . .
Edward II*, written *c.* 1627–8, pub.
1680 (for her authorship, see Donald
A. Stauffer in *Essays in Dramatic
Literature: The Parrett Presentation
Volume*, ed. Hardin Craig,
Princeton University Press, 1935, pp.
289–314; Isobel Grundy in *Bodleian
Library Record*, xiii, October 1988,
pp. 82–3). Lady Falkland read, says
her daughter, 'history very
universally' ([Anne or Mary Cary],
The Lady Falkland: Her Life, ed.
R[ichard] S[impson], London
Catholic publishing and bookselling
company, 1861, p. 113).
3 The Falkland daughter wrote
after 1639 (Imperial Archives, Lille);

*The Life of William Cavendish,
Duke of Newcastle*, 1667; Delarivier
Manley, *The Secret History of
Queen Zarah . . .*, 1705, and other
works (see Ballaster, p. 94); Anne
Clifford, *Lives of Lady Anne
Clifford . . . and of her Parents,
Summarized by Herself*, ed. J. P.
Gilson, Roxburghe Club, 1916;
Cassandra Willoughby, later
Duchess of Chandos, MSS at
Nottingham University Library,
Gloucestershire Record Office,
North London Collegiate School,
and BL (some pub. in HMC
Reports, 69, 1911; and in Alfred
Cecil Wood, ed., *Continuation of
the History of the Willoughby
Family*, Shakespeare Head Press,
1958).
4 *Lady Falkland: Her Life*, p. vi;
Donald A. Stauffer, *English
Biography before 1700*, Harvard
University Press, 1930, p. 149. See
also Marie B. Rowlands, 'Recusant
Women 1560–1640', in Mary Prior,
ed., *Women in English Society
1500–1800*, Methuen, 1985.
5 Research by Susan O'Brien has
ended the near-invisibility of the Bar
Convent at York, which, although
illegal, flourished uninterruptedly
from 1686 and managed the longest-
running girls' school in Britain (see
study of English nuns by O'Brien,
forthcoming). For the attraction of
the conventual idea to non-Catholic
women, see Bridget Hill, 'A Refuge
from Men: The Idea of a Protestant
Nunnery', in *Past and Present. A
Journal of Historical Studies*, 117,
1987, pp. 107–30.
6 See Roger Thompson, *Unfit for
Modest Ears*, London, 1979, pp.
132–57.
7 Shirley's life of Clement at the
Priory of Our Lady, Hassocks,
Sussex: excerpts printed with
material about Shirley in John

Morris, *The Troubles of our Catholic Forefathers* [sic] *Related by Themselves*, vol. I, Burns and Oates, 1872, repr. 1970; and in Dom Adam Hamilton, ed., *The Chronicle of the English Augustinian Canonesses Regular of the Lateran, at St Monica's in Louvain (Now at St Augustine's Priory, Newton Abbot, Devon)*, Edinburgh: Sands and Co., 1904. A second volume, 1906, takes the chronicle to 1644. Hereafter in text as Morris and as Hamilton.

8 Winefrid Thimelby letters in Arthur Clifford, ed., *Tixall Letters: or The Correspondence of the Aston Family, and Their Friends, During the Seventeenth Century*, Longman, Hurst, Rees, Orme and Brown, 1815, vol. II, pp. 1–109; life of Falkland excerpted in the *Rambler*, 1857 (1861 ed., p. v); Thomas Hunter, *An English Carmelite*, compiled from the writings of Burton before 1725, ed. H. J. C[oleridge], Burns and Oates, 1876 (MS then owned by Carmelites at Lanherne in Cornwall), hereafter in text as Burton; Holland, 'Narration', in C. S. Durrant, *A Link Between Flemish Mystics and English Martyrs*, Burns, Oates and Washbourne, 1925, pp. 272–305, hereafter in text as Durrant; St Monica's Chronicle in Morris and in Hamilton.

9 [Edward Scarisbrick], Life of Trevor Lady Warner, 1691, in Henry Foley, ed., *Records of the Society of Jesus*, Burns and Oates, 1871, pp. 84, 151, 230ff.

10 *Tixall Letters*, vol. I, p. 184 (179–200). Hereafter in text as Tixall.

11 Tixall (Constance Aston), vol. I, pp. 85–138.

12 Morris thinks that the earliest part was written about 1631, presumably by a different hand (vol.

1, p. 7; Hamilton, vol. I, p. xii).

13 Luce Irigaray, *This Sex Which Is Not One*, trans. Catherine Porter and Carolyn Burke, Cornell University Press, 1985, p. 205. This element in the chronicles goes against Gail Malmgreen's claim that 'the historiography of Roman Catholic laywomen . . . is almost non-existent' (*Religion in the Lives of English Women, 1760–1930*, ed. Malmgreen, Hull University Press, 1986, p. 2).

14 Anonymous early life of Mary Ward: see Mary Catharine Elizabeth Chambers, *The Life of Mary Ward (1585–1645)*, 1882, vol. I, p. 68.

15 Another fascinating intersection was recorded by Mother Mary Augustina More, after the nuns of St Monica's were made refugees by the French Revolution (Durrant, p. 353ff).

16 Nithsdale, in *The Book of Carlaverock*, ed. William Fraser, Edinburgh, 1873, vol. II, p. 224.

17 *The Book of Carlaverock*, vol. II, p. 234.

18 In Sheffield Grace, ed., *Transactions of the Society of Antiquaries of Scotland*, J. Rider, 1827.

Purkiss

I would like to thank Julia Briggs, Hero Chalmers, Ivan Dowling, David Norbrook, Nigel Smith, and my editors Sue Wiseman and Isobel Grundy for their help, and for illuminating comments on an earlier version of this piece.

1 *Strange and Wonderful Newes from Whitehall*, 1654. Often attributed to Trapnel (for example in Wing) but appears to be a paraphrase of her writings. Hereafter cited in text as *Strange*.

2 *Anna Trapnels Report and Plea*,

1654; *The Cry of a Stone*, 1654; *A Legacy for Saints*, 1654. Hereafter cited in text as *Report, Cry, Legacy*.

3 Seventeenth-century taxonomies of prophecy include John Smith, *Of Prophecy*, in *Select Discourses*, 1660. For a full discussion of the genre of prophecy in radical sects, see Nigel Smith, *Perfection Proclaimed: Language and Literature in English Radical Religion 1640–1660*, Clarendon Press, 1989, pp. 25–32.

4 In her checklist of women's writings in the seventeenth century, Patricia Crawford shows that prophetic writings made up 72 of 230 first editions of works by women during the Interregnum, making prophecy the largest single genre in which women wrote. See her 'Women's Published Writings 1600–1700', in Mary Prior, ed., *Women in English Society 1500–1800*, Methuen, 1988.

5 For Marchamont Nedham's report on Trapnel and other Fifth Monarchists, see *Calendar of State Papers Domestic*, 1653–4, p. 393; for Trapnel's identification of Cromwell with Gideon and her vision of horns, see *Cry*, p. 5 and pp. 13–14, and Austin Woolrych, *Commonwealth to Protectorate*, Clarendon Press, 1982, pp. 387–9; for Trapnel's arrest, see *CSPD*, 1654, pp. 86, 134, 436, 438. For Trapnel's biography, see Richard L. Greaves and Robert Zaller, eds., *Biographical Dictionary of British Radicals in the seventeenth century*, 3 vols., Harvester, 1982–4, and Bernard Capp, *The fifth monarchy men: a study in seventeenth-century millenarianism*, Faber, 1972.

6 Ann Kibbey, *The Interpretation of Material Shapes in Puritanism: Rhetoric, Prejudice and Violence*, Cambridge University Press, 1986; Phyllis Mack, 'Women as prophets

in the English Civil War', *Feminist Studies*, 8, 1982.

7 Mary Poovey, *The Proper Lady and the Woman Writer: Ideology as Style in the Works of Mary Wollstonecraft, Mary Shelley and Jane Austen*, University of Chicago Press, 1984, pp. 41–2.

8 I borrow the term 'making a spectacle of oneself' from Mary Russo, 'Female grotesques: carnival and theory', in Teresa de Lauretis, ed., *Feminist Studies/Critical Studies*, Macmillan, 1986. Throughout, my use of the term 'surveillance' is based on Michel Foucault's *Discipline and Punish*, trans. Alan Sheridan, Penguin, 1979.

9 Puritanism's discourses of the body are discussed in detail in Kibbey; David Leverenz, *The Language of Puritan Feeling*, Cornell, 1980; and Richard Bauman, *Let Your Words Be Few: symbolism of speaking and silencing among seventeenth-century Quakers*, Cambridge University Press, 1983. For Douglas's occupation of the bishop's chair at Lichfield, see *CSPD*, 1637–8, p. 219; for Prynne, Burton and Bastwick, see Michael Wilding, *Dragon's Teeth: Literature in the English Revolution*, Clarendon Press, 1987, p. 16, and Brian Manning, *The English People and the English Revolution 1640–1649*, Heinemann, 1976.

10 For further discussion of this point, see Kibbey, and Keith Thomas, 'Women and the Civil War Sects', *Past and Present*, 13, 1958, pp. 42–62.

11 Peter Stallybrass, 'Patriarchal Territories: the body enclosed', in Margaret Ferguson *et al.*, eds., *Rewriting the Renaissance: the discourses of sexual difference in early modern Europe*, University of Chicago Press, 1986.

12 Jane Lead, *A Fountain of Gardens*, 3 vols., 1696–1702, vol. II, sig. A₃ᴿ, hereafter cited in text as *Fountain*, and Bodleian Library MS Rawlinson A. 21, fol. 325ᵥ: letter, dated 21 December 1654, signed BT. For another comment on Trapnel's voice while in a trance, see *Several Proceedings of State Affairs*, 12–19 January 1654: 'she is heard and understood very plainly by all when she prays, but when she sings, very little is to be understood'.

13 Hester Biddle, *Wo to thee city of Oxford*, 1655. In arguing that Biddle's voice is erased, I differ from Elaine Hobby, who argues that 'God's voice and Hester Biddle's voice are one and the same' in this passage: Hobby, *Virtue of Necessity: English women's writing 1649–88*, Virago, 1988, p. 41.

14 For the *ars moriendi* tradition and the prophecies of Sarah Wight, see Barbara Ritter Dailey, 'The visitation of Sarah Wight: holy carnival and the revolution of the saints in civil war London', *Church History*, 55, 1986, pp. 438–55, especially p. 443. Dailey gives several instances of minor transgressions, but does not record any cases of women commanding God.

15 See Lucinda McCray Beier, *Sufferers and Healers: the Experience of Illness in Seventeenth-Century England*, Routledge, 1987, chapter 8, especially p. 214. For the complex relations between illness and Puritanism, see Andrew Wear, 'Puritan perceptions of illness in seventeenth-century England', in Roy Porter, ed., *Patients and Practitioners: lay perceptions of medicine in pre-industrial society*, Cambridge University Press, 1985.

16 Elinor Channel, *A message from God (by a dumb woman)* . . . published according to her desire by Arise Evans, 1654, p. 7.

17 Henry Jessey, *The exceeding riches of grace advanced by the Spirit of Grace . . . in Mʳⁱˢ Sarah Wight*, 1647, p. 132. All further references to Wight's utterances are from this edition, with page numbers given in the text. Nigel Smith also discusses Wight's and Trapnel's fasts in *Perfection Proclaimed*, pp. 45–52. For a very different example of the relations between gender, religion and food, see Isobel Grundy's essay, p. 137 above.

18 James Fisher, *The Wise Virgin: Or, a wonderful narration of the various dispensations of God towards a childe of eleven . . .*, 1656, hereafter in text. Nigel Smith also discusses Hatfield's fasts in 'A Child Prophet: Martha Hatfield as *The Wise Virgin*', in Julia Briggs and Gillian Avery, eds., *Children and their Books*, Oxford University Press, 1989.

19 For the debate about whether religious inedia can be equated with anorexia nervosa, see Rudolph Bell, *Holy Anorexia*, University of Chicago Press, 1985, and Caroline Walker Bynum, *Holy feast and holy fast: the religious significance of food to medieval women*, University of California Press, 1987. In this discussion of fasting, I also draw on Susan Bordo, 'Reading the Slender Body', in Mary Jacobus *et al.*, eds., *Body/Politics: Women and the Discourse of Science*, Routledge, 1990, and Joan Jacobs Brumberg, *Fasting girls: the emergence of anorexia nervosa as a modern disease*, Harvard University Press, 1988.

20 Keith Thomas, *Religion and the Decline of Magic*, Penguin, 1971, pp. 571–81, and 590–1.

21 Katharine Evans and Sarah Cheevers, 'A Short Relation', in Elspeth Graham et al., eds., Her own life: autobiographical writings of seventeenth-century Englishwomen, Routledge, 1989, pp. 120–1; Henry Jessey, op. cit., p. 45.

22 Women are characteristically the bearers of this kind of knowledge. There is an illuminating discussion of the politics of such historical returns in Clair Wills, 'Upsetting the public: carnival, hysteria and women's texts', in Ken Hirschkop and David Shepherd, eds., Bakhtin and cultural theory, Manchester University Press, 1989.

23 Caroline Walker Bynum, op cit., pp. 189–91.

24 For women's responsibility for food purchase and preparation, see Kate Mertes, The English Noble Household, Blackwell, 1988.

25 Nigel Smith also suggests that Wight's inedia was part of an imitation of Christ, though he does not consider the implications of this in gender terms, in Perfection Proclaimed, p. 48.

26 Though not known to have fasted, Jane Lead uses similar food imagery; see Fountain, vol. II, 1697, pp. 202–3.

27 John Reynolds, A discourse on prodigious abstinence, 1689. The case of Martha Taylor is reported in J. Robins, Newes from Darbyshire, 1668, and The wonder of the world, 1669, where it is understood in providential terms.

28 Bodl. MS Rawl. A. 21, fol. 325ᵛ.

29 Denise Riley, 'Am I That Name?': Feminism and the Category of 'Women' in History, Macmillan, 1988.

30 Elizabeth Poole, A vision: wherein is manifested the disease and cure of the kingdome, 1648, p. 7. Hereafter in text.

31 Jane Lead, The revelation of revelations, 1683, p. 53.

32 Elizabeth Hincks, The poor widows mite, cast into the lords Treasury, 1671, p. 24.

33 Elaine Hobby, op. cit., p. 42.

34 Eleanor Douglas, The Restitution of Prophecy, 1651, 'To the Reader'. The text is written from the Fleet, which may explain Douglas's references to its rejection.

35 See, for example, Ben Jonson's 'On My First Son', and Margaret Cavendish's 'An Excuse for So Much Writ Upon My Verses' ('Condemne me not for making such a coyle/About my book, alas it is my childe') in Poems and Fancies, 1653.

36 The Ranters Monster, 1652, repr. in Joseph Arnold Foster, ed., Reprints of English Books 1475–1700, East Lansing, 1940. Christine Berg and Philippa Berry also connect Adams's case with women prophets in 'Spiritual whoredom: an essay on female prophets in the seventeenth century', in Francis Barker et al., eds., 1642: literature and power in the seventeenth century, University of Essex, 1981. Joan Robins also claimed to be pregnant with Christ.

37 Ambroise Paré, On Monsters and Marvels, trans. Janis L. Pallister, University of Chicago Press, 1982, pp. 38; 40. See Marie-Hélène Hunt, 'Living Images: Monstrosity and Representation', Representations, 4, Fall 1983, pp. 73–98; and Keith Thomas, Religion and the Decline of Magic, pp. 105, 109, 124, 125.

38 See Kibbey, op, cit.; S. Williams, Divine Rebel: the life of Anne Marberry Hutchinson, Scribner, 1981.

39 John Winthrop, The short story of the rise reign and ruin of the antinomians, 1644, 'The Preface',

sigs. B₃ᵛ–B₄ᴿ. For another account of
Dyer's monstrous birth, which does
not relate it to religion, see *Newes
from New-England of a most
strange and prodigious birth*,
1642.

40 George Puttenham, *The Arte of
English Poesie*, ed. Gladys Doidge
Willcock and Alice Walker, 1936, p.
261.

41 Thomas Hobbes, *The English
Works of Thomas Hobbes*, ed. Sir
V. Molesworth, 1839–45, pp. 398–9;
see also Edward Coke, *Institutes*,
vol. III, chapter 5, cited in Keith
Thomas, *Religion and the Decline
of Magic*, p. 470. See H. Rusche,
'Prophecies and propaganda, 1641
to 1651', *English Historical Review*,
84, 1960, pp. 752–70.

42 Catherine Gallagher, 'More
about "Medusa's Head"',
Representations, 4, Fall 1983, p. 56.
See also Patricia Parker, *Literary Fat
Ladies: rhetoric, gender, property*,
Methuen, 1987, chapter 1, especially
p. 15.

43 Neil Hertz, 'Medusa's Head:
Male Hysteria under Political
Pressure', *Representations*, 4, Fall
1983, pp. 27–54.

44 For the status of the virgin body
in the Renaissance, see Philippa
Berry, *Of chastity and power:
Elizabethan literature and the
unmarried queen*, Routledge, 1989,
and Peter Stallybrass, 'Patriarchal
territories', op. cit. In describing the
reproductive female body as
grotesque, I am drawing on Mikhail
Bakhtin, *Rabelais and his world*,
trans. Hélène Iswolsky, Indiana
University Press, 1984.

45 See *A Legacy for Saints*, and the
untitled poem in the Bodleian
Library, Oxford (Shelfmark S. 1.
42), not paginated, not dated.

46 Jane Lead, *Divine Revelations
and Prophecies*, 1700, repr. 1830, p.

21. Hero Chalmers, 'Jane Lead:
Prophecy and the Female Subject in
the Late Seventeenth Century',
unpublished paper, September 1989,
also makes this point. I am grateful
to Hero for sharing her illuminating
work with me. See also Catherine
Smith, 'Jane Lead: mysticism and
the woman cloathed with the sun',
in Sandra Gilbert and Susan Gubar,
eds., *Shakespeare's sisters: feminist
essays on women poets*, Indiana
University Press, 1979.

47 Philippa Berry, op. cit., chapter
1. See also Marina Warner,
*Monuments and Maidens: the
allegory of the female form*,
Weidenfeld and Nicolson, 1985.

Wiseman

Thanks to Helen Cobb and Diane
Purkiss who ran the 'Women, Text
and History 1500–1750', in Oxford
in 1988 and to the participants in
the seminar at which this essay was
given as a paper, especially Sophie
Tomlinson and Kate Lilley.

1 Thomas Scot, *Philomythic*,
London, 1616, p. 24.

2 Margaret Cavendish, *Playes*,
London, 1662, sig. A11r. Subsequent
references in text. The distinction
between Cavendish's insistence on
the relationship of theatre with
aristocratic status and her husband's
interest in popular theatre is
signalled by the fact that during the
Interregnum he also theorized about
the restoration of the theatre. He
wrote to Charles Stuart advocating
the restoration of public and more
'popular' theatres and festivities. See
S. Arthur Strong, *A Catalogue of
Letters and Other Historical
Documents . . . at Welbeck*, 1903,
pp. 226–7, quoted in Douglas Grant,
Margaret the First, Rupert Hart-
Davies, 1957, pp. 149–50.

3 See Denise Riley on the problem of interpellation versus agency in the category 'women', '*Am I that name?' Feminism and the Category of 'Women' in History*, Macmillan, 1988, pp. 1, 10–11.

4 Caroline Neely, 'Constructing the subject: feminist practice and the new Renaissance discourses', *English Literary Renaissance*, Winter 1988, vol. 18, no. 1, p. 5. Neely notes this incidentally, in an argument primarily concerned with other issues.

5 Catherine Gallagher aims to link Cavendish's 'singularity' to a political and implicitly psychoanalytic figure of relations based on those of monarch/subject. However, the equation between an 'absolute' monarch and an 'absolute' subject can only be problematically resolved through the use of the linking term 'absolute', where 'absolute' is both a political and a psychoanalytic term. See 'Embracing the Absolute: the Politics of the Female Subject in Seventeenth-Century England', *Genders*, no. 1, Spring 1988, pp. 24–39.

6 Samuel Pepys, *The Diary*, ed. R. C. Latham & W. Matthews, G. Bell & Sons, 1974, vol. 8, pp. 242–4. See also Douglas Grant, *Margaret the First*, pp. 15–19.

7 Dorothy Osborne, *The Letters of Dorothy Osborne*, ed. G. C. Smith, Clarendon Press, 1928, pp. 37, 41. John Evelyn, *The Diary of John Evelyn*, ed. E. S. de Beer, Oxford, 1955, Vol. III, p. 481.

8 Letter from Charles North to his father, 13 April 1667, Bodley MS North c.4, fol. 146. Thanks to Professor Robert Jordan for showing this to me.

9 See, for example, Jacqueline Pearson, *The Prostituted Muse: Images of Women & Women Dramatists 1642–1737*, Harvester, 1988, and Kathleen Jones, *A Glorious Fame: The Life of Margaret Cavendish Duchess of Newcastle*, Bloomsbury, 1988.

10 Sara Heller Mendelson, *The Mental World of Stuart Women: Three Studies*, Harvester, 1987, pp. 5–6.

11 Natalie Zemon Davis, '"Women's History" in Transition: The European Case', *Feminist Studies*, 3, no. 3/4, Winter 1975/6, quoted in Joan Kelly, 'The Social Relations of the Sexes', in her *Women, History and Theory*, University of Chicago Press, 1984, p. 9.

12 *Playes*, 1662, sig. A2r, Douglas Grant, p. 161.

13 Thomas Killigrew, for example *Thomaso, or, The Wanderer*, and *Bellamira* in his *Comedies and Tragedies*, London, 1664. Killigrew regarded his plays as produced by the 'leisure' of 'Twenty Years Banishment'.

14 Two-part pamphlet plays include *The Committee Man Curried*, 1647, and *Newmarket Fayre*, 1649.

15 See also Clifford Leech, 'Private performances and amateur theatricals (excluding the academic stage) from 1580 to 1660. With an edition of "Raguaillo d'Oceano", 1640', unpublished Ph.D. dissertation, University of London, 1935, pp. 363–6.

16 Richard Luckett, 'Music', in *The Diary of Samuel Pepys*, ed. Robert Latham and William Matthews, vol. 10, pp. 258–82, p. 263.

17 'The Concealed Fansyes', ed. Nathan Comfort Star, *P.M.L.A.*, 1931, vol. XLVI, pp. 802–838; 'A Pastorall', MS Bodl. Rawlinson poet. 16; see ff. 49–50 for the sisters' dedications of the 'Pastorall' to their

father. Jane Cavendish writes, 'Now let my language speake, & say/If you be pleas'd I have my pay', fol. 49; and Elizabeth Brackley echoes the dedication and the figure of submitting the work to Newcastle's 'judgements of pure wit', fol. 50. Subsequent references in text.

18 Sandra A. Burner, *James Shirley: A Study of Literary Coteries and Patronage in Seventeenth Century England*, University Press of America, Lanham, New York, London, 1988, pp. 146–7.

19 *Cupid's Banishment*, ed. C. E. McGee, *Renaissance Drama*, vol. XIX, 1988, pp. 226–64. For a further analysis of the problematic status of women as masque performers in the pre-1642 masques, see Suzanne Gossett, '"Man-maid begone!" Women in Masques', *English Literary Renaissance*, Winter 1988, vol. 18, no. 1, pp. 96–113.

20 See, for example, Cavendish's *The Blazing World*. Sophie Tomlinson, 'My Brain the Stage: Margaret Cavendish and the Fantasy of Female Performance', in C. Brant and D. Purkiss, eds., forthcoming.

21 See also *Playes*, 1662, sigs. A3r–B2r.

22 Elaine Hobby's suggestion that the scenes are for the reader to 'act out' can be used to point towards the questions of the subject positions of the reader during such a process, but the aim of this essay at this point is to consider the acting out in terms of fantasy and theatre in relation to the idea of the world and the theatre. See Elaine Hobby, *Virtue of Necessity*, Virago, 1988, pp. 110–11.

23 *The Female Academy*, *Playes*, 1662, pp. 652–79. See Denise Riley, '*Am I that name?*', p. 25.

24 *Poems, or Several Fancies*, London, 1668, frontispiece.

25 Sigmund Freud, '"A child is being beaten", a contribution to the study of the origins of sexual perversions', *Works*, 24 vols., vol. 17 (1917–19), ed. James Strachey, Hogarth Press, 1955, pp. 175–204.

26 *Poems, or Several Fancies*, London, 1668, p. 131. Cavendish does not write with any consistent attitude or programme about war. In some ways, like the relationship between femininity and power, the question of war splits her texts; in this case, the division might be characterized as between a royalist voice and a pragmatic, Machiavellian voice, each of which is at moments endorsed. See note 43.

27 *Sociable Letters*, London, 1664, pp. 406–7. Subsequent references in text.

28 *Love's Adventures*, scene 36, *Playes*, p. 75. Subsequent references in text.

29 Lisa Jardine, *Still Harping on Daughters: Women and Drama in the Age of Shakespeare*, Harvester, 1983, p. 31. Recent articles on pre-war significances of gender and cross-dressing include Laura Levine, 'Men in Women's Clothing: Anti-theatricality and Effeminization from 1579 to 1642', *Criticism*, Spring 1986, vol. xxviii, no. 2, pp. 121–43; Phyllis Rackin, 'Androgyny, Mimesis, and the Marriage of the Boy Heroine on the English Renaissance Stage', *P.M.L.A.*, vol. 102, 1987, pp. 29–41; Kathleen McLuskie, 'The Act, the Role, and the Actor: Boy Actresses on the Elizabethan Stage', *New Theatre Quarterly*, 1987, part 3, pp. 120–30. My argument is that these plays do foreground gender transformations in such a way as to supply a reader with a number of alternative pleasures. However, in this respect,

The Convent of Pleasure seems to be a very different case from *Love's Adventures* and the role of cross-dressing and disguise would appear to change according to acting ethos (private or public?) and the way in which each material instance discursively reworks codes already present. For a full analysis of gender and codes of performance, see Sophie Tomlinson, 'My Brain the Stage' (see note 20).

30 Kathleen McLuskie, 'The Act, the Role . . .' p. 124.

31 Ann Rosalind Jones, 'Nets and Bridles: early modern conduct books and sixteenth century women's lyrics', in Nancy Armstrong, Nancy and Leonard Tennenhouse, eds., *The Ideology of Conduct: Essays in Literature and the History of Sexuality*, Methuen, 1987, p. 44.

32 See Sherry B. Ortner, 'Gender and sexuality in hierarchical societies: the case of Polynesia and some comparative implications', in Ortner and Harriet Whitehead, eds., *Sexual Meaning: the Cultural Construction of Gender and Sexuality*, Cambridge University Press, 1981, p. 359.

33 *Kissing the Rod*, ed. Germaine Greer, Susan Hastings, Jeslyn Medoff, Melinda Sansone, Virago, 1988, e.g. p. 1 where all women poets are characterized as people 'who tried to storm the highest bastion of the cultural establishment, . . all *guerrilleras*, untrained, ill-equipped, isolated and vulnerable' (p. 1). This disturbingly dehistoricizes the problems, aims and conditions of early modern, cultural production. See also my discussion of Kathleen Jones and Jacqueline Pearson, above.

34 Diane H. Coole, *Women in Political Theory*, Harvester, 1988, pp. 71–84. She notes patriarchal

assumptions remaining in Hobbes's theory of consent, p. 84. Thomas Hobbes, *De Cive*, IX, p. 3, in Molesworth vol. 2, p. 116, quoted in Coole, p. 80.

35 Gordon J. Scochet, *Patriarchalism in Political Thought*, Blackwell 1975, for example pp. 158–164, on Hobbes p. 165 and chapter XII.

36 Margaret J. M. Ezell, *The Patriarch's Wife*, University of North Carolina Press, 1987. Ezell is right to point to the difficulty in mapping dominant discourse on the subjective experience (as 'revealed' equally problematically in texts), see pp. 161–3, especially p. 162. However, her comment that, 'The twentieth-century interpretation of domestic life in seventeenth-century England restricts the patriarch's wife more than the actual practice did', seems to underestimate the power of dominant ideals.

37 Brian Manning, *The English People and the English Revolution*. Heinemann, 1976, p. 229.

38 Edward Hyde, Earl of Clarendon, *The History of the Great Rebellion*, ed. W. D. Macray, 6 vols., Oxford, 1888, vol. III, p. 381. Clarendon notes that 'nothing could have tempted him out of the paths of pleasure . . . but honour, and ambition to serve the king.'

39 Ann Rosalind Jones, 'Surprising Fame: Renaissance Gender Ideologies and Women's Lyric', in Nancy K. Miller, ed., *The Poetics of Gender*, Columbia University Press, 1986, p. 80.

40 Margaret Cavendish, *The Worlds Olio*, London, 1653, p. 41.

41 Elizabeth Poole, *An Alarum of Warre*, 1648, BL E 555(23), pp. 5–6. Quoted in S. D. Amussen, 'Gender, Family and the Social Order 1560–1725', in Anthony Fletcher and John

Stevenson, eds., *Order and Disorder in Early Modern England*, Cambridge University Press, 1985, p. 199.

42 Catherine Gallagher, op. cit., pp. 24–33.

43 For example, she asserts that a usurper is likely to be a better governor than an hereditary prince because: 'A Prince that is born to a just title becomes carelesse, as thinking his rights to his Crown, is sufficient warrant . . . for the loyalty of his Subjects which makes him trust the conduct of his greatest affairs to those he favours most . . . whereas an usurper dare trust none but himself which makes him more wise in governing' (*The Worlds Olio*, p. 48). This, for a moment, contradicts the monarchist ideologies so often central to her texts.

44 Margaret Cavendish, *Bell in Campo*, in *Playes*, London, 1662.

45 Thanks to Sophie Tomlinson for this suggestion; see her forthcoming article, above.

46 Kathleen Jones, *A Glorious Fame: the Life of Margaret Cavendish, Duchess of Newcastle 1623–1673*, Bloomsbury, 1988, p. 90. There are, as Sophie Tomlinson notes, also moments of 'social inclusivity' in Cavendish's feminist drama; such as the masque in *Convent of Pleasure*. See her article, above.

47 Margaret Cavendish, *The Matrimoniall Trouble*, in *Plays Never Before Printed*, London, 1668, Act I scene 2, p. 424. See also the representation of citizens' wives in *The Convent of Pleasure* Act III scene 6.

48 Sara Heller Mendelson, *Mental World of Stuart Women*, p. 5.

49 Margaret Cavendish, *The Presence*, in *Playes, Never Before Printed*, London, 1668.

50 Peter Stallybrass, 'Patriarchal Territories: The Body Enclosed', in Margaret W. Ferguson, Maureen Quilligan, Nancy J. Vickers, eds., *Rewriting the Renaissance*, University of Chicago Press, 1986, p. 134.

51 S. D. Amussen, p. 216. Recently her conclusion that 'The radical groups of the civil war challenged the class order not the gender order' has been qualified – see D. Purkiss in this volume; E. Hobby, *Virtue of Necessity*. See also Natalie Zemon Davis's 'The Reasons of Misrule' and 'Women on Top', in her *Society and Culture in Early Modern France*, Polity, 1987.

52 Anthony Fletcher, *Reform in the Provinces: the Government of Stuart England*, Yale University Press, 1986, p. 357.

Rumbold

1 Mrs Caesar's book is now in the British Library, catalogued as Add. MSS 62558. It is used as a political source in the account of Charles Caesar by Eveline Cruickshanks, in Romney Sedgwick, *The House of Commons, 1715–54*, 2 vols., The History of Parliament, H.M.S.O., 1970; and in Linda Colley, *In Defiance of Oligarchy: The Tory Party, 1714–60*, Cambridge University Press, 1982, pp. 58, 99. Mrs Caesar's friendship with Pope was first explored in Howard Erskine-Hill, 'Under which Caesar? Pope in the Journal of Mrs Charles Caesar, 1724–1741', *RES*, 33, 1982, pp. 436–44; and I pursue the topic in *Women's Place in Pope's World*, Cambridge University Press, 1989, chapter 8.

2 'Journal' is the term adopted by the British Library, 'Diary' by Cruickshanks.

3 Add. MSS 62558, fol. 25. Mrs
Caesar's correspondence is
preserved at Rousham Park in
Oxfordshire, in unpaginated
volumes lettered A–H; and I am
grateful to Mr and Mrs Charles
Cottrell-Dormer for their kindness
and hospitality in making it possible
for me to study the collection.
Letters about the elopement are C,
17 October 1729 (Lord Strafford); F,
4 October 1729 (Lord Oxford);
undated (Lady Strafford); undated
(Lord Dupplin). See also *The
Correspondence of Alexander Pope*,
ed. George Sherburn, 5 vols. Oxford
University Press, 1956, vol. III, p. 56;
and Helen Sard Hughes, 'A
Romantic Correspondence of the
Year 1729', *Modern Philology*, 37,
1939, pp. 187–200 (pp. 197–8).
4 The ballad is printed in
*Additions to the Works of
Alexander Pope*, [ed. George
Steevens], 2 vols., Dublin, 1776, vol.
I, pp. 131–4.
5 Rousham Letters, C, 16 and 18
December 1740; F, 13 September–1
November 1730; F, 6 and 15 April
1731; Cruickshanks, p. 517.
6 Add. MSS 62558, fol. 82.
7 Add. MSS 62558, fol. 1.
8 Lucy Hutchinson, *Memoirs of
the Life of Colonel Hutchinson*, ed.
James Sutherland, Oxford
University Press, 1973, p. 10. I am
grateful to Neil Keeble for sharing
with me his forthcoming paper,
'The Colonel's Shadow: Lucy
Hutchinson, Women's Writing and
the Civil War'. For reflections on
female limitations by the Duchesses
of Marlborough and Buckingham,
see *Women's Place in Pope's World*,
chapter 7. For an ironic disavowal
of political involvement on the
grounds of gender by one who had
formerly been a zealous activist, see
The Complete Letters of Lady Mary

Wortley Montagu, ed. Robert
Halsband, 3 vols., Oxford
University Press, 1965–7, vol. III, p.
157. For Charles Caesar's letter, see
Rousham Letters, F, 15 April 1731.
9 Add. MSS 62558, fol. 55.
10 Add. MSS 62558, fol. 17.
11 Rousham Letters, F, 4 October
1729; G, 20 January 1736.
12 Add. MSS 62558, fol. 55.
13 Add. MSS 62558, fol. 56. The
allusion is to the conventional
grouping of commendatory verses
prefaced to Pope's *Works* of 1717.
14 Cruickshanks, pp. 516–17.
15 Add. MSS 62558, fol. 6;
Cruickshanks, pp. 513–14.
16 Rousham Letters, D, 1 February
1717–11 October 1718 (Charles
Caesar), D, 20 October 1717 (Lady
Ormonde); Add. MSS 62558, fol. 6;
DNB, entry under Robert Harley,
first Earl of Oxford.
17 Rousham Letters, F, undated.
18 Rousham Letters, C, 26
September 1731; see also G. E.
Cokayne, *Peerage*, entry under
Thomas Hay, ninth Earl of
Kinnoull.
19 Rousham Letters, G, 7 February
1733; Cokayne, *Peerage*, entry under
William Capell, third Earl of Essex.
The allusions, too complex to cite
here, are quoted and discussed in
Women's Place in Pope's World, p.
235.
20 *Calendar of the Stuart Papers*, 7
vols., Historical Manuscripts
Commission, H.M.S.O., 1902–23,
vol. IV, pp. 301, 414–15, 547, 554;
Add. MSS 62558, fol. 3.
21 *Calendar of the Stuart Papers*,
vol. IV, p. 554; Add. MSS 62558, ff.
15–16.
22 Add. MSS 62558, fol. 62.
23 Add. MSS 62558, fol. 51.
24 Add. MSS 62558, fol. 45; Pope,
Correspondence, vol. II, p. 293.
25 Mrs Caesar compared

Bolingbroke (who had deserted the Jacobite cause) unfavourably with the Jacobite Wharton, whom Pope had denigrated: see Add. MSS 62558, fol. 69; Erskine-Hill, 'Caesar', pp. 441–2.

26 Add. MSS 62558, fol. 83.

27 These lines were first satisfactorily explained by Erskine-Hill, 'Caesar', pp. 442–4. Mrs Caesar proclaims her authorship in her scrapbook (now in the Wren Library, Trinity College, Cambridge) where she preserves Pope's couplet in her own hand (fol. 4).

28 Add. MSS 62559 (Caesar family papers preserved with Mrs Caesar's book), ff. 15–16. No poems by Prior to her are now known.

29 Add. MSS 62558, fol. 8.

30 Add. MSS 62558, ff. 3, 61.

31 Add. MSS 62558, fol. 51.

32 Add. MSS 62558, fol. 11; see also George Sherburn, *The Early Career of Alexander Pope*, Oxford University Press, 1968, pp. 221–8.

33 Add. MSS 62558, fol. 51. For a clearer account, see Cruickshanks, p. 513. There is a family tree at the front of Edmund Lodge, *The Life of Sir Julius Caesar*, London, 1827; but most of the activities of Charles Caesar are mistakenly attributed to his cousin of the same name, both in the table and in the text, pp. 62–3, 70–4.

34 Add. MSS 62558, fol. 52.

35 Details are given in Edward, Earl of Clarendon, *The History of the Rebellion and Civil Wars in England*, ed. W. Dunn Macray, 6 vols., Oxford University Press, 1888, vol. I, pp. 64–7 (Book I, 112–14).

36 Add. MSS 62558, fol. 53. For 'Tullibardin' and his services to an earlier generation of Caesars, see Clarendon, loc. cit.

37 Add. MSS 62558, fol. 53.

38 Entries under Henry Caesar, Sir Charles Caesar by E. R. Edwards, Geoffrey Jaggar and M. W. Helms, in Basil Duke Henning, *The House of Commons, 1660–90*, 2 vols., The History of Parliament, H.M.S.O., 1983.

39 Add. MSS 62558, fol. 54.

40 Sir Henry Chauncy, *The Historical Antiquities of Hertfordshire*, London, 1700, pp. 122–6, 345–6; entries under Ralph Freman [*sic*], Hertfordshire constituency, by E. R. Edwards and Geoffrey Jaggar, in Henning; entries under the same heads by A. N. Newman in Sedgwick.

41 Add. MSS 62558, ff. 25, 60; Rousham Letters, C, 17 October 1729; D, 8 May 1723; F, 23 October 1730 (Charles Caesar).

42 All the verse cited is preserved in Rousham Letters, A.

43 Add. MSS 62558, fol. 61.

44 Cokayne, *Peerage*, entry under Thomas Wentworth, third Earl of Strafford.

45 Add. MSS 62558, fol. 81.

46 Cruickshanks, pp. 515–17.

47 Add. MSS 62558, fol. 39.

48 Add. MSS 62558, fol. 40; Cruickshanks, p. 517.

49 Add. MSS 62558, fol. 49.

50 Add. MSS 62558, fol. 82; Lodge, p. ii.

51 Add. MSS 62558, fol. 84.

52 Robert Clutterbuck, *The History and Antiquities of the County of Hertford*, 3 vols., London, 1815–27, vol. II, p. 285.

53 Add. MSS 62558, fol. 86.

54 *The Works of John Sheffield . . . Duke of Buckingham*, 2 vols., London, 1723, vol. I, p. 189.

55 *The Correspondence of Jonathan Swift*, ed. Harold Williams, 5 vols., Oxford University Press, 1963–5, vol. V, p. 206 (Lord

Orrery to Swift).

56 Rousham Letters, G, undated (Mary Barber to Mary Caesar).

57 Sir Charles Firth, 'Burnet as an Historian', in *Essays Historical and Literary*, Oxford University Press, 1938, pp. 192–3.

58 Add. MSS 62558, fol. 2.

59 Add. MSS 62558, fol. 63.

60 Clarendon, *The History of the Rebellion*, vol. I, p. 3.

61 *Bishop Burnet's History of his Own Time*, 2 vols., London, 1724–34, vol. I, p. 2.

Index

INDEX   239

Tonson, Jacob, 38
Tories, 57, 58
   and Jacobites, 179–98 *passim*
   women write for, 42–3, 95, 103, 104, 105–6
Trapnel, Anna, 24, 26, 139–51 *passim*, 156–8, 202
Travers, Rebeckah or Rebecca, 23, 212
Trotter, Catharine, later Cockburn: *Agnes de Castro*, 40, 42, 47, 102–3
   career of, 39–49, 53–4
   Fatal Friendship, 44, 45, 46, 47
   Love at a Loss, 47
   Olinda's Adventures, 40, 47, 48
   philosophical works, 41
   poems, 41–2, 75
   The Revolution of Sweden, 47, 56
   The Unhappy Penitent, 45
Trotter, David, 41
Trotter, Sarah (Bellenden), 41
Tullibardine, John Murray, Earl of, 189
Turner, Jane, 29, 32
Twisden, Sir William, 79
Tyrrell, James, 74 and n. 5

universities, 18, 21, 25, 26–7, 142
Upon the Royston Bargain, 179
Utrecht, Peace of, 185, 192

Valois, Marguerite de, 199
Venn, Anne, 29–30, 31–2
Venn, John, 29–30
Villedieu, Marie de, *see* Desjardins
Virgil, 136–7
Vivers, Margaret, 24
Vives, Juan Luis, 171

Waller, William, 200
Walpole, Sir Robert, 193, 194, 195
Ward, Mary, 136
Warner, Trevor, Lady, 129
Warren, Mercy Otis, 126
Watts, Isaac, 50 and n. 52
Waugh, Dorothy, 24
Weamys, Anna, 200
Wharton, Anne, 34, 41; poems by, 76–7, 86, 92 and n. 29
Whigs, 42–3, 95, 104, 181–5, 190, 196
White, Dorothy, 23, 24, 25
Whitehead, Anne, 81
Whitrow, Joan, 212
Wight, Sarah, 31, 32, 145–50 *passim*, 224
William III, 198
   and stage, 33
   and women writers, 50, 53, 79, 186, 187
Willoughby, Cassandra, 126
Wimpole, Cambs, 181
Winchilsea, Anne Finch, Countess of: elegy by, 79, 81, 82, 83
   'The Introduction', 54, 110
   publications by, 81, 82
Winthrop, John, 154, 156
Wiseman, Mary, 136
Wiseman, Susan, 12, 159–77
Wogan, Anne (Barlow), 78
Wollstonecraft, Mary, 220
Woodford, Samuel, 76
Worthington, Mary, 136
Wycherley, William, 43

Xavier, Francis, St, 130
Xaviera, Mother Mary, *see* Burton, Catharine